How to Live Through Junior High School

Since its first publication, *How to Live through Junior High School* has given invaluable practical guidance to thousands of parents, teachers, and students in matters of living and dealing with the new awakenings, emotions, and problems of early adolescence.

Completely rewritten and updated to reflect the contemporary scene and the considerable new research in the fields of adolescent education and psychology, *How to Live through Junior High School* is now more useful and informative than ever. Based on the author's twenty-five years of experience as a middle school teacher, counselor, and administrator and spiced with quotations drawn from several hundred questionnaires completed by students, teachers, and parents, this book discusses in frank detail the academic, social, family, and sex problems of young people between the ages of ten and fifteen—problems concerning study and work habits, motivation,

(Continued on back flap)

Also by Eric W. Johnson

SEX: TELLING IT STRAIGHT

V.D.

LOVE AND SEX IN PLAIN LANGUAGE

with coauthor Corinne B. Johnson

LOVE AND SEX AND GROWING UP

(Continued from front flap)

cliques, drinking, smoking, drugs, allowances, chores, sex education and behavior, divorce, respect for property, lack of self-confidence, anger, moodiness, and many other areas.

Eric W. Johnson's wise, witty, and reassuring advice will provide students, teachers, and parents with a better understanding of, and a fresh perspective on, that crucially important period when young people pass from childhood to young adulthood.

new edition

How to Live Through Junior High School

A Practical Discussion of the Middle and Junior High School Years for Parents, Students and Teachers

ERIC W. JOHNSON

J. B. LIPPINCOTT COMPANY
Philadelphia and New York

The chart on page 223 first appeared in W. A. Marshall and J. M. Tanner's "Variations in the Pattern of Pubertal Changes in Boys," Archives of the Diseases of Childhood, *45 (1970), 13, and is reproduced with permission of the authors.*

New edition
Printed in the United States of America

U.S. Library of Congress Cataloging in Publication Data

Johnson, Eric W
How to live through junior high school : a practical discussion of the middle and junior high school years for parents, students and teachers.

Bibliography: p.
SUMMARY: Discusses such teen-age problems as grades, cliques, parents, divorce, motivation, anger, allowances, chores, reading, lack of confidence, and many more.
1. Child study. 2. Adolescence. [1. Conduct of life. 2. Adolescence]. I. Title.
HQ772.J63 1975 301.43'15 75-829
ISBN-0-397-01076-1

Preface

Over the years, as teacher of English, history and sex education, as junior high school principal and as adviser, I have talked with hundreds—no, I guess it's thousands—of students in grades five through nine and their parents and teachers. For this book, I have supplemented the knowledge and impressions gained from all this talking and listening by asking a number of students, parents and teachers to reply in writing to some questions about the life, ideas, joys, sorrows and problems of middle and junior high schoolers and of their parents and teachers. This I did by distributing questionnaires, each either seven or nine pages long, through seven schools in the greater Philadelphia area, to not quite a thousand students, of whom about four hundred replied; to over five hundred sets of parents in three schools, of whom just over a hundred replied; and to a few teachers in the schools, of whom not quite forty replied. The questionnaires were answered anonymously and returned to me in sealed envelopes. They were read by only one assistant, not connected with any of the schools, and me.

Of the seven schools, six enroll students from primarily middle-class families (a few wealthy; most, I should judge, comfortable; and a very few impoverished—financially, at least), and one enrolls students from a crowded urban area where most of the families have low incomes. I found that the responses from students in the last school were so different in many respects from those of the other six schools that I did not include them in the totals given in the book, because it is written primarily for the personal interest, guidance and help of people likely to read a book like this. The book makes no pretense to be a sociological study of a cross section of society.

Although there were quite a few questions calling for yes/no/maybe answers that were easily tabulated, most of the space in the questionnaires was given to free-response answers, and many of the students, parents and teachers wrote quite fully in response to my *why*'s and *explain*'s. These responses constitute a remarkable set of quite open-ended utterances written in a great variety of moods, manners and language. Reading them is a bit like having confidential, somewhat jumpy conversations with several hundred people, mainly students. The responses will not satisfy the statistically minded. Their greatest value is as a set of subjective replies, many very deeply felt, which I have added to my own experience and that of others to illuminate and give life and balance to the ideas in the book, and as a source of information and suggestions. I don't know of any other such extensive collection of free responses from groups of students, parents and, to a lesser extent, teachers. What they lack in neat, sterile objectivity I hope they make up for in revealed experiences, feelings and opinions.

The replies to the questions, as one would expect from nonproofread, not-to-be-graded written utterances, displayed the normal range of deviations from standard English spelling and punctuation. Being an English teacher, I had no difficulty in understanding them, but the common reader might not have found it easy. Therefore, I have corrected the spelling (except in a few cases where I thought the errors were funny) and the punctuation. I never changed the thought of any reply, although occasionally I have excerpted or slightly condensed.

An unsolvable problem in writing the book was what to call people who are in grades five through nine. "Boys" and "girls" sounds too young for some eighth- and ninth-graders, although they often call themselves that. "Children," in some circumstances, sounds even more demeaning, although they often call themselves that, too, and, after all, even I, at fifty-six, am a child of my parents. Some object to the term "adolescent," which has clinical overtones, although in reading the book you will see that I have a high regard for the condition of mind and spirit called adolescence and believe that it may be a renewed state of adolescence which will save our world. "Student" is a nice, neutral word, and I've used it most often, even though there are situations where it is not appropriate, as for example when young individuals (there's *another* term) confront not-so-young individuals amid the mess the bedrooms of the former are usually in. I've also used the terms "teen-agers," "youngsters," "kids," and "young people," but none does well in every situation. One boy opted for "men" and "women," a girl wanted me to use only "females" and "males" throughout, and another girl cried, "For God's sake, why not just call us people!"

Another problem that has arisen of late to plague people trying to write clear sentences is that of the sexist pronoun. I share people's objections to using the masculine *he, him* and *his* when referring equally to *she, her* and *hers*. However, I find that my distaste for the awkwardness of "he-or-she"ing outweighs my distaste for the sexist domination of the masculine singular pronoun, so deeply rooted in our language. Therefore, when it was unavoidable, I have gone the "he" route and hope that readers will add their own "or she" if they wish to.

Each chapter is preceded by five brief quotations from students, and the large figures *5, 6, 7, 8, 9* refer to the grade in school of the person quoted. Here and there in the book where I felt it was helpful I have indicated by *B* or *G* whether it was a boy or a girl who wrote a certain passage quoted.

Acknowledgments

I am most grateful to the hundreds of students, parents and teachers who gave time and thought to replying to the questionnaires, and to the principals, teachers and secretaries of the seven schools which cooperated in the project. I refrain from naming the schools here only, as the kids say, "to protect the innocent."

The following individuals, none of whom has read the entire manuscript or is responsible for any errors of fact or interpretation, gave valuable help.

For the sections on mathematics:

Georgia M. Elgar, Charlottesville, Va.; teacher and consultant in mathematics; most recently, Associate Professor of Mathematics and Data Processing, City Colleges of Chicago.

William H. Cromley, Jr., Philadelphia; head of the department of mathematics, Germantown Friends School; formerly Assistant Professor of Mathematics, Thiel College, Pa.

For ideas about the passage from childhood to adulthood:

George M. Goethals, Cambridge, Mass.; Department of Psychology and Social Relations, Harvard University.

For help in preparing, reading and tabulating the student questionnaires and for good general advice:
Mary Solis-Cohen Keller, Philadelphia; Director of Volunteer Resources, Philadelphia Child Guidance Clinic; formerly specialist in learning and reading problems, and adviser, Germantown Friends School.

For careful review and correction of the chapter on drugs:
Charles P. O'Brien, M.D., Ph.D., Philadelphia; Associate Professor of Psychiatry and Director, Drug Treatment and Research Center, University of Pennsylvania.

Mary-Jo Bryan Wolsky, Philadelphia; formerly trainer and counselor, Addiction Services Agency, City of New York; now with ACT (Achievement through Counseling and Treatment).

For help with the section on reading and reading problems:
Mary Gray Ornston Stoner, Philadelphia; reading and learning specialist, Germantown Friends School; formerly of the Beauvoir School, Washington, D.C.

For help and advice in many sections of the book:
E. Gelett Ketchum, Educational Consultant, Psychological Services, the Institute of the Pennsylvania Hospital.

Lastly, I thank Barrie Van Dyck, my editor at J. B. Lippincott, for her taste, judgment, clarity and tact.

ERIC W. JOHNSON

Contents

How to Live Through Junior High School

1

The Sleeping Lion Awakes: An Orientation to This Book

"**5** Why write a book? We get along OK, but I guess I'll read it.

6 Give plenty of facts and keep out the opinions.

7 You asked me some pretty personal questions, you know, so this ought to be a pretty good book.

8 I feel that adults are inferior.

9 If you give shitty advice like the newspapers I swear I'll burn your book after the first page."

Why should anyone write or read a book about grades five through nine, ages ten to fifteen? What is so special or difficult about middle or junior high school? Well, in my experience in schools and with parents and teachers, I have found that there is no period during the journey from kindergarten to twelfth grade as difficult as these years during which most boys and girls reach puberty and begin that period of life for which, in our culture, we have invented the term *adolescence*. Peace, calm and confidence at home often terminate, and there is a bewildering onslaught of problems. The years of junior high school

Note: Figures at chapter openings refer to grade levels of students quoted.

are the most difficult ones to find good teachers for; many parents are perplexed and troubled; and the girls and boys, while experiencing new and exciting feelings and understanding, are also experiencing puzzlement, frustration, and sometimes anguish.

Typically, fifth grade—ten years old—is a time of stability and contentment and a relatively pure enthusiasm for whatever is good and new and interesting. The troubles—and they are healthy and necessary troubles—usually begin in sixth grade, progress vigorously through seventh, reach their peak in eighth grade and only begin to taper off in ninth. There is no more puzzled parent than a parent of an eighth-grader.

About thirty-five years ago, the psychiatrist J. Lander wrote:

> With the advent of puberty, the sleeping lion awakes, stretches, and, as though fortified and rejuvenated by his long rest, proceeds to tear apart that elaborate structure which has apparently kept him so satisfactorily under control. . . . The youngster is suddenly immersed in a war, a war he thought he had won when he succeeded in controlling those aspects of his behavior which had so violently displeased the adults around him—his pleasure in exposing himself, the joy of examining others, the delights of dirt, the gratifications of gluttony, the pleasure of masturbation. . . . He had suffered much to erect barriers [to his instincts] . . . , the incentive . . . being to achieve peace within himself and peace with those around him. Now all this peace is lost, and the barriers totter.*

* Quoted by Harvey Stanford Waxman, "The Psychological Manifestations of Puberty Among Adolescent Boys," Harvard University, April, 1974, p. 5, from J. Lander, "The Pubertal Struggle Against the Instincts," *American Journal of Orthopsychiatry,* 1942, 12, 456–461.

Perhaps Lander is a little overdramatic; and the stretching lion is a good and necessary lion, even if he is not always a friendly one. Probably most girls and boys, or their teachers and parents, do not recognize in themselves, or in their students or children, the waking lion or the tottering cage. But essentially a breaking of barriers and a new reaching out is what happens, conspicuously or not so conspicuously, during the years we are discussing.

In this book I am speaking to daughters and sons and students, to mothers and fathers and teachers. The book concerns the ideas, feelings and lives of girls and boys at school and at home and how they relate to those of parents and teachers. In the main, I have tried in what I write to be practical and concrete, not abstract, keeping in mind the mother who, when I asked her to set down her reasons for predicting she'd neither buy nor read my book, wrote:

It is impossible for the author of such a book to set up the concrete problems *I* will meet, and then tell *me* how to solve them. The author can only generalize, and I can get only generalized advice. Long ago I gave up listening to one-shot lectures by psychiatrists.

A ninth-grade boy, faced with the questionnaire I asked several hundred students to answer to provide part of the material for the book, wrote in somewhat the same vein:

I didn't answer the questions. I am strongly against "guide books." I think if a parent or child cares enough to want to have a good relationship, they can talk to each other, which is much better than using the intermediary of a book. Furthermore, a book is general, and each child and parent is different.

Well, neither the mother nor the boy dissuaded me from writing the book. What other parents have written and said to me, and what many students have written on their questionnaires and have told me, make it clear that there is still a place for a book about the stormy, entertaining, complicated, difficult period of early adolescence and the years just before it. As you will see in the pages that follow, scores of teen-agers have not hesitated to generalize about themselves, their parents and their teachers. You may find their generalizations instructive; you will see that many of them are mutually contradictory and deeply tinged with self.

What I write is based on a variety of experience and information: my own work in schools during about twenty-five years mainly with grades five through nine; several hundred long, rather open-ended questionnaires; over a hundred somewhat more structured questionnaires completed by parents and teachers; and, to a small degree, experience with my own children and their classmates, all of whom have now passed beyond grade nine.

I think that it is often—not always—best when the problems of families and schools are being discussed for the child, the parents and the teacher all to be present. Such talk gives all of them a common experience, an experience that may lead to a better understanding than having to rely on secondhand reporting to those who were not present. Of course, there are subjects best discussed more privately, and there are sometimes feelings and thoughts that parents, teachers or children wish to express without "the other side" knowing. Well and good—and the ideas and facts in this book will be seen and reacted to in the blessed privacy of reading, though later they may be discussed with others.

Communication with Parents

The first question I asked the students on the questionnaire concerned communication: *Is it difficult for you to talk satisfactorily with your parents about questions important to you? Yes — At times — No —.* About two thirds answered *yes* or *at times* it is difficult; one third said *no,* it's not. Somewhat more boys than girls found it difficult; fifth-graders had much less difficulty than ninth-graders.

How do they express their difficulties? In fifth grade it tends to be in simple terms: "I was afraid they might get mad"; "sometimes I'm ashamed"; "I feel funny sometimes"; "I don't know how to begin"; "I'm embarrassed." Eighth- and ninth-graders put it a little differently: "My parents are very old-fashioned. They don't seem to understand that the world has changed"; "they get upset, then I get upset, and it turns into a shouting contest"; "their viewpoints are closed, they are set upon their ways, and a child should follow these ways"; "I'm about the best talker at school but at home I shut up." And, on a different level of concern: "They are *too* interested"; "I'm afraid they might blab."

Judging from the advice that girls and boys write on their questionnaires, both to their parents and their teachers, I would say that one of their most intensely felt needs is to be listened to and heard; they don't want to be asked questions, which they so often perceive as prying, but they do want to be listened to. This, of course, is very frustrating to parents who, faced with their non-communicating daughters and sons who so often seem to have nothing much to say except when they are asking for food, service and transportation, are reduced to asking those turn-off questions: "How was school today?" "How did the party go?" "What did you and your friends do?" "Have you got any homework?"

Concerns of Parents

If the need to be heard is high on the list of problems of young teen-agers, what are the areas that are of greatest concern to parents and teachers? In the questionnaire for parents, I listed over fifty possible areas, some related especially to school, some to home and some to primarily social problems and attitudes. I asked parents to rate their degree of concern about the problems on a five-point scale from "very concerned" to "no problem at all." The twenty-five areas that *most deeply concerned or interested* the parents are these, in a descending order of "count" based on frequency of mention combined with intensity of concern:

Rank	*Count*	*Area of Concern or Interest*
1	81	study habits
2	80	how to motivate study and homework
3	79	what to do when child is in academic or other difficulty
4	59	attitude and behavior toward brothers and sisters
5	56	cliques at school
6	55	low concept of self
7	53	carelessness and sloppiness
8	53	understimulation of child (boredom)
9	50	grades and reports
10	47	teachers' attitude toward child
11	44	child's attitude toward classmates
12	43	lack of adequate knowledge of child's ability
13	40	home arguments

Rank	*Count*	*Area of Concern or Interest*
14	38	family and household chores and duties
15	36	moodiness of child (ups and downs)
16	35	emotional outbursts
17	35	lack of adequate knowledge of child's progress
18	35	child's attitude toward teachers
19	33	arranging enjoyable joint family activities
20	32	reconciling standards of behavior, dress, etc., at school and at home
21	31	lack of respect for property
22	30	child's lack of friends
23	30	attitude and behavior toward parents
24	29	how to help child make friends at school
25	27	lack of good manners at home
	27	attitudes and actions of other parents
	27	use of TV
	27	the sort of friends the child has

You can see that the top three places go to very practical matters of school and learning. Perhaps this is because the parents knew that the questionnaire came from me, a teacher, not a family counselor or psychiatrist.

And what were the areas felt to be of *small concern?* Here they are, starting with the least, with a count of only 1, and proceeding upward to a count of only 12:

Rank	*Count*	*Area of Concern or Interest*
1	1	lack of interest in opposite sex
2	2	too many parties, etc.
3	3	school puts too much responsibility on parents
4	4	possibility of child's developing homosexual tendencies
5	6	use or suspected use of drugs

Rank	*Count*	*Area of Concern or Interest*
6	7	sexual behavior of child
7	8	use or suspected use of alcohol
8	8	dating, going steady, etc.
9	10	smoking
10	11	too few parties, etc.
11	11	bedtime
12	12	gossiping
13	12	overactivity of child
14	12	child has too little to do
15	12	overstimulation of child

Since most of the readers of this book, I guess, are likely to be parents, I have taken seriously their lack of concern and do not deal much with the areas that rate very low, except for three: sexual behavior, alcohol, and drugs, because I think parents ought to be concerned about these areas. Perhaps some are like the mother and father of the teen-age girl in a *New Yorker* cartoon who said to a friend, "My folks don't care what I do so long as it doesn't come to their attention."

Concerns of Teachers

In the questionnaire for teachers, I listed twenty-six areas of concern and rated the responses in the same way as I did those for parents. Here are the ten areas of *deepest concern* to teachers, in descending order of importance:

Rank	*Count*	*Area of Concern or Interest*
1	57	disrespect for property
2	56	how to develop steady motivation on the part of students
3	55	how to develop interest on the part of students

Rank	*Count*	*Area of Concern or Interest*
4	49	how to help students who have few friends
5	47	lack of good manners and respect on part of students toward each other
6	38	how to improve communication with students
7	34	how to develop an atmosphere of lively participation by students
8	34	cliques at school
9	32	how to develop an adequate knowledge of students' personalities, backgrounds, out-of-school influences, family situations, etc.
10	32	use of alcoholic beverages by students

The ten areas of *least concern* to teachers were: interference by parents in the life of the school (count of 7); disobedience on the part of students (16); lack of ability on the part of students (19); how to maintain good order and discipline (20); reconciling standards of behavior, dress, etc., at home and at school (20); sexual behavior of students (20); how to develop fuller participation of parents in life of school (23); students' lack of knowledge of sex information and issues concerning sexual behavior (24); smoking by students (25); and competition of TV with homework and reading (26).

It is interesting that the problems of interest in schoolwork and motivation rank very high on the lists of both parents and teachers. However, the number-one concern of teachers, disrespect for property, ranks twenty-first from the top on the parent list.

The Questionnaires

The questionnaires on which parts of this book are based were sent to students and teachers in six schools, and to parents in three of the same schools, whose population is predominantly, but not entirely, middle class. The several hundred responses do not, therefore, represent a cross section of the population of the United States—far from it. However, they are, I think, a pretty good sampling of the daughters and sons and mothers and fathers who are likely to read a book like this. But even all of this group may not be represented, since only those who chose to do so took the time and made the effort to complete the questionnaires. Those who, for whatever reason, did not reply are not represented. However, the tremendous variety of the replies, in opinions expressed, in ability to write, in attitude toward home, school and world—and toward the idea of the book itself—makes me believe that the material from the questionnaires does provide some useful information and some authentic insights.

Many of the questionnaires were remarkably complete, helpful and self-revealing. I have tried to measure the material in them against the background of my own experience and the common sense that comes, I hope, from having worked for years in different classrooms and with different grade levels. However, my experience has limits, even if it is long. I know little about the most serious problems of juvenile or parental delinquency and crime, or about the needs of seriously retarded children. I have, therefore, not tried to deal with these subjects. The families that I know about are those whose members are, by and large, trying to do their best—but A-for-effort doesn't always mean A-for-performance, as my readers will know for themselves and as the material from the questionnaires shows. Lots of people feel they need more help than they are getting to do the best job they can of being successful, happy children and students and parents and teachers during the middle and junior high school years.

And this leads to a word on one of the most wasteful, corroding, misguided practices I know of among teachers, guidance people and writers: that of blaming parents. (It doesn't help much to blame kids either, but that's not what I'm talking about right now.) Among all the thousands of parents I have met over a good many years, I can think of very few that needed any blaming, which only makes people feel more anxious and puts them on the defensive so that they are more likely to mishandle their problems. Plenty of parents need guidance; plenty are eager for good ideas and specific remedies. And some are in various ways at the root of their children's troubles and need insight. But almost all want and try to do the best they can for their children. They don't need to be told, "It's your fault"; they need to be told, "Here, try this; it might work."

The Independence and Durability of Children

The way many people talk and write, you might think that children are spineless, characterless clay to be molded entirely by parents, and a bit by teachers, and that only when they reach adulthood do they become in any way self-directing. This is a harmful idea. Children, even from the day of their birth, have potential characters all their own, and much of their future development is predetermined by the genes they were born with. They'll be greatly affected by their environment, of which their parents and their school are major parts, but they are in considerable measure *independent beings,* and it is a delusion for parents and teachers to think that they alone are responsible for how a child turns out. This delusion may cause children, over the years, to dismiss their own responsibility by blaming their parents.

All of this is only common sense. Anyone who has

had babies will know that some, from the first moment, are highly sensitive to sounds, light, heat and changes of position, while others seem placidly unaware of these stimuli. One child may seem almost to be born with good study habits. From a very early age he goes right at a project, tackles it systematically section by section and keeps at it until it is completed; whereas another child may be highly impetuous, intuitive, unpersistent, yet original and pleasingly provocative. I cannot feel that these differences in their characters are the parents' "fault."

In addition, children are surprisingly durable. If we parents and teachers consciously watch every word or action while we are around them, we may turn ourselves into nervous wrecks, and it is probably healthier for children to associate with parents and teachers who can be themselves most of the time. We can expect to make plenty of mistakes in dealing with our children and pupils —certainly our parents and teachers did with us—and both the young and we will undoubtedly learn much from these mistakes. Aside from the traumatic experience (that is, one that is exceptionally deep and shocking), it is only *serious mishandling over a protracted period* that will permanently damage a child.

One more thing: we mustn't expect our children to be perfect. Too many of us do, and consequently we are usually disappointed. Disappointed parents and teachers are not pleasant to live with, no matter how bravely disappointed they may be. I suppose it's good and natural that we hope our children and students will be better than we are, but let's face facts and recognize that they may turn out to be worse—or at least very different and less "successful." Certainly, human history does not plainly confirm the view that each generation excels the preceding one.

I think we must be satisfied to give birth to our children, to feed and clothe them, to love them (most of the time), to advise them when we feel sure about something, to answer their questions if we think we know the answer, to set up some guideposts for them, to provide for them the best school-teaching we can and to enjoy them (at least some of the time). If we do these things consistently, we must have some faith that they'll turn out more or less satisfactorily.

All human beings are a perplexing mixture of good and evil. If you can know this and not expect perfection, perhaps your daughter will never have to say as the girl in a cartoon in an old *Saturday Evening Post* said to her friend as they were confiding in each other, "You know, the trouble with me is I'm the sort of person my mother doesn't want me to associate with." A pretty good piece of advice, I think, especially for parents and teachers of ten- to fifteen-year-olds, is to try to spend more time developing, encouraging and praising the good we see than in struggling to put down, discourage and punish the bad. Respect and acceptance from adults are necessary first steps to *self*-respect and *self*-acceptance, and nothing is more pleasant for parents and teachers than to feel respected and accepted by boys and girls. Certainly self-respect is a necessary basis for respect of others. To do well and be reasonably happy, we must feel good, not bad; we must like ourselves (quite a different thing from feeling satisfied with ourselves). This truth isn't a bad one for boys and girls to remember about their parents and teachers, either. Most adults need encouragement.

For parents, their children's adolescence should be a time for gradual retirement from the center of their children's universe, and if the retirement isn't voluntary, a healthy adolescent will assist it with a series of not too tactful nudges or shoves. If parents manage to adjust to these shifting relationships without feeling injured, *and without abdicating,* they will be better able to contribute to their children's healthy development.

A leading psychologist and father of five children, after I had discussed this book with him, wrote:

Many problems of this age are *not* avoidable; they are part of a stage in parent-child relations, and attempts to remove the problems may create worse ones. Restrict your advice for the most part to how parents and teachers can find ways of easing the strain on themselves and the kids—to palliative measures (like taking aspirin). Adolescents don't have problems in the South Seas, if Margaret Mead is right, but then they don't have to try living in our culture either.

2

The Passage from Childhood to Adulthood

"**5** I like my life right now, even speling.

6 I try to be nice but it isn't natural for a 6th grader to be nice all the time.

7 Remember there is not just one kind of kid. Tell about many kinds of kids.

8 When your child asks for help, help them. Don't say, 'You should know that.'

9 This book would be useful because parents need a realization of what's going on."

It helps us to understand growing up if we consider life as a journey with recognizable stages. The typical voyager passes through the stages in a fixed order; the transition from one to the next is gradual. We are talking about the progress of a journey, not a game of sudden moves.

Some people strongly object to the idea of stages, and I sympathize with parents who gripe about teachers' saying, in effect, "Don't worry, she's just going through a stage." Several parents, in reply to my question *What is the most* un*helpful thing a school person ever did or said in relation to a child of yours?* referred to remarks such as these: "He'll grow out of it"; "they all behave this way in this grade." If the "don't-worry-it's-just-a-stage" is said as a cop-out, then I think parents have a right to feel dissatisfied and even resentful. But when such a comment is made by an experienced and perceptive teacher, one should take comfort.

All of us—parents, teachers and boys and girls—can be helped in our understanding of life if we are aware that *developmental stages* exist and if we use this knowledge and perspective as a help in deciding what to do or, often, what not to do.

Freud's Stages of Development

Sigmund Freud emphasized the crucial importance of the first few years of human life in determining the future health and happiness of all individuals. He observed that babies and very young children go through a series of overlapping stages: the *oral stage,* when the mouth and sucking are the source of most pleasure; the *anal stage,* when infants experience the special pleasure of the anus and of bowel movements and feces; and the *phallic stage,* when both little girls and little boys become strongly aware of the pleasurable feelings in their genitals. The phallic period is sometimes called the period of *infant sexuality.*

For all of us, memories of the events of these early periods, their pleasures, their pain, and how these were dealt with by our parents and others close to us have gone into the *unconscious* part of our mind. I think I am typical when I say that my own "common sense" always has had difficulty accepting the reality and importance of these stages because, like most of my readers,

I am now entirely unaware of them. Oral period? Anal period? Phallic period? I don't remember any of that. It sounds like elaborate jargon unconnected with reality, much less with any reality that *I* had anything to do with.

I think this reaction is natural, for how, short of going through psychoanalysis, can we be conscious of what is buried in our unconscious and well defended there? But, unconscious as we are of them, we passed through these early stages of life's journey, and how we made the passage influences very strongly how we will view and deal with our selves and our world from then on. Freud believed, and I think most students of human behavior agree with him, that the first five or six years of life, and the unconscious but nonetheless real memories, are the predominant influence working upon us for the rest of our lives.

After the phallic stage, according to Freud, we move into a period called *latency,* during which the strong instinctive drives, especially the sexual drive, are less active, more hidden, more controlled. This is the period when "that elaborate structure" of which Lander writes keeps boys and girls "so satisfactorily under control." However, delightful as the controlled and relatively optimistic and cooperative living during the latency period is for boys and girls who are passing through it and for the parents and teachers who live and work with them during this time, it is not nearly as latent as Freud apparently thought it was. Even before puberty, boys and girls are quite interested in each other and in sexual feelings and behavior.

If it is true that the early years of life determine so much of our future behavior, and if it is true that the unconscious part of our minds influences us so strongly—in short, if most of the formation of personality and character is well established before boys and girls reach middle school—why pay all this special attention to grades five through nine, ages ten to fifteen? I see two reasons. The first is that we all know that we never stop being influenced by our present environment: our friends, our family, our teachers; books, plays, movies and events. We experience minor and sometimes major conversions and changes of conviction and new understanding. We soften, harden, become more broad-minded, or less so. In a sense, each day can be, potentially, a new one with the possibility of a fresh start. "Too late for man is early yet for God," an ancient Quaker friend told me, and he was not talking only about the state of the world.

The second reason for paying attention to this period is that with the coming of puberty, the tearing apart of the elaborate structures of control, the loss of peace and the tottering of barriers, many of us go into a sort of second infancy—back to the drawing boards, so to speak, for possibly major alterations. In some ways, eighth-graders seem much less mature than fifth-graders. Really they are not, of course, for they are grappling anew with the deepest issues of life—how to achieve self-respect, how to deal with their inner urges, how to win independence from childhood, how to shift from the family to the world outside. Adolescence, as no one needs to be told, is a period of turmoil and rapid movement. During this stage, teachers and parents and especially friends strongly influence the course of the future journey.

Piaget on the Development of Thinking

Another scientist, somewhat later than Freud, who observed that human development comes in stages was the Swiss psychologist Jean Piaget. He made extraordinarily brilliant observations of the *thought processes* of children, especially of their ability to think logically. He noted that "intelligence," whatever that may be, does not increase at a steady rate but in spurts. Therefore, the conventional IQ score (of which I shall write more in Chapter 4) often is not an accurate measure of intelligence because people shift from one stage of thinking to a higher stage at different ages. Another significant observation of Piaget's is that children and young people develop their capacity for logical thinking independently of their emotional environment.

Piaget called the first stage the *sensorimotor period,* when children's perception of the world is obtained directly by the physical senses. By about age two, the child has learned that actions have physical consequences and that he and his environment are not the same.

The second stage is called the *period of prelogical thought* and lasts, typically, from ages two to five. The thinking of children during this stage contains a sort of "magical" element, in that children are not able to distinguish well between events and objects that they experience and those that they imagine.

The third stage is called the period of *concrete operations.* During this stage the child learns to observe, count, organize, remember and reorganize concrete objects and to do mental operations without losing the distinction between real and imaginary. This stage lasts until perhaps age eleven or twelve, *if* the person involved is going to move on to the fourth stage of development of thought. Many never do.

The fourth stage is called the *period of formal operations.* When people enter this stage they begin to be able to deal with abstractions, to reason about the future, to understand and construct systems of thought, to put forth theories and to test them. The fourth stage comes with adolescence, typically between ages eleven and fifteen or sixteen, though it may come much later. It is interesting that, according to studies, almost half of all Americans never reach "adolescence" in their capacity to think. That is, they never learn to think abstractly, never reach the stage where they reexamine their world, the people in it (especially their parents, siblings and teachers), and themselves. It is important to know this, because to require a person who has not reached the period of formal operations to think in abstractions is to require the impossible. (My guess is that almost all the children of readers of this book would, indeed, reach the fourth stage during their middle and junior high school years. Such, usually, is the case with the children of readers of books.)

Kohlberg's Stages in the Development of Moral Reasoning

Yet another set of stages that we pass through on our journey from childhood to adulthood is stages of *moral reasoning*—the ability to think about right and wrong, truth and falsehood, good and bad. Lawrence Kohlberg, a psychologist at Harvard, has observed and identified these stages, and his ideas are especially helpful in understanding the development of girls and boys in middle and junior high school.* People go through the stages in a fixed sequence; it is not possible to skip a stage. However, different people proceed at different speeds, and people stop at a certain stage and proceed no farther. The environment at home and at school directly influences the *rate* of progress through the stages and also *how far* a person's ability for moral reasoning will develop.

* "The Adolescent as Philosopher: The Discovery of the Self in a Postconventional World," by Lawrence Kohlberg and Carol Gilligan, *Daedalus,* Fall, 1971, pp. 1051–1086.

As you read the explanation that follows, it will help you to look at the chart of stages shown below.

Kohlberg Stages of Moral Reasoning	*Typical Age*
Stage 0: The good is what I like.	0 to 4
I. Preconventional Level	
Stage 1: Avoid punishment	4 to 7
Stage 2: You be nice; I'll be nice.	7 to 10
II. Conventional Level	
Stage 3: Good boy, good girl	9 to 11
Stage 4: Law and order; rules and obedience	11 to 15 and up
III. Postconventional Level	
Stage 5a: Voluntary agreements, determined for self and faithfully held.	adolescence (about 14) and up
Stage 5b: Individual sense of right and wrong; conscience as a higher law	after adolescence
Stage 6: Sacredness of life as a universal value	rarely shown; fullest moral maturity

During the first four years, approximately, there is no "moral" reasoning. The child simply knows or feels that "what I want and like is good." Then, at perhaps age four, children enter the first of three major levels, the *preconventional level.* This is the level before the rules of group living or of society become a direct force upon the young person's life. There are two stages in this level. *Stage 1* is simply based on the avoidance of punishment: If I am frowned at, scolded or hit, I don't do it; if I am smiled at, praised or pleasantly stroked, I do it. The child in Stage 1 simply defers to superior power. *Stage 2* of moral reasoning is based on a simple sense of the fairness of sharing: I'll be nice to you because then you'll be nice to me; I'll scratch your back, you scratch mine.

Typically among middle-class American children, the preconventional level lasts up through grade four or five. However, some people never go beyond Stage 2, and many regress to it in times of stress. Some go beyond it earlier than grade four or five.

The second level of moral reasoning is called the *conventional level,* and this is composed of Stages 3 and 4. During the conventional level, people reason in terms of what they think society expects of them. *Stage 3* is "the-way-I'm-supposed-to-be" stage. The child at this stage wants to be a good girl or good boy. "Moral" is what receives approval and gets one liked. *Stage 4* is the law-and-order stage. People in this stage believe in fixed rules, in respect for authority. Theirs is the moral reasoning of the Ten Commandments rather than of the Golden Rule. Probably most Americans do not go beyond this stage, including very intelligent and successful ones who would argue that there is no better way to arrange society than on the basis of law and order.

The third level of moral reasoning is called the *post-conventional level.* Those who enter this level do so through a process of questioning the accepted rules and conventions and working out for themselves moral principles to which they hold on the basis of their own convictions rather than because they were told by someone else that the principles are right. Again, there are two stages in this level, Stage 5 and Stage 6. Agreements and obligations freely entered into and faithfully held would be characteristic of *Stage 5*. The writers of the United States Constitution, in general, seem to have operated on the basis of this stage of moral reasoning. Obviously, teaching and reading and discussion would help a person move on to Stage 5 from Stage 4.

Kohlberg found it necessary to make two divisions in Stage 5: 5a is that which I have just described; 5b is a morality demonstrated by decisions based on individual conscience, an inner sense of right and wrong, even though the actions it dictates may go against the morality based on a concept of community welfare or the rules of society.

Stage 6 morality is seen only in rare individuals and is based, says Kohlberg, on "belief in the sacredness of human life as representing a universal human value" and a deep commitment to that belief. Such figures as Gautama Buddha, Jesus of Nazareth, Hillel the Elder, Mohandas Gandhi and Martin Luther King come to mind as representatives of this highest stage of morality; doubtless there are many others, probably most of them living or having lived out their lives without ever becoming famous.

Kohlberg's stages of moral reasoning relate to Piaget's stages of logical thinking. As you might expect, it is impossible for people to pass beyond Stage 4 morality, that of law and order, until they have moved into Piaget's period of formal operations, the period when abstract thinking and a high order of questioning are possible. This passage is likely to come with the passage through adolescence. The "adolescent" thinker is one who, finding old barriers tottering, is having to rebuild, to think anew, to find himself again, to establish new relationships with all aspects of his world, including the world inside himself, both the physical part and the mental part. The process makes waves, a rough passage—much rougher for some than for others. The breakdown of the desire to look like a good boy or good girl and of the established order of rules and respect causes *stress* for the individual. We all know that under stress we often regress to more childish behavior. So early adolescents, under the stress of the rough passage, may seem to regress to earlier stages of moral reasoning, a sort of relapse into what appears to be Stage 2. But it is Stage 2—"You scratch my back, I'll scratch yours"—for only a brief period, a sort of backsliding necessary for a move forward to new levels of maturity. Some have suggested that Kohlberg should have included a Stage 4½, the stage of the adolescent relapse, the relativistic crisis.

However, the Kohlberg stages are steps in the development of moral *reasoning*, not necessarily moral *behavior*. The ability to reason in the Kohlberg sense is a necessary condition to moral behavior, but our behavior does not always come up to the best we know, no matter how old we are.

A Somewhat Orderly Progression

The passage from childhood to adulthood is not quixotic; as I have said, it is a progression with a sort of order. This is true of the physical passage—from girl to woman, from boy to man—of the passage in ability to think logically, and also of the passage through the stages of moral reasoning. In our culture, at the beginning of the stretch of rough water, the children's love, loyalties and interests are centered mainly in their families, which provide most of their support and guidance. At the end of the passage, the adults have established their own "families" of some sort, their own loyalties and interests, which are much more independent of those of their families, their own means of support and their own new (or possibly only extended) love relationships.

In some societies (we often call them "primitive," but these days we are feeling less confident about pinning this pejorative label on them when we see the problems that our "advanced" societies cause and suffer from), the passage is quick, clear and sure. There are definite rites —or ceremonies—of passage. Before the rites one is a child; after the rites one has been admitted to the company of women or men. These rites include such events as, with girls, the celebration of the arrival of the first menstruation, a formal training in the skills of providing sexual satisfaction to one's husband, the donning of new apparel or certain symbols of maturity, and even such a radical action as a clitoridectomy. With boys, for whom there is no such spectacular, defined and observable event as the first menstruation (for who is to say when a boyhood erection and orgasm has become a full-fledged ejaculation with semen?), there comes an age or time when the young male may be taken off into the company of men, perhaps circumcised, tutored in the duties and privileges of manhood, and allowed to emerge a man. Among American Plains Indians the boy goes out alone on a "vision quest," finds a spiritual helper and returns, reborn, with a new name, his name as a man. These rites of passage are generally recognized by the society, and there is no doubt when the passage has been completed. It is more like crossing a river than negotiating a run of white water.

In our society, for better or worse, the passage is not so clear-cut or brief. In some groups, however, the passage is quite strictly controlled by social convention and expectation—what the psychologist George Goethals calls *"The Late George Apley* passage." The Apley of J. P. Marquand's novel hardly doubted, nor did those around him doubt, that he would go to one of certain schools and colleges, enter one of certain proper occupations, marry one of a certain group of women, and thus proceed down a smooth social canal from childhood to manhood.

In less privileged segments of our society, as for example in the gangs of Brooklyn, spontaneous rites control and mark the passage.

However, in those parts of our society which we call "middle class," in which most of my readers and I have our being, the transition from childhood to adulthood is long, often tormented, and not clearly defined. It can last for ten years or even longer; it usually involves some sort of "moratorium," as the psychoanalyst Erik Erikson calls it, a time of doing what one doesn't have to do. In speaking of this phase of adolescence, Goethals says, only half joking, "There is nothing better than a misspent youth," and "Woebetide the adolescent who does not rebel!"

Of course the height of adolescent rebellion usually does not come until after the middle and junior high school years. But we experience the beginnings of it in these years often strongly and spectacularly, and it is good to understand the place, forms and functions of rebellion in the scheme of development and, whether we be child, parent or teacher, to consider how best to cope.

3

From Ages Ten to Fifteen: A Closer Look

What do you worry about most?

"**5** My rabbit, dog and cat.
6 I'm getting smaller and the girls are getting bigger.
7 *When* am I going to get my period?
8 Will I ever have a boyfriend?
9 I'm smart enough but what am I going to do with it?"

Sometimes, in my worst moments, especially in February and on rainy days, I tend at school to become a bit irritated by the noisy foibles of junior high school girls and boys and to lump them together as an inconsiderate bunch, bent on trouble, disrespectful of teachers, property and each other. I know that many parents often feel the same way about their adolescents at home. But whenever I take the time to sit down and talk with my students, in a group or especially with an individual, I realize that they are human beings like myself, struggling with their problems, trying hard to make the best of themselves and their surroundings, truly puzzled by the stresses upon them, usually ready to respond to humor with humor, to sympathy with sympathy, and trying to give some fun to life and get some fun out of it. If we discuss the state of the world, the school or their families, I find them, most of the time, trying in the best way they know to make things better. Reading the several hundred questionnaires that the boys and girls in grades five through nine completed and returned to me, usually anonymously, I was vividly reminded how deeply these young people care, even those who put on a show of not caring.

Ten-Year-Olds

In Chapter 2, I described in somewhat general terms the developmental stages that we all go through, especially the changes that occur during the period from ages ten to fifteen. It's very dangerous to generalize about people, but, for a moment, to achieve some perspective, let's compare the typical ten-year-old with the typical fifteen-year-old, recognizing that no girl or boy will totally resemble the description.

Ten-year-olds have not reached puberty: only very few girls have menstruated and even fewer boys have had their first ejaculation with semen. Their lives have not yet been disturbed by the onslaught of sudden growth. In Piaget's terms, they are well established in the period of concrete operations, not so good at abstract thinking and theorizing, great at learning facts and picking up information. There is a positive, unsentimental realism about them, perhaps not as interesting as the later, more complex feelings, but to be enjoyed while it lasts. They tend to be optimistic, happy, pleasantly but simply humorous, enjoying jokes and laughter more than wit and chuckles. They are as easy to get along with as they ever have been or will be again for a decade, or perhaps ever.

They feel good about themselves and about those around them. They can accept reasonable authority and discipline without complicated reactions.

In Kohlberg's terms, they are in Stage 3 of moral reasoning: good boy, good girl—not goody-goody, but good, desiring the approval of their parents and teachers and acting rather realistically, even naturally, to win that approval. They rather expect to be nice to people (although a desire for adventure and mischief is active), and they assume that people will be nice to them.

Boys tend to run with boys, girls to move with girls, but there are some girls who can run faster than some boys, and many of the girls don't particularly like to be cast into the girl mold.

Ten-year-olds like their parents, like their teachers (if they are competent ones), like being at school, like being at home. If they are in trouble, or if there is a conflict of interest between home and people outside, they tend to rely on home and parents for their support and reassurance. The family is still their center.

Physical Growth and Development, Ages Ten to Fifteen

During the interval between ten and fifteen there is usually a radical change in the rate of growth. As far as we know, the pattern of this change has not altered over the generations. Girls, in general, have always developed physically about two years earlier than boys. However, some boys develop earlier than some girls. Even more important is the fact that some boys have completed their physical adolescent development before others have even started theirs. For example, some boys have completed their adolescent spurt in height by age thirteen and a half (having started at perhaps age ten and a half), while others have not even started theirs until age sixteen and will not complete it until age seventeen and a half. A similar variation, although not quite so great, exists for girls. (See the chart of sequence of events at adolescence on page 223, Chapter 10.)

Thus, says J. M. Tanner, Professor of Child Health and Growth of the University of London and an authority on the physical growth of children: "The statement that a boy is fourteen is in most contexts hopelessly vague. All depends . . . on whether he is preadolescent, midadolescent, or postadolescent." Typically, girls reach their *top rate of growth* at about age twelve, boys at age fourteen, but there is the same individual variation I spoke of above. Also, it is interesting to note that the average age for going through the turmoil of physical growth has lowered over the past century at a rate of three to four months each decade. So today people reach puberty about three years earlier than people did a century ago.

While there is a ground plan of growth characteristics of the human species as a whole, each person has a style of growth of his or her own. Boys and girls need lots of reassurance about this. Some are afraid of it and embarrassed by their early and rapid development; an even larger number are terribly concerned that they are behind most of their classmates and will never make it to normal physical adulthood. It is a comforting fact that the late maturers among both boys and girls will not be less manly or womanly, whatever these adjectives may mean to readers young or old, than those who mature early. Take an example in the simple matter of height. Dick (not his real name) at age eleven was a fraction of an inch shorter than John. At age twelve, he was just a little taller. By age fourteen, however, he had grown to be four inches taller than John. You can imagine how disturbing this was to John, who may have felt himself now to be a shrimp. However, by age fifteen, Dick's rate of growth began to slow while John's reached peak velocity. By the time both were seventeen, they were the same height.

The same sorts of differences in maturing occur in girls. The average period of time from the first sign of puberty, when the breast buds begin to appear, to menarche (the first menstruation) averages two and a half years, but it ranges from six months to five and a half years. The span from the beginnings of puberty to full physical maturity varies from one and a half to six years. Physically, some people bloom early, some late, some slowly, some fast, but all eventually bloom.

An interesting, perhaps minor, point is that in many people even the face doesn't mature evenly. They pass through periods of seeming to be all nose or all teeth and almost chinless. But usually the horsey or rabbity phase passes, and it is well not to jump to conclusions.

In the typical growth spurt, the legs reach their peak of growth first, but the trunk grows more than the legs. The breadth of the body follows leg length, and shoulder width comes last. "Thus," says Tanner, "a boy stops growing out of his trousers (at least in length) a year before he stops growing out his jackets." The parts of the body that reach adult size first are feet, hands and head.

The physical awkwardness that results from these rather sudden and diverse spurts in growth of different parts of the body can be embarrassing to adolescents and annoying to adults. These boys and girls, especially boys, upset chairs, knock over desks, try to walk through tables, and step on toes. They are not at all sure just where their physical extremities are located. They seem to have increased enormously in size and strength and not at all in judgment.

The question arises among girls and boys and their parents: Is it an advantage or a disadvantage to be an early maturer? The answer is mixed. Larger, stronger boys tend to become the leaders of their group. They are not necessarily more popular, but they tend to dominate. They appear to be more confident; they are more often chosen for positions of responsibility. The early-maturing girls tend also to be leaders; they are more sought after by boys, especially by older boys. (They can be quite terrifying to their less-developed male age-mates. In this connection, it has been suggested that the gang activity of preadolescent boys is a sort of collective defense against the more mature females. The boys need to cluster to protect their feelings of masculinity.)

By comparison, the late maturers seem to have a somewhat poorer concept of themselves during adolescence; they tend to hold onto their families longer, and their parents hold onto them longer, probably because both realize that they need each other longer. In general, they are more sensitive, both toward others and in their own feelings.

One disadvantage that the early maturers suffer is that since they enter at an earlier age the turmoils that come with adolescent growth, they have had less life experience to prepare them for these shaking events.

How does it all come out later on? Studies of people in their early thirties suggest that those who matured early tend still to be dominant men or women; they tend to be well settled into their vocations, to be in managerial situations, and to be somewhat more rigid and controlled than average people. The late maturers, on the other hand, tend to be more flexible, more oriented to activities of the mind, somewhat freer in their orientation to the world, and to maintain a more playful stance toward things. There is no difference in the marital status of the two groups. (Please note the words *suggest* and *tend to* rather than *show* and *are;* there are so many exceptions to the general statements I have made that any firm predictions about how later life will be for an individual, if they are based only on the age of physical maturing, are unsafe.)

I have just said that parents should not be concerned, and should do their best to help their child not to be concerned, if their child's development seems too early or too late. In a few cases, where a child's growth and development are drastically out of step with those of his classmates and where this may be causing feelings of inadequacy or oddness, a general physical checkup is a good idea, with endocrinal studies if the doctor thinks them desirable. If one parent or both parents were quite early or late in physical or sexual maturing, it is quite likely that their children will be, and it can be a comfort to physically immature children to know that their parents, who are obviously physically and sexually mature adults, also developed late.

Fifteen-Year-Olds

On pages 42–43, I described the "typical" ten-year-old. Now we are ready for a look at the typical fifteen-year-old, not that there is any such being. I described the ten-year-old without differentiating much between girls and boys, but that would be impossible for fifteen-year-olds. Physically, the majority of the girls are quite mature. They have passed puberty; almost all have passed their period of greatest speed of growth. However, there is a minority who still look much more like children than young adults. The contrast with boys is striking. While there are some boys who are already "men" and may have been shaving a couple of times a week since seventh grade, most are still in the midst of their growth spurt, and a few haven't started it yet.

Socially, the girls are much more mature. Most are interested in the other sex, more often in boys who are older. Their interest is rather more social than sexual. Very soon after boys reach puberty, they begin to have an active sex life, most of it involving masturbation, wet dreams and fantasy, much less of it involving outright sexual contact with girls. By the time they are eighteen, almost all boys have experienced frequent orgasms, while most girls have not. Even at age fifteen, the boys are much more active sexually than are the girls, if we measure activity in terms of what Kinsey called "sexual outlets"—that is, orgasms. Kinsey found that females do not reach a level of orgastic sexual activity equal to that of late adolescent boys until they are well into their thirties, and perhaps not then.

By age fifteen, most middle-class American girls and boys have entered or are entering Piaget's period of formal operations. They are critically examining themselves and even more critically, so it would seem, everything and everybody around them that at age ten they had taken pretty much for granted. Subjects for examination include especially their parents, other members of their family and their school. Many fifteen-year-olds display a newly sensitive eagerness and responsiveness to people. There is a fresh burst of intellectual enthusiasm and congeniality with adults. The sense of humor now takes on a new richness and depth, and there is a hunger for serious discussion of important questions. Further, if parents get satisfaction from being needed, never are they more needed than during these adolescent years when more and more often there are glimpses of a new, deeper dimension of parent-child relationships. Child and parent begin to enjoy each other as people who can know each other well and respect each other.

A Period of Turmoil

Adolescents are no longer mere children. They are beginning to assert their individualities and need to be appreciated as increasingly self-directed individuals. If they can know that parents and teachers are trying to understand them and help each of them as a unique person with unique problems of supreme importance to him or her, then adults will find them at times responsive, for they have a great hunger to be understood. However, they still, though they will consider it childish to ask for it openly, strongly desire the approval of adults, and parents and teachers should approve wherever they sincerely can.

Whether or not they show it, most adolescents are at times quite insecure and frightened; everything is so new. A seventh-grade girl confided to her mother: "Sometimes I get scared; I'm not a leader, and I don't like to be a follower. What am I?" This question is typical of the hunger of the adolescent for self-understanding. Yet adolescents are clever at concealing their hungers and their worries. The direct, probing question from the adult will seldom elicit a cordial response and almost never a revealing one. Frequently, adolescents appear callous, indifferent, insensitive and even hostile. But it is safe to assume that, actually, each one is sensitive, probably easily hurt, and longing for support and someone to confide in. It's safe to assume that they are uneasy and worried. But they often cover up their surges of feeling, which embarrass and puzzle them, with an I-don't-care attitude. They may appear to be thoughtful and distracted, but they won't tell you their thoughts if you ask. They may be dreaming about a triumphant role on the stage or screen, or a homerun they're hitting, about the approving roars from the crowd, about sex, about how to impress a boy or girl, or about how much their families would appreciate them if they ran away or were killed. But they'd be mortified if they found that parents knew their thoughts —even more, probably, than adults would be if their secret thoughts were known.

As I have said, fifteen-year-olds have begun, often quite suddenly, to reject authority. Such rejection is usually an essential and constructive part of growing up. They no longer look automatically to their parents and teachers as the standard-setters but will often flout the standards of adults and turn feverishly toward their peers for approval.

Interest in cliques becomes much more intense. Their members have a compulsion to cluster and conform. For some adolescents, the clique serves important functions. It is a small group of congenial friends in whom they can confide and upon whom they can count for understanding and consolation. With their fellow experimenters and fellow sufferers they can try out their new ideas and attitudes. It gives them a feeling of security, which they crave as they flounder along the passage between childhood and adulthood. Certainly, annoying and cruel as adolescent cliques may sometimes seem, membership in a clique is a quite normal step toward maturity, much healthier than a continued dependence upon parents would be. It will help parents through this trying period to see the clique in perspective and to treat its members with respect, even while enjoying some of its humorous aspects.

By age fifteen, adolescence has become a time of emotional ups and downs for many. Elation and optimism are often followed by sullen moods and depression. Boys and girls go through periods when they won't talk to their parents or when they seem utterly and wretchedly disgusted with adults and all they stand for. Then suddenly will come a period of cheerful confiding and appreciation. There is no small amount of screaming and temper, and many adolescents will on occasion rush out of the room or away from the table in a surge of anger, possessed by a feeling that the world is too much for them and that no one, but no one, understands. Sometimes the indignation of adolescents can be devastating to the composure of their parents, who feel they can forgive the anger but assume, since they see themselves as the conscientious parents that they are, that right is on the parental side. However, righteous indignation may be even less acceptable to parents than the attitude of sullen defiance exhibited by some boys and girls who seem to be saying by their injured expression and attitude, "Go on, hit me!" Adults should remember that adolescent instability helps make possible the development of good new understandings. Better to emote into maturity than to stagnate in placid conformity.

Sloppiness becomes spectacular in many adolescents. Bedrooms are a mess, and so are desks and classrooms if the teacher permits them to get that way. Well over half of the eighth- and ninth-graders replying to my questionnaire reported that their parents thought that their room was "rather messy" or "very messy," whereas only a third of fifth-graders said that, and 86 percent of eighth- and ninth-graders agreed that their parents were right, because "things pile up after a while"; "I leave my stuff all over the place. There is a trail where I have been"; "I have a lot of stuff and a small room and I can find things better on the floor"; "I feel more relaxed if things are scattered around naturally"; and, most commonly, "because I *am* messy." Many boys and girls at this age seem carefully to cultivate sloppiness of dress, perhaps to avoid being conspicuous away from home. Yet this sloppiness is combined with a developing painstaking concern about hair and complexion. One of the curses of adolescence is acne, which in some children is unavoidable, no matter how carefully the face is cleansed and medicated and the diet controlled. A word of reassurance will help: almost all bad complexions improve after a year or so—often sooner—and bad skin is much more noticeable to the person who wears the face than to those who look at it.

Earlier, I said that self-respect and self-understanding are an essential basis for respecting and understanding others. It is well to see the self-centeredness of adolescence in this light. These years are years of turmoil and self-examination. There are so many things to understand about oneself that there is little energy and imagination left over for considering others. And this self-examination, especially if sympathetically encouraged, will often lead to a much deeper quality of unselfishness and appreciation of others than is possible to the fifth- or sixth-graders, who may still be unselfish because they have been taught that this is a good way to be.

Before going on to talk more specifically about school, I want to report on how the girls and boys in grades five through nine responded to three questions about themselves, because I think the responses will shed some light on what it's like to be of these ages; and to know better what it's like can help parents and teachers understand the young and relate to them. The questions are:

1. *Would you say that you find your life in the grade you are now in a happy time in general?*

2. *What would you say are the two or three things in life that worry you most?*

3. *If you could change two or three things about your life, what would they be?*

Are You Happy?

On the happiness question, I was rather surprised to find that most boys and girls in these grades consider themselves happy. Seventy-nine percent of the entire group consider themselves either "very happy" or "rather happy"; only 6 percent (and twice the proportion of girls as of boys) consider themselves "very unhappy." As one would expect from our general knowledge of developmental stages, fifth-graders, 90 percent of them, put themselves in the very-or-rather-happy category, while only 80 percent of the sixth-graders do, 70 percent of the eighth-graders, and 75 percent of the ninth-graders. Not a single fifth-grader chose the category "very unhappy" for himself or herself.

What Worries You?

It is not easy to put responses to this question into categories because the answers are expressed in such a variety of terms and language. However, here's a list roughly in order of frequency of mention and by grade.

Fifth grade. The most common response was "nothing," but well over half of the fifth-graders could think of something that worried them, the most often mentioned being death, sickness and injury, with a scattering centering on family problems. One boy worried about "being a thief" and a girl about "Will we have to get rid of our dog?"

Sixth grade. Almost all the sixth-graders had worries, and "school" and "marks," in one aspect or another, topped all the others, with death and dying a close second. The girls are beginning to worry about boys, and the boys about girls. Family problems loom fairly large, and there is some mention of crime, sexual attacks (girls) and sexual intercourse (boys). One girl expressed her worries as "having my period, getting married and having a baby," while another worried about "getting overly plump." Yet another was bothered about "being invaded by insects or something." Generally the girls expressed more worries, or expressed them more fluently, than the boys.

Seventh grade. School and death (nobody mentioned taxes) are again the most frequently mentioned worries. "My future" in one way or another worried many, as did making it socially or with friends, both among girls and boys. The boys were worried by their appearance ("I have big ears"; "my complexion disgusts me"), while girls more often mentioned some aspect of sex, usually social.

One boy said he worried about "being beat up by this kid—or being a burguraler"; another about "our country's health"; and yet another said, "I try to analyze death. Is it when the heart stops or the brain stops?" A girl wrote, "I want life not to be a big bustle and hurry but just to go along easily," but another was concerned "that I'll die without ever really living." Two other girls said, "I worry that I'll be frigid" and "Will my parents find out I've been kissed?"

Eighth grade. Worries in this grade become much more numerous and more fluently expressed. School, grades and death are at the top but frequently joined by concerns about social acceptance or popularity. College and career begin to loom as a concern of boys; personal appearance worries both boys and girls; and some girls say they are troubled by sex, especially the possibility of sexual attack on the streets.

A boy said, "I keep thinking about school and thinking that if I did better in school maybe I'd be more liked by everyone and not just teachers." One said he feared "math teachers and many-legged creatures that hang onto the ceiling over my bed." Yet another boy worried about "how we can all get along in our house without so many arguments and fights which are giving me a pain." A girl wanted "not to have this school messed up so I can say I was proud I went here." Two comments about personal appearance were: "I would like to be beautiful and have a figure you can wear under a sweater" and "I am worried that I am not handsome (but my aunt told me I was but nobody else ever said so)." Another boy had a quite specific worry: "So much land being closed to motorcycles." Yet another said he worried about "girls, the first day of school, and failure, in that order."

Ninth grade. School is by far the greatest worry among the boys, with future—especially career—a close second. For the girls, death is a major concern. Both boys and girls worry about popularity and about drugs.

A boy expressed the worry when he asked, "Will I make it?" Other boys said they worried about "my parents finding out about my smoking, drugs and drinking"; "money" (this subject was not mentioned at any grade level as often as I expected it would be); "getting a girl pregnant"; and "dying a painful death."

Some girls expressed their worries thus: "I worry that I'm being cruel to people without knowing it"; "what my parents are going to do to me next"; "living—I live dangerously"; and "I wonder if I'm going to be something special or nothing."

Although these few quotations are by no means a scientifically chosen sampling, they do, I think, give a valid general impression of the worries of these young people.

What Would You Like to Change?

Perhaps the most frequently mentioned desire for change is *"to be more popular,"* the older girls and boys mentioning it most frequently: "I'd fit in perfectly with everyone"; "I'd have mobs of friends"; "I'd be able to talk more freely with people."

The second most frequent desire for change is *"my appearance,"* which was mentioned often by all grades and both sexes: "I'd change little parts of my body"; "I'd bulge out my biceps more"; "I'd be prettier"; "I want to have decent legs and skinnier feet."

In one way or another, many girls and boys wanted to change *their personality.* "Give me a cooler head"; "to like myself"; "to be less rigid and more bouncy"; "to act my age and not 5 years older"; "I wouldn't be a snob."

The area of *family relationships* was very often listed: "Get rid of my sisters"; "that my little brother didn't wear glasses so I could hit him"; "we'd live near a lake and my father would like fishing"; "we'd make our home-life more happy even at the risk of making it stereotype"; "I would adjust and edify my mother to a state of near sanity"; "have mom trust me again"; "that Mom was not so old-fashioned." Many of the children whose parents were divorced wished that the divorce had never happened or "that I'd have my dad back again."

Perhaps most frequently mentioned, but not as urgently as the changes listed above, were *school and marks.* Several students wanted to change schools, especially those in grades seven and eight, but most often it was a desire to have higher grades or simply to "be smarter." Many expressed their wish "not to be lazy," usually as if laziness were a condition with which one is afflicted rather than something a person might do something about.

Quite a few people wanted to move, usually to the country; many wanted more money; a number wanted to do better with the opposite sex; a sprinkling would change the condition of the world. Several girls wished they were boys; no boy said he wanted to be a girl. In general, the older the adolescents, the more introspective were their comments.

Here is a group of comments about desired changes which, even though quite individual and not expressed in ordinary language, do, I think, reflect the state of mind of more people than just those who wrote them. In this series of quotations and most of those that follow, I have started with fifth-graders and ended with ninth-graders. People said they'd like to change: "My comic collection"; "how my classmates refer to me"; "I'd eliminate school and replace it with money"; "get a new mother, change my personality, and get ten cats"; "my school, my bust, and have my toenails stop smelling"; "I'd be at the top of my class so I wouldn't have to worry about friends"; "I'd be a boy and not quite so smart"; "that I studied harder in my earlier years"; "not so nervous talking about girls to my parents"; "spend my earlier years in a better school, like the one I'm in now"; "get better grades with hardly working"; "get rid of war and hatred"; "less drug use for social and mental crutches"; "I would never have fallen in love with this boy"; "that I hadn't told my parents I drink."

The teacher or parent who reads these comments must often feel, as I felt when I read them, "I'd like to talk with that boy or that girl." That's a good feeling, provided that the preposition is *with* and not *to,* and provided that the talk involves listening. Too many of us older people are too ready—with the very best intentions—to take advantage of the boy's or girl's brief moment of self-revelation to make a speech, to give advice or to say something like, "But you really shouldn't feel that way," and then go on to say how the teen-ager should feel. No matter how people *should* feel, how they *do* feel is the fact and a fact that doesn't change by being denied. If we are able to find some words to show that we really do understand how the girl or boy feels, that we sympathize, then the young person is more likely to express further feelings. This is communication, perhaps the principal basis for understanding.

And if sons and daughters can find the strength and unselfishness to show that they understand how their parents and teachers feel (for parents and teachers are often insecure, deep-feeling people who also are longing for understanding, especially from those younger than themselves), how much happier and more satisfied we all would be together.

4

In School: Grades Five through Nine

"**5** This is my happiest year in school!

6 Teachers sometimes like act like they never went to school and had problems.

7 Never scream at a growing child.

8 Teachers try to scare the lesson into us and not teach.

9 He's a good teacher. He treats us like people with feelings, not dogs or cats."

If you asked a committee of fifth-graders to go out and count how many gravestones there were in the nearby cemetery (the school in which I teach happens to be surrounded by graveyards) and how many of the people there died between 1800 and 1900, they'd rush right out, bright-eyed, pencil in hand, to do the research. They'd return breathless, eager to report the results of their counting. The class might well whip out their notebooks and conscientiously write down the figures and have the feeling they were doing something important. Ask some seventh-graders to do the same thing and they'd groan, object and, if necessary, procrastinate, but probably not bother to formulate the reasons why such an activity would be worthless. But ask ninth-graders to do it, and their first reaction would be (unless they thought you were joking) to inquire why the job should be done and what relation it might have to the purposes of the course.

To older junior high school students even more than to most people, concentration on details is painful, and they have a low tolerance for pain. It could well have been a teacher of eighth grade in a bad moment who said that the human brain is the least-used muscle in the human body, at least if you construe "use" to mean "employ for the purpose of acquiring or memorizing strictly academic knowledge." Yet the increased powers of analysis and synthesis, the deepening sense of humor, and the really passionate interest in people and their relationships make junior high schoolers rewarding to reach *if* teachers and parents do not become despondent, disgusted or angry when the earlier conscientiousness disappears and seemingly sloppy, incompetent work takes its place. For a high percentage of early adolescents, this messy stage is an essential part of growing up.

From Enthusiasm to Relapse

According to Erik Erikson, during the years between the end of the period of infantile sexuality and the arrival of puberty, the young person's mind is very ready for acquiring information and the skills of learning. It is a time for schools to capitalize on, for the mental soil is fertile and cultivated by a good deal of experience, and it is less disturbed than it has been or ever will be again by weeds noxious to academic growth.

Therefore, grades five, six and, to a degree, seven are especially good ones in which to emphasize the development of skills of language and number, and habits of learning. These, unfortunately, often are dull, but they do not have to be. A skilled, enthusiastic teacher who uses ingenuity (and a variety of tasks, games, activities, rewards and appeals to the students' pride in achieved competence) can be the motivator and facilitator of great accomplishments. If there is ever a time for memorization and rote learning—and it's a bit risky to admit that there is, because such admission is likely to bring out the worst in unimaginative teachers—this is it.

Soon after the arrival of puberty, the Kohlberg "Stage 4½" of adolescent relapse (poor academic performance, in a narrow sense) becomes quite typical, and antischool feelings are soon likely to reach their height. One of the greatest frustrations for parents is to watch their children seemingly disintegrate academically and not know what to do about it. All too often it appears that the school doesn't know what to do about it either. A conscientious mother complained to me: "Last week, on Tuesday and Thursday, Mary told me she'd done all her homework at school. The other nights she just dashed off her math in ten minutes, and it was a disgrace. Now, when I used to go to school I would never have gotten away with that. But when I asked Mary about it she said, 'Oh, it's just homework, and the teacher doesn't mind as long as we think we understand.' Then, her English papers were terrible. She just scribbled down anything and handed it in."

The mother was right in complaining that her daughter was not working to capacity. A constant challenge to school and parent—and it's been left mostly to the school—is trying to stimulate the best possible work from junior high school students. The boys and girls themselves are aware that they are not working well, as replies to my questionnaire show. I asked, *Do you think you are working up to capacity in school—that is, doing as well as you can?* Among boys the percentage of *yes* replies declines from 67 in grade five to 20 in grade nine, and among girls from 74 in grade five to 35 in grade eight, after which it rises to 50 in grade nine. There is an almost identical grade-by-grade decrease of *yes* answers to two other questions: *Do your parents think you are working up to capacity?* and *Do your teachers?* It's interesting, too, that the students believe that their parents are more likely to think they are working to capacity (57 percent) than are teachers (47 percent).

The low quality of schoolwork, often combined with loud and uncouth behavior, explains why so many teachers can hardy wait to find an escape from junior high school teaching and move to the calmer, nobler realms of the upper grades, and why so many elementary school teachers observe with alarm their formerly tractable, pleasant pupils now hanging around the junior high halls, and wonder what's wrong with the teachers "up there."

Why Such Poor Performance?

Of course, the reason that the quality of schoolwork goes down is the emergence of the major distractions I have already described: the sudden physical growth, the rapid sexual development, the readjustment of relationships with adults and peers, and the surge toward independence. To expect a smoothly competent academic performance when such turmoil is going on is, in most cases, to expect the impossible. It's a rare teacher who can make history, science, writing, spelling and punctuation consistently fascinating enough (or who has the physical and emotional stamina necessary to apply sufficient pressure) to prevail over these other urgencies.

Wishing to please the teacher is a rather low order of motivation anyway, quite extraneous to the matters being studied, and commonly it is not until ninth grade, and sometimes much later, that the simple desire to please is replaced by a genuine, steady realization that good schoolwork helps you to get into college or to get a good job. Further, many students are as yet innocent of, or have forgotten, the satisfaction that comes from hard brainwork and the discipline of learning. It is only in ninth, tenth or even eleventh grade that many will develop a driving, genuinely intellectual curiosity and a pleasure from dealing with ideas. Thus seventh-, eighth- and ninth-graders tend to be between motivations, and this makes designing a good educational scheme for them a challenge to all involved.

Can We Prevail over "Other Urgencies"?

Some teachers, backed by strong groups in many communities, try to prevail simply by holding the academic line and applying superior force. They would seem to agree with that opinionated genius Samuel Johnson, who complained about boys' education in England in the late eighteenth century: "There is now less flogging in our schools than formerly—but then less is learned there; so what the boys get at one end they lose at the other."

However, some schools have taken another tack and have made creative efforts to deal directly with the other urgencies by making them a major part of the curriculum. Such programs are planned so that more initiative and choice are put into the hands of the students; the materials for the courses in science, history, literature, writing, and even mathematics, are chosen for their direct relevance to the felt needs of young adolescents; the walls of academic departments are to an extent breached; and the "lockstep schedule," as the opponents of tradition call it, is unlocked so that students, in effect, march more to their own drummers rather than to the rhythm of bells. Many of these programs have great potential and some seem already to be working well. At this writing it is too early to say for sure whether in the long run they will succeed when the verve of experiment has gone out of them.

When they don't work, and where a firm, planned, orderly, demanding, rather traditional scheme of education is replaced by a well-intentioned but inadequately thought-out "openness," the results are very bad, I think. As T. S. Eliot once said, "So many of us in our day suppose that we are emancipated when really we are merely unbuttoned."

If parents, teachers and students are involved in an educational plan that has replaced a traditional one with a less-structured and quite possibly more productive one, all should be alert to the need for *monitoring*—keeping track of—the progress of each student. Monitoring the development of skills, achievement in various subjects, behavior and degree of interest is not easy to manage. It probably requires a more complex structure, more carefully worked out and conscientiously administered, than the old-fashioned, simple structure of thirty-kids-and-a-teacher with a migration to another room every forty-five minutes.

What Makes a Good Teacher?

In the questionnaires, I asked students, *What are the most important qualities of a good teacher?* Here are their answers, listed in order of frequency of mention:

nice, kind, helpful, etc.
strict, firm, in control
interesting, makes learning fun
patient
not overly demanding

knows subject
fair, has no pets
understanding
good balance between control and freedom
relates well to students

When I tabulated the replies in two groups, one for grades five, six and seven, and one for grades eight and nine, I found that the younger students rated "understanding" much higher than the older ones. The older students rated firmness or being in control very high, while the younger group did not often mention it. It is not at all surprising that students in adolescent turmoil feel the need of being well controlled by teachers no matter how much they may complain about the control. However, if teachers who are prone to strictness take too much heart from this statistic, they may find themselves exerting excessive external control, which looks good in the classroom and to the class but which also can retard the development of self-control and maturity.

Here are some comments made by students about what makes a good teacher: "Gets ideas from class so she can improve herself"; "harsh and gentle at the right times"; "thinks before yelling"; "forceful in the subjects but agreeable to the kids"; "doesn't teach all by control"; "teaches you to learn from your mistakes"; "knows about a young mind"; "no wishywashyness"; "not inflicting personal problems on the class"; "one who is serious when it is time to be serious and clowns around when it is time to clown around"; "not an old square goat."

What Makes a Poor Teacher?

I also asked the question, *What are the most important characteristics of a poor teacher?* Some students simply said, "The opposite of the good qualities," but many listed bad qualities with considerable enthusiasm. Here are the items on which significant numbers of the students agreed, again in descending order of frequency of mention:

can't keep order
boring
yells, gets angry easily
unfair, has favorites
mean, not helpful
doesn't know subject
lacks intelligence
mind rigid and closed
too strict

The younger students objected most to teachers' anger and yelling, while the older ones were most put off by teachers who were boring or unable to control the class, two defects which are usually closely related.

Some of the comments about poor teachers seem harsh, especially when one realizes that probably the teachers involved are for the most part unaware of the effect of their actions and attitudes on the students: "Lets the kids do whatever they want"; "stops talking whenever there's the slightest noise"; "treats you like animals"; "doesn't explain things"; "intolerant of mistakes"; "covering up own mistakes"; "not willing to face up to the students' criticism"; "cries in class"; "grinding—too powerful, rules the kids like prisoners"; "always trying to find the bad in what kids do"; "too quick and rushy"; "he just wants the money."

Parents' Views on Teachers

I asked parents exactly the same questions about teachers as those I asked the kids. They rated the good qualities in this order: fairness, being interesting, caring, patience, knowledge of subject, and being loving. The poor qualities were unfairness, poor discipline, impatience and dullness.

Some parents expressed some frustration and annoyance at teachers. One said, "Oh, my God!—rigid, humorless, self-hating, needing to have ego nourished at all times." Another said: "A poor teacher usually 'knows it all' and won't listen to either students or parents. They talk too much about too little, or about their own experiences, sounding as though each student should fit into the same patterns they have previously encountered. Worse yet, some teachers pretend to listen and say 'yes' to every suggestion and then ignore them all."

What Teachers Say and Do That Is Helpful

Teachers who read this book will be interested in how students answered this question: *What is the most helpful thing a teacher ever said or did to you?* By far the most frequently mentioned remarks were of teachers giving the student encouragement: "Told me I was doing excellent"; "encouraged me up." Here are other comments or actions: "Try your hardest and don't worry"; "said to ignore teasing"; "told me about life"; "taught me how to be free in my own classroom"; "told me if I didn't start to care, I'd flunk"; "told me I had ability" (a frequently mentioned comment); "talked to you as if you were equal"; "agreed with me that grades are as artificial as the dollar"; "if you ever have a problem, come back and see me"; "work when you work, play when you play"; "found time to help *me;* made me feel I was not just another student"; "gave me support when my life was going downhill (or so I thought)"; "asked me why I was so sad"; "thought I looked sick and sent me to infirmary. I was glad"; "I was mad and a certain teacher told me about his childhood and was honest with me"; "kicked me out of class"; "gave me a book that gave me a whole new outlook on life."

Parents also replied to the same question about helpful teacher comments or actions. They agreed with the kids that words of encouragement are the most helpful. (Of course, encouragement must be based on facts, not on wishful thinking, but I have seldom seen a student about whom there was nothing encouraging to say.) Here are some parent comments: "Strangely enough, it was to say that the child should repeat a grade. Finally he is in the right slot"; "that our 13-year-old became frustrated easily"; "the advisor gave us an objective evaluation" (this comment was made frequently); "recognized that our son had more intellectual energy than was being sopped up in classwork and fashioned a special course for him without anyone, including our son, even noticing"; "told us to get him to talk to someone besides us about his problems"; "a concrete piece of evidence (test scores) that my daughter was bright instead of general assurances"; "school psychologist told us that we *can* solve our problems if we set aside some time for sharing and exploring"; "told me my son had done no work for a month"; "told our son he was a bright boy. It seemed to make him even brighter"; "no. 2 son looked sad for grades 4, 5 and 6. A fifth-grade teacher said, 'Individualistic children are very often unhappy at this age. Nothing you can do can help. By high school these individualists become more content.' It was true!"

I asked parents a question not asked of the students: *What was the most* un*helpful thing a teacher ever did or said?* Here are some replies that are either typical or instructive or both: "A teacher delighted in making damaging personal remarks. Parental intervention marked the child for additional abuse. 'Dummy' was her favorite epithet—also 'fatty,' 'shrimp,' etc. (Would you believe it, she is now a guidance counselor!)"; "told me the sixth-grade booklist contained 'every good book for sixth-grade reading' "; "a far too unstructured, permissive lower school teacher permitted kids to fall behind in basic disciplines"; "said to our child, 'Your brother was a trouble-maker' "; "telling me our daughter was so *cute* I should not worry that she couldn't read."

Advice to Teachers

Another question I asked students about teachers was, *If you were writing a book for teachers, what advice would you give them?* Here are some replies that seem to me to give aptly expressed good advice or an understanding of the state of mind of the student writers:

Fifth grade. "Try to be understanding"; "don't pick on one person"; "always try to help and encourage your students"; "don't get angry at kids when they do little things"; "be strict if they get bad"; "try to act more like a kid."

Sixth grade. "Don't pick on favorites or crack stupid jokes"; "make it fun to work and don't yell"; "don't be so mean by embarrassing students in front of the whole class."

Seventh grade. "Try to help with everything, not just schoolwork"; "take a course in adolescent psychiatry"; "listen and learn and like us."

Eighth grade. "As long as you're learning from the students you're teaching fine"; "present good behavior with rewards, not bad behavior with punishment"; "stick to threats"; "be mindful of our workload"; "befriend the whole class, not just the attention-seekers"; "don't talk all the time, let the students make their points"; "talk to a kid, try to find out their problems. That's the biggest thing"; "be like a teacher and adult friend, not a student"; "act the same way all year. Don't start soft and pleasant and then go back to your normal grisly selves."

Ninth grade. "Get the message across, no matter how"; "bring things down to our level without being phony"; "don't let your more articulate students bullshit too much."

How Teachers Annoy

There's no doubt that some teachers can greatly annoy some students and parents. To find out how, I asked, *What annoys you most about teachers?* Here are some replies that may be helpful to teacher-readers of this book, either because they can think, "Well, I never do *that,*" and be satisfied, or, "Uh-oh, that's me!" and be more careful.

Fifth grade. "They talk too much, no time to ask questions"; "when they misunderstand you and scold you for it"; "talking when I want to talk"; "they're so goody-goody"; "when they're nicer to someone else"; "when they tell you not to do something and then they do it."

Sixth grade. "When they tell other people you're bad or rude or compare you to other people who are really smart and she's good so why can't you be like her"; "they don't let you make up your own mind"; "our teacher tells us about her boyfriends and it really bugs me"; "they act big because they think they have control over me"; "when they walk off while talking."

Seventh grade. "They don't seem to have any feelings"; "they don't admit they're wrong"; "some goof instead of teaching"; "constant cry of 'shut up!' "; "they joke when I want to be serious" (I was surprised at the large number of students who objected to teachers' joking); "not to stick to threats"; "to jump to conclusions"; "they can do anything they want"; "blindness to how poorly the class is doing"; "yelling" (by far the most common annoyance at all grades).

Ninth grade. "Some are most unfair and don't realize the pressure of a young teenager"; "when they're wrong and you know it and they get all pissed off if you try to tell them"; "if we give any grief to them we get in trouble"; "sound like computers."

And some parents say: "They think they know more about your child than you do—usually after the first report period when they've seen the child 5 hours per week with 20-plus other children"; "saying one thing to parents, another thing to children"; "won't admit they make mistakes"; "being told what *they* think I want to hear"; "when they speak but don't listen"; "a wariness toward parents; often reluctant to discuss child in real terms"; "too easily influenced by 'smooth talkers'—both parents and students"; "some make me feel as if they all belong to some country club and I don't—intellectual snobbery"; "they do not listen to the wisdom of mothers"; "when they're not completely truthful in reports. It can be hard to be critical but it is important for a teacher to give warning signals."

If Parents or Students Are Dissatisfied with a Teacher

What should parents or students do if they are so dissatisfied with a teacher that they feel they would like to change? First, before they come to even a tentative conclusion on the matter, they should try to be sure of their feelings. They should never forget that a teacher who may seem to be a disaster for one student (perhaps for a friend or older child in the family who had the teacher in a previous year) could well have great success with another, for students have different styles of learning and relating.

Also, fortunately, it is very rare that a single year with a teacher has a really damaging effect on a student—much rarer than most parents and students seem to think. In fact, maturing and learning often result from adversity and the need to adjust to a new sort of person in authority (or perhaps failing to exercise authority).

Second, students and parents must remember that it is almost always impossible to allow students to have free choice of teachers, for there are always some teachers who will be more popular than others, and obviously all students cannot get the popular teachers. Even if it is ultimately shown to be possible and desirable to arrange a change of teachers, the school must, in self-defense, say no at the outset. So parents and students should not feel discouraged too soon.

How best to go about investigating the possibility of a change will depend on how the lines of communication and authority are set up in the school. In general, though, if I were a parent who thought he wanted a change, I would first confer with the teacher involved. I'd carefully explain my concern in terms of the child's reactions and needs, and I'd ask the teacher what to do about them. I'd scrupulously avoid complaint but keep the discussion in terms of the child's education. This has several advantages: it doesn't put the teacher on the defensive; it alerts the teacher to the child's needs and is likely to enable him to meet them better in case no change is made (intelligent squeaking does get grease; shrill squeaking may put sand in the bearings); it enables parents and perhaps the student, too, to know the teacher a little better and perhaps to appreciate him more and to see how to benefit from whatever strengths there may be.

If this first step brings no improvement, then I'd go to the person next up the line of authority, particularly one who has both schedule-changing powers and some knowledge of teachers and students. I'd quietly, factually express my concern and make my case, expressing my recognition of how nearly impossible it must be for the school to meet such requests. Good administrators will admit that all teachers are not perfect, will probably defend the teacher involved and express doubts about the possibility of making a change. But at the same time they will leave the door open.

Then I'd wait, keep a prudent silence, especially not talking with any other parents, for a groundswell of opinion makes change impossible. In a week or ten days, if the change hasn't been made, I'd call back to inquire. If the answer is no, I'd stop trying unless you are convinced that disaster for your child is likely.

It is not a good idea to go, first off, to the principal (unless the school is a small one or the principal has encouraged such direct approaches). Principals tend to have to uphold their teachers and to stick to standard procedures. Further, having the entire school as their responsibility, they may not know the student or circumstances and may find it a real burden—unfair to the rest of the school, for their time is limited—to have to learn the details. You're more likely to achieve success at a low or middle level of authority. Also, if the principal acts to allow such a change, it is more likely to make big waves and to be harmful to relationships among students, teachers, parents and administration.

What Parents Should Find Out from the School

If a child isn't learning well, parents should not conclude that it's necessarily the fault of the teacher. There are limits to what a teacher can do, and no teacher is good for all types of children. As a matter of fact, it is a strength to a school to have many kinds of teachers in it, and consistency of method and approach in a faculty is a very pallid virtue. Teachers are important, but there are many things parents can do to support the efforts of teachers to improve standards.

In addition to getting to know teachers, one of the first steps parents should take is to inform themselves about just what sort of work the child is expected to do. If the school doesn't tell you in its reports or grade meetings, then try to find out—although usually the answer is not a simple one. Here are some of the other things parents probably ought to know about their children:

What is the school's impression of the child's behavior? Is he liked by his classmates? Is he a leader or a follower, or both? Does he cause more than the normal amount of disturbance or trouble? Is he too quiet? Does he make good use of his time at school?

What is the school's estimate of the child's capacity —his academic aptitude as distinguished from his academic achievement? How well does he read? (Many schools will give you scores for standardized reading tests, which give comprehensive and vocabulary ratings.) How adept is he with numbers? Can he reason well? Does he understand basic concepts?

In general, is his ability according to intelligence tests below average, average, or above average for the national population and for the students of the school he attends? Most schools, I think wisely, do not give out IQ scores because they are so easily misinterpreted and because laymen—and, too often, teachers—tend to tag students as IQ 102, or IQ 138, and think they have the whole story. The term used should be "IQ score," not IQ, to make it clear that we are referring to a score on a test, perhaps a very good and important test, not to an absolute condition. The school will probably be willing to tell you whether your child's scores show him to be very able, somewhat above average, average, or below average in relation to others in his school and to the general population. It is important to remember that all tests are fallible, especially those administered to a group, where so much depends upon the atmosphere, the attitude of the child and his physical state. IQ scores can vary from twenty to thirty points in a week on some of the shorter group tests. I know a boy whose dog had been run over and killed the morning of an important aptitude test. He was so distressed that his IQ score was 98; two weeks later it was 131.

In addition to aptitude, you will want to know what your child's actual subject achievement is. Do his teachers think he is doing good work? How does he compare with others in his grade? What do standardized achievement tests show about reading, vocabulary, language usage, mathematics, etc.?

Seeing Test Scores in Perspective

I should say a word about the meaning of test scores. On aptitude tests, the scores are frequently given in percentiles. To establish percentiles the developers of a test list all the scores of those who have taken the test, from the lowest score to the highest. They then divide the scores into a hundred groups, each group a percentile (a one-hundredth). If there were 3,000 students who took the test for purposes of standardization (that is, establishing norms of performance to which individual performance can be compared), the 30 top scores would be in the 100th percentile, the next 30 in the 99th percentile, and so on down to the lowest 30, which would be in the 1st percentile. An indication of the 55th percentile does not mean that the student got 55 percent of the answers right. That's quite a different thing.

If the 3,000 students taking the tests were from independent (private) schools, then the percentiles would be based or "normed" on the performance of the independent-school population. If your child's scores were in the 75th percentile in the verbal section and 24th percentile in the numbers section, it would mean that his linguistic aptitude as measured by this test was fairly high (about one quarter of the independent school students would score above him and three quarters below), while his numerical aptitude was fairly low (slightly over three quarters of the same group would score above him). Incidentally, a major difference in verbal and number scores *may* indicate some sort of personality disturbance which is interfering with learning.

In the most commonly used *achievement* tests, as distinguished from aptitude tests, scores are often given as "grade equivalents." If your child is in eighth grade, for instance, he might, on a test like the Stanford Achievement Test, get a grade-equivalent score of 7.9 in vocabulary, 8.4 in reading comprehension, 10.2 in arithmetic reasoning and 9.0 in arithmetic computation. This would mean that *on this test* he performed in vocabulary like a seventh-grader in the ninth month of school in the average public school, in reading comprehension like an eighth-grader in the fourth month, and so on.

If a school is willing to give you test scores, be careful not to put too much faith in them. They are important evidence, yes, but not all-important. Every year in schools where I have been teaching, we have had a few children who test consistently low and yet do good work; and, more frequently, there are those who test high, yet do poor work. If you have one of the former, be thankful that he is able to make the best of his ability; if you have one of the latter, you may find some of the suggestions later in this book helpful.

Accept the Facts, Good or Bad

An objective picture of your child's capacity and achievement is important to you, since it will show you how much to expect from him and will help you adjust his own attitude toward his work. Many parents (some persistently flying in the face of facts, others because they do not have access to the facts) err in believing their children are near geniuses and therefore expect academic excellence when such excellence is impossible. Such unrealistic expectations lead to frustration for both parent and child and to hostility between them.

I could mention several cases like Gloria, an eighth-grader whose mother, a brilliant doctor married to a professional linguist, was bitter about her daughter's merely average performance in school. She kept nagging at the girl through sixth and seventh grades: "You ought to get A's and B's. You're perfectly able to. We're going to limit your social life and TV unless your next report is better than this one. You can do better and you know it." The unspoken overtones were: "We are ashamed of you. You are lazy. We don't value what you value. You're not being honest when you claim you cannot do better." Actually, it was the parents who were not being honest, because the school had pointed out to them clearly that all the tests showed that Gloria had a good but not brilliant mind and that she ought to be getting just about average marks in a group where the academic competition was pretty keen. The result was that Gloria, without knowing just why, went on a sort of academic strike, and in eighth grade, instead of doing average work, was close to failing.

She became a problem at school—sullen, uncooperative and often dishonest. Between her and her parents there was almost no communication; her only interests seemed to be boys, rock bands, going into the city, and "fast" behavior. Thus a mother's unrealistic insistence helped to spoil a fine youngster who could have been a credit to her family, her school and herself. When things became impossible, the father and mother at last came in for conferences. Psychological help was enlisted, and after a while the parents achieved a realistic perspective on their daughter. The girl was able to come back to normal, but only after much unhappiness and expense.

On the other hand, there are parents who consistently underestimate the ability of their children and who are content to have them be "happy, normal children." I have had parents say to me: "Thank heavens Mark isn't a genius! I just want him to be friendly and get C's." These parents share the common misconception that genius children are queer, unhappy, undesirable. This is not so, as Lewis Terman showed in his monumental work on exceptionally able children, *Genetic Studies of Genius.* His findings have been confirmed by later studies and by commonsense observation of many teachers. It may seem unjust, but genius children tend to be more successful all around than are average children. They have bigger bodies, better health and more friends; they are better with their hands, more musical and generally better adjusted; they are happier. When they graduate from school they go to better colleges, hold more offices, have more dates, get better marks; and after graduation they are likely to marry sooner, have more children (today, perhaps, these two are not considered so admirable), make more money and live longer. So don't pray to be spared a genius in the family.

And if you have one, recognize it. Don't be like the father and mother I knew who insisted that their Charles, a very able student, was "just a good average American boy," didn't want him to take extra courses and discouraged him from independent study at home. Having no support at home for his naturally curious and creative mind, Charles turned his exceptional intelligence to devising ways of getting out of work, disobeying his parents and attracting attention by spectacularly obnoxious behavior. However, he never got into serious difficulties and has turned out to be a mediocre person with a sharp, biting wit and an unhappy sense of frustration.

Parent-Teacher Conferences

Now, getting back to how parents can work with the school to help their children achieve the best possible academic performance, I must say a word about parent-teacher conferences, which, if well used, are a most fruitful way of sharing ideas and information. After all, your child is one person, but his life is divided into at least two parts: home and school. If you and the teachers can work together with a good understanding of each other, your child is likely to benefit. Therefore, if possible, confer with your child's homeroom teacher, or counselor, or guidance person, at least once a year to see how things are going. Here are some suggestions for getting the most out of your conference:

1. Call the school for an appointment. A well-organized school will leave a message for the teacher, who will return your call. It's not fair to seize a teacher in the hall when he has other duties or when he's preparing for a class in a seemingly unoccupied moment in an empty classroom; in any case, you probably won't get much satisfaction from a conversation that occurs under such cir-

cumstances. If you do happen to run into him, at least give him an out by saying: "I know you're terribly busy. When would be a good time to see you about Frank?" Then he can say, "Oh, right now. I happen to be free," and thus save both of you the bother of scheduling a time; or, "I'm terribly busy right now. How about next Thursday at 10:20, when I have a free period?"

2. If you have any specific questions in mind, leave word in advance what they are so that the teacher can prepare to answer them, looking up records and scores and perhaps conferring with other teachers. A prepared teacher is much more useful to you in a conference than an unprepared one.

3. Come ready with definite questions to ask, but don't insist on sticking only to those questions, or, if you have no definite questions, then say frankly that you are generally concerned and would like to know how your child is getting along.

4. Plunge right into the subject of the conference. I have wasted many hours in past years talking with parents about the weather, politics, the recent school play, or other irrelevant topics, instead of spending time on what the parents really wanted to talk about. Now I make a point of saying, almost right away, something like, "Well, let's see, we were to talk about Bob's difficulty in mathematics," or "Do you want to start with your comments or questions about Julie, or shall I say a couple of things we have on our minds?"

5. Ask teachers for their frank, plain opinion, and when you get it be very careful not to appear to be on the defensive. If you do, and the teachers feel they must handle you with kid gloves, you are much less likely to get full, accurate information about your child. If a teacher says, "I've been wondering whether perhaps Sue isn't be-

coming a little too dependent on her mother for help in mathematics," don't jump to the defense of mothers, but rather say something like, "Oh, really? That's interesting. What makes you feel that?" Then, after you show that you really want to know what the teacher means, you can explain, if it seems helpful, exactly to what extent aid is being given or why you think it is needed.

6. If you're in doubt, confer sooner rather than later. Usually problems are more easily solved if the school knows about them early, before they become aggravated and while there is still plenty of time left in the school year to do something about them. For instance, if you are aware that Jim is so afraid of ridicule from a larger, brighter boy that he doesn't dare speak up in class or even ask questions about homework assignments, it's best for the teacher to know this as soon as possible. A good teacher may quite often easily improve such a situation, perhaps by a word to the other boy, perhaps by calling directly on Jim and making sure his answer gets approval, by judiciously arranging committee or learning groups so that Jim is with people who will bring him out, or, if necessary, by arranging a resectioning of the class. If you think your problem is a small one which can be dealt with quickly, it is often a good idea to telephone the school and ask them when you may talk with the teacher briefly or when it would be convenient for the teacher to call you. For instance, if you think you are sending Alice off in ample time to reach school before the opening bell and yet you have the impression from what other children say that she is often late, and if you can't get a straight answer from Alice, you might just want to ask the simple question, "How many times has Alice been late in the past few weeks?" There would be no point in scheduling an appointment just to find that out.

7. Remember that most school problems are rather complicated, and simple answers are likely not to be useful. Therefore, don't say, "I need only five minutes of your time." You're almost certain to need more; if you don't get more, you will leave the conversation unsatisfied. Once a mother saw me in the hall and asked "for just five minutes," sat down with a sigh and said: "We are convinced my daughter can't spell and doesn't understand what she's reading. What should we do?"

8. If possible, keep the conference focused on the future and what specific things can be done to solve the problem under discussion. Avoid long descriptions of what Miss Cleaver back in second grade did to Pam's attitude toward learning. If it's important, bring it up, but only to help the present teacher know better what to do next. We teachers make some serious mistakes, and schools are often at fault and need to be told so, but it's better to tell the teacher who's making the mistake at the time it's being made (or the grade head or principal if you have valid reasons for not wanting to say it directly to the teacher) than to complain later.

9. Except in emergencies, or upon specific suggestion from the teacher, confer only during school hours. It's not good to telephone a teacher at home in the evenings or over weekends unless he or she has told you definitely that it's all right to do so. Teachers need their free time for preparation, reading, recreation, and, all too often, housework; and they are unlikely to have at hand all the data they need to deal usefully with your question.

10. Remember that most schools are crowded these days, and teachers' lives are overloaded. It may well be that some schools will be unable to give enough time for conferences such as those I suggest. If so, be understanding, but keep trying for your conference.

After the conference, what happens? You should consider carefully the information you have gathered and act upon any suggestions the teacher may have given, provided you approve of them and think they will work. If you don't, be brave and say so during the conference so that the teacher will know where you both stand.

Since some teachers have as many as 100 to 150 pupils to teach during a day, occasionally they may need a reminder about a point agreed upon during a conference. For instance, I appreciated this note I received from a mother: "Thanks very much for our helpful conference. We're already trying the plan of letting Ike go out to play baseball before supper instead of coming right in to do his homework. We appreciate your offer to talk with him about tutoring camp this summer." Thus I am appreciated and reminded. And being human, like all teachers, I need both.

One other relatively minor matter: usually when children go from one grade to another they have new teachers, and some of the successful methods worked out with previous teachers may be forgotten, or not communicated, and thus not used by the new teachers. Many schools have faculty meetings early each year where the teachers of each grade share their ideas and experiences in dealing with individuals in the class, but schools are large and even important matters are sometimes overlooked. Therefore, it is a helpful precaution to write a note early in the year to the homeroom teacher or some person in touch with the student's teachers if there's any point that you particularly want to be sure isn't forgotten. For example: "Please be sure to seat Barry near the front of the room where he can see the board. He won't sit there unless you tell him to"; or "Maud had math tutoring all summer. If she shows a need for more, we're ready to supply it and would appreciate knowing it right away. Last year this got her through quite well."

Earlier, I said that in recent years I've found it's often more helpful to include the student in the parent-teacher conference rather than having the parents and teachers talking about the student in his or her absence. When students aren't present, it means that parents or teachers must explain later what went on, and the explanations will often not be as accurate or impressive as hearing it all firsthand. If students are present, they will be unable to play off teacher and parent against each other. Also, many students feel it's not quite fair for adults—even if they are loving, intelligent ones—to talk about them in their absence. They sometimes perceive it as a ganging up of the establishments of home and school against the defenseless student. Students may not need or want to defend themselves, but they often can do some very helpful explaining and expressing of feelings right in the conference.

If the student is to be present at the conference, parents and teachers must not act, or seem to act, as a powerful double hammer of authority. The student needs a chance to talk and explain and react.

Obviously, having a ninth-grader present at a conference will probably be more appropriate that having a fifth-grader. Also, there are feelings (for example, anger, deep discouragement, distrust) and topics (such as the methods used by a teacher, fundamental objections about the school, suspected need for psychiatric evaluation or treatment) that are better discussed, at least in the early stages, when the student is not present.

Cheating

In all schools, as far as I know, occasional cheating is a quite common practice in the middle and junior high school years (and I have no reason to believe that it is not in the earlier and later grades too). In answering my question *Do you ever cheat?* the percentage of *yes* answers increased with each grade, thus: fifth grade, 31 percent; sixth grade, 39 percent; seventh grade, 45 percent; eighth grade, 51 percent; and ninth grade, 67 percent. According to the questionnaires, more girls (53 percent) cheat than boys (36 percent).

The number of times that cheating took place varied from once per year to hundreds of times, with greater frequency in the later grades. My own experience is that some class groups cheat much more than others, they cheat more in some subjects than in others and with some teachers more than with others. Some people argue that a good way to end cheating is to remove academic pressure from students and to give up marks. There is little doubt that these steps would radically reduce the amount of cheating—for why cheat when there's no pressure and no mark?—except for those who'd cheat just to have the satisfaction and approval of a good performance, even though unearned. However, eliminating the pressure and marks would not teach honesty; it would merely remove the motivation to cheat in school. The real challenge for schools and parents is to develop ways to teach honesty even when good performance is very important and when a reasonable amount of competition is present, which it always will be in many segments of life.

On the questionnaire I asked the students why they cheated or did not cheat. The replies showed that there are a number of common reasons. Those given *for cheating:* "To get the answer"; "when the answers are right under your nose and the problem is much too hard, you don't want to waste time asking a teacher, so you just look"; "it's a game, when the person's not looking it's their fault"; "when I know how to do it and it gets boring (not on tests)"; "I want a good grade" (the most commonly mentioned reason); "I'm scared if I flunk my parents will punish me"; "I forgot to study" (the second most commonly mentioned reason); "French is such a hack the whole class does group tests but the teacher doesn't know it"; "I gave out a few answers because of group pressure"; "everybody was doing it, I protested a few times, nothing was done, so I tried it"; "I don't have to but if I did I might."

The reasons most commonly given *for not cheating* are that cheating is wrong (the most frequently given reason); that by cheating, students are only hurting themselves; that cheaters get into trouble; that the student doesn't need to cheat to do well; and that the student didn't know how to go about it.

These replies, and my own experience, show that cheating is likely to take place when one or more of the following conditions are present:

1. Seats are too close together, the teacher is not alert, and the test is such that cheating is possible.
2. The work tested or assigned seems pointless or unreasonable to the students.
3. The work is hard and not well taught.
4. There is tremendous emphasis on marks for their own sake.
5. There is a strong dislike of or disrespect for the teacher or a general feeling of hostility in the classroom.
6. There is little moral sense in the families from which the students come.

I asked the students what they think teachers and parents should do about cheating. Many simply said, "Punish!" Some suggestions quite frequently made were: "Flunk the student on the test"; "talk to the kid and find out why he's cheating and then help him (or her)"; "explain why it's wrong and how cheaters are only cheating themselves."

As for what parents might do, a few students recommended punishment (nothing specific suggested). Most said that parents should talk it over and try to get at the root of the problem and explain their own feelings or standards on such matters. I think this is sound advice but not easy to do, especially if parents are not entirely honest themselves. If parents are certain (sometimes it's only rumored) that cheating is going on in a class, they would do well to talk the problem over with their children and then with the teacher of the class.

As for teachers, the following is a set of policies that works fairly well:

1. Try to keep the work interesting and convince the students that it's important to learn it; make it challenging but never beyond the capacities of over half the class.

2. Admit frankly to the students before the first test of the year that cheating often occurs in school and that therefore it's only sensible to move desks apart and cover easy-to-see answers. I don't think this makes students feel that you don't trust them, but rather that you recognize what's what.

3. Keep alert during tests (this doesn't mean a constant glare) and, when marking papers, watch for verbatim similarities. Don't be blindly trusting.

4. Find an early opportunity for a class discussion of reasons for cheating and its effects. It's surprising how many students haven't ever thought much about it.

5. Quietly take away the paper of any student who is clearly cheating, fail him for the test and confer inconspicuously after class to arrange for a time to talk at greater length privately. "Setting an example" by drastic,

conspicuous action is not only unnecessary (word gets around without a show) but often creates such bitterness and alarm that no moral lessons can be taught.

6. Find out from the student, when you talk privately, why he cheated and try to help him overcome the need for it; then explain, or get him to explain, how cheating is self-defeating and how it affects a person's reputation; but explain also that cheating is quite frequent and that the episode under discussion, although serious, does not mean a permanent blot on the person's record, especially if it doesn't happen again.

7. Ask the student whether he would like to have the teacher tell his parents what happened or whether he'd prefer to do it himself. I explain that parents should know when a child is in trouble so they can help him and also because they share the responsibility for the child's growing up good and strong. If a child is obviously afraid of his parents (a surprising number of children who cheat are), I may let him off this time without informing the parents. If he says he will talk to his parents, then I ask him in a day or two what their reaction was.

In general, it seems to me, no teachers—or parents, insofar as they have knowledge of it—should let an accident of cheating or any other dishonesty pass undealt with. If people succeed in cheating (or stealing, or lying, or whatever it may be), they're more likely to cheat, steal or lie the next time and to be less honest people. It pays to deal promptly and definitely with cheating and to take enough time to do it understandingly and well. In the long run, it will save the adult's time by preventing future incidents, and, more important, it will save the morale of the offender and of the group involved.

Honesty does not grow naturally. It is developed little by little as we, parents, teachers and students, speak and act in situations where honesty is tested. Of course, honesty grows well in an honest atmosphere at home and at school. It is always cheering to observe that there is in almost any group a good fraction of girls and boys who will not cheat under any circumstances, who believe in honesty and who have the character to be honest.

The School's Part in the Development of Moral Behavior

I have been talking about what teachers and others can do to help develop honesty in students. It would be nice to know how to train children to tell the plain and simple truth, although, as Oscar Wilde wrote, "The truth is seldom plain and never simple." The way to teach honesty or any other moral value is not simple either. In Chapter 2, I spoke of Kohlberg's stages in the development of moral reasoning. Are there ways that schools can help accelerate the progress of young people through these stages and help more of them arrive at higher stages? There is no question that teachers can help students speed up their cognitive development, help more of them reach the stage of formal operations—the ability to think in and deal with abstractions—and develop the habit and skill of deep questioning. We do this by giving children experiences—such as the reading of books, the discussion of issues, the challenging of canned answers—that cause them to keep restructuring their own thinking and its relationship to the people and things around them. We do this, whenever the students can take it without undue confusion and bewilderment, rather than simply imposing moral and cultural patterns directly upon them—something traditional teachers are all too likely to do. If an eighth-grade girl asks, "Is it all right for a boy and a girl to have sex if they are in love and know what they are doing?" we don't say yes or no, but we turn the question back on the class and ask them to discuss the issues involved: What do we mean by "all right"? All right with and for whom? What do we mean by "have sex"? Has that phrase only one meaning? What does "in love" mean? How can people tell if they are in love? What are the symptoms of "love"? How do people who love each other behave toward each other? What is "true love"? Is there untrue love? And what do you mean by "if they know what they're doing"? What *are* they doing—physically, emotionally, in relation to the other person? What are the consequences of their actions?

Mental exercises like these around a question like this are likely to accelerate cognitive development, I think, and help students arrive at the higher stages of moral reasoning.

If students are encouraged in school to discuss the moral issues involved in the actions and thoughts of characters in books and stories read for history and English and current events, in the discoveries of the social and physical sciences, in sports, and in the behavior and actions of students and teachers in the community and in the school itself, it is likely that their moral reasoning will be strengthened, which in turn may develop moral behavior. And what is "moral"? I'm not going to tell you. That's a good educational question for the readers of this book to start discussing right now.

Talking with Teachers

Discussing important questions of life and morals involves talking. How easy do students find it is to talk with teachers? I asked them this question: *Is it difficult for you to talk satisfactorily with your teachers about questions important to you?* Twenty-two percent of the students in grades five through nine answered *yes,* 44 percent *at times,* and 34 percent *no,* with only slight overall differences in percentage among the grades and between girls and boys.

I asked, *If it is difficult, why?* Here is a sampling of the reasons given:

Grades five through six. "She doesn't have time, the room's not very private, and she often doesn't understand a word I say"; "they're too busy"; "I'm shy"; "I'm afraid"; "they're not my father or mother."

Grades seven through nine. "They don't care"; "they'd get mad and yell"; "they don't really listen"; "I don't know how they'll react"; "they're always right"; "they don't talk seriously about anything"; "I've never considered talking to a teacher about anything"; "they jump to conclusions"; "I wouldn't want them to know about me"; "I'm afraid of their authority"; "they aren't really young"; "I don't ever bother with teachers"; "to me teachers seem to be for teaching"; "although you might like them, it's still hard to talk to strangers"; "they're all so square."

I also asked, *What important subjects have you discussed individually with any of your teachers in the past few months?* As one would expect, most students listed academic subjects like spelling, history, science, homework, or quite specific matters of behavior at school. In answer to the question *What subjects have you felt you'd like to talk about but have not done so?* the answers were almost identical with the subjects that *were* discussed, except that quite a few students said they would have liked to discuss the way teachers conduct their classes but did not quite dare to.

The answers to the questions above show that there is a readiness on the part of many students to talk individually with teachers but that many others need encouragement. However, it does not often occur to students in grades five through nine, and especially not to those in the lower grades, to discuss the broad moral questions and issues that are likely to develop and improve moral reasoning and behavior.

One last point: the foregoing paragraphs have concerned individual discussion with a teacher. The very good teachers that I know find that students are greatly interested at all levels, but especially as they enter adolescence, in talking about moral issues as a group in the relatively ordered atmosphere of a guided, or at least well moderated, discussion. If teachers plan and allow time for this sort of discussion, related but not strictly limited to "facts" of the academic area being taught, they can contribute to the moral and ethical reasoning and maturing of their students. Parents can help too—and so can students if they bring up questions of right and wrong in class and at home.

5

Learning How to Learn: Study Habits, Homework, Marks

"**5** I like to get it over with in little packages.

6 We're the seniors of the bottom so we better learn to do it ourselves.

7 The teacher pested me into doing better things.

8 She explained that getting bored with routine in the middle of the year was normal.

9 I got a lamp and dictionaries but I don't open up my head."

Perhaps the most common complaint of parents about their sons and daughters at school is that they don't know how to "study" and that the school should devote more time and intelligence to teaching them "study habits." One parent, commenting about school, home and learning, put the question very well, in terms more realistic than the simplistic notion of study habits: "Problem: how to instill organization without quenching the internal fire? And: how to kindle the internal fire?"

Two other parents wrote comments which, together, illustrate how nearly impossible it is for any ordinary school system to meet the needs of every student. Parent 1: "We are on a creativity kick. The school has abolished report cards and grades in favor of conferences and 'satisfactory-unsatisfactory.' I feel that the children are being asked to work without precise goals. Even most adults need strong, immediate goals to encourage their best work." Parent 2: "Our son is a creative type who goes into marvelous frenzies of interest about projects. This doesn't jibe with the sequential progression of schoolwork. I wish it could." Yet another parent expressed an idea which ought to be obvious to every student, parent and teacher, but isn't. She said: "The greatest lesson each student can learn in school is how to educate himself."

The term "study habits" is somehow not fully connected with reality. What we all really need in life is not study habits, but to know *how to learn,* because if we are to be successful in the modern world we have no choice but to keep learning. There is no definite body of facts and concepts the mastery of which will mean that we now "know," for example, science. Students have to learn to *do* science. The same is true for mathematics and for English. It is true even for history. Of course, there is a body of information and a sense of historical time that it is important for people to acquire, but the main thing in history is to learn how to read and interpret data, to use sources and to weigh the significance of evidence. Whether it is the data and sources of Ancient Greece or of U.S. current events does not make a crucial difference. What students should consider is how to answer such questions as these: What did men and women do then? How did they organize? How were they affected by what went before? What were their ideas of what was coming next? How did their words and actions relate to the words and actions of people elsewhere? How do we test whether what we read about human behavior in the past and now is true? How is new information found and what do we do with it? And how does the present require us continually to rewrite the past? Dealing with questions like these is "doing" history, and it can begin in fifth grade, or earlier.

So schools should be teaching how to deal with areas of human behavior and thought, not how to master prewrapped packages of "fact." However, this kind of education isn't very popular with lots of teachers and parents. There is nothing that mediocre teachers like better than some neat packages of information which they can unwrap in front of the students, require the students to "master," and then neatly test the mastery. Some parents like that too, and so do some students, because it gives an illusion of accomplishment. It is true that to learn how to master facts is an important skill, and the only way we can discover whether it has been acquired is by testing. But the testing must be seen as a part of our main task, which is to teach each student to educate himself. The subject matter we use, the departments we organize into, the assignments we set and perform, and the tests we give and take should all serve the goal of self-education.

Some Study Techniques

From the foregoing, it must be clear that "how to study" is not a simple, easily taught lesson. Basically, study is a process of independent learning, and it requires *concentration;* concentration requires *motivation,* and motivation—or the lack of it—is an extremely complex problem. Our best psychologists certainly would not claim they could easily answer the question "How can a person be taught to learn?" if for some reason he is not learning well.

However, there are some routines and practices that may help some people. But no set of techniques is appropriate for everyone. Each has his own style. Some work in bursts, some plod. Some reason in straight lines of logic, some leap intuitively from insight to insight. However, those students who are not doing well at school, or who are doing well but should be doing even better, may be helped by this list of study techniques. Few will want to use them all, and no one, I should guess, will reject them all. For simplicity's sake, however, I state them almost as commandments—not ten, but seventeen:

1. *Write down your assignments* with date due, clearly, promptly, in a regular place, preferably a small homework notebook, not on just any available scrap of paper. If you aren't sure what the assignment means, ask the teacher.

2. *Have a regular schedule for home study.* In junior high school you should probably allot one and a half to two hours a day for schoolwork at home, although, since work and projects come in spurts, a fixed routine cannot always be held to. You can probably work better after dinner than before; when you return from school, your mind needs a rest and your body some food and exercise. However, styles and rhythms of brainwork and body work differ.

3. *Have a regular place for study* equipped with pencils, pen, paper, scissors, ruler, dictionary, calendar, and a good lamp.

4. *Be certain of the purpose of an assignment before you do it.* Ask yourself, What am I supposed to learn from this? Why was it assigned to me? Teachers almost always have something in mind when they give assignments. What is it? I have seen hundreds of students doing their lessons mechanically without ever knowing why they were

doing them, except out of some habit of duty. If you have a clear purpose you will work much harder and more intelligently. If you don't know the purpose of the assignment, ask the teacher. (Not "What's the point of this, anyway?" although that's a good question and deserves an answer, but more tactfully, "What are the main things you want us to get out of this assignment?") A very good student may see purposes far beyond those of the teacher, but it never hurts anyone to know the teacher's purpose.

5. *Skim over any reading assignment rapidly before reading it closely.* Don't read it first; just glance at the main headings and titles, or paragraph beginnings, to get a general idea of what it's about and to help you relate the ideas to the main topic and to the rest of the course, and to whatever other knowledge you may have, when you read the chapter closely later. This skimming oughtn't to take more than four or five minutes for a fifteen- to twenty-page chapter.

6. *Use any study aids in the book* if you have some close reading to do. Note the chapter title, which will probably give you the main idea, and the headings of the main sections. If there are italicized words, read them with especial care. Look closely at any lists of points numbered 1, 2, 3, etc. Be sure you know why the authors included whatever charts, maps and pictures there are. Go over any questions and exercises at the end of the chapter; they will usually bring out the main ideas.

7. *Pause after each paragraph or section of the book to see if you can recall the main ideas.* If you cannot, reread the passage. This pausing for recall and review is one of the best ways to fix the ideas in your mind. (Of course, you do not do this if you are reading a novel or story, as that is quite a different activity from reading for mastery of facts.)

8. *Mark your book if you own it.* (Don't mark a book that isn't yours. If the book belongs to the school, keep it clean.) Reading should be an active process. Don't just sit back and let the words come in your eyes and be absorbed into a sort of mental fog. Instead, read with a pencil in hand, and make circles, underlinings, squiggles, etc., to emphasize the main points. If you can afford it, buy your own copies of the major texts you use so that you can mark them. Don't try to save a few dollars a year by keeping a pristine book which can be sold to another student. Your education is too important for this. (And don't buy a book already marked by another reader. Marking is no use unless you do it yourself.) If you cannot mark the book, you may want to take notes, although this can be very time-consuming.

9. *Look up new words if you need to.* Always keep a dictionary at your place of study. After you've looked up a word, try to use it a couple of times in the next day or so to implant it in your mind. Of course, it is not always good to look up new words. It can break the train of thought of the passage; often the context—the sentence and passage in which the word appears—will give enough clues for you to get the meaning. All of us learn most of our vocabulary through context clues, not from dictionaries. But don't let a key word get by if you can't make sense out of the passage without looking it up.

Choose your dictionary with care. For able junior high students a collegiate dictionary may be best, but for most students it will contain so many uncommon words that the words they need will be hard to find, and the definitions will be difficult to understand. So, a dictionary can provide more frustrations than meanings. You may want two dictionaries, one simple and one more complete. Three good paperback dictionaries are *The Amer-*

ican Heritage Dictionary of the English Language, Popular Library; *The Merriam-Webster Dictionary,* Pocket Books; *Webster's New World Dictionary,* Popular Library. Two shorter, easier dictionaries are *Dictionary 4,* Pyramid Publications; *Webster's New World Quick Reference Dictionary,* World Publishing.

10. *When you've finished an assignment, think back and try to recall the main ideas.* This is a quick way to fix ideas in your mind and to show you where you need to reread. Don't just heave a sigh of relief and close the book when you reach the last word.

11. *Remember, there are different kinds of reading for different kinds of assignments.* Get your mind set for the kind of reading you think applies:

a. Skimming—to get a general idea or to locate a specific bit of information you need.

b. Rapid, relaxed reading—to enjoy a story.

c. Close, active reading—to study textbooks and encyclopedias in order to master the material.

d. Word-for-word reading (perhaps aloud)—for directions, mathematics and science problems.

e. Poetry reading (best aloud)—for levels of meaning, metaphor, feeling, sound.

12. *Note and study all corrections and suggestions made to you in class and on your papers.* If your teacher makes a correction on your paper or a suggestion to you in class, that's important. You may well be tested on it later, and you know it's something directed at you which the teacher thinks you personally need. Don't let it pass. *Note also any suggestions made to the class in general.* If the teacher thinks something is worth taking time to mention particularly, it's probably important, and teachers have a way of emphasizing in class what they are likely to give tests on later. (Keep a notebook open and

pencil available all the time in class.) You don't have to agree with the teacher's suggestions, corrections or opinions of what's important or not important, but it's wise to understand the teacher's thinking as well as you can.

13. *Plan your time* if you have a long-term assignment. For instance, if you have three weeks to do a report on a large subject, such as the caste system of India, divide up your time, perhaps spending a week doing rough organization and collecting materials, another week reading the materials and taking notes, and a third week reorganizing and then writing up your report and proofreading it. Don't put off the work until the last few days. You may find yourself without material and without time to search for it.

14. *When doing an assignment, note down any points on which you aren't clear* and raise them in class at the beginning of the next period. This is not only a good way to learn; it also makes a wonderful impression on teachers.

15. *Learn to make a rough outline,* a most valuable tool for organizing your ideas or reviewing materials you have studied. If your teachers have not taught you how to do this, you can find a section on outlining in almost any English textbook. I think it's a waste of time to spend hours making a perfectly formed outline for an ordinary assignment or review. The important thing is to get the main ideas and subideas briefly stated and arranged in logical form.

16. *When you review for tests, don't reread all the materials.* Instead, use the study aids in the book, the marks you have made and any notes you may have taken on your reading or on what the teacher has emphasized. Spend your time on the parts you don't know.

17. *Your basic obligation to your work is to be in-*

terested in it. Don't set up a block between you and your education by crying, "I'm bored!" or, "It's *stu*pid!" You have a perfect right to feel that way, but if you let the feeling control your actions, you may fail to learn. Instead, require yourself to find something in the work that interests you. Keep alive and curious.

Using these seventeen points in studying will take a little more time when you first go over your material, but the total amount of time taken will be less, and your mastery of the work will be more efficient. Of course, if you have a system of your own that you think works better than this one, and you are doing well in school, ignore my suggestions and go on using your own system.

Why Homework?

"Homework" is really a misnomer. A better label would be "independent work." It should have four main purposes:

1. To give the student a chance to practice and master skills or content taught at school.

2. To encourage or require independent creativity, such as writing, doing projects, research, or crafts and art.

3. To encourage or require wide independent reading.

4. To provide time for reading "study" material in courses like history.

The purpose of homework, at least in middle and junior high school, should generally *not* be the learning of new concepts, new lessons or new skills. These should be taught in school, and homework should be used to reinforce them. Unfortunately, there are too many teachers who spend so much time "hearing" students "recite" on the previous night's homework that they haven't enough time left to discuss and teach the new material and consequently throw the responsibility for new learning on the student at home, where, if the young person is puzzled, the buck is passed to the parent. If this is happening frequently in your school, a conference with the teacher, grade head or principal would be in order so that parents may find out how they can help and, incidentally, call attention to a condition of which the school may have been unaware.

Homework and the Parent

It can be said quite dogmatically that parents should never *do* homework *for* students. If parents err, they should err on the side of giving too little help rather than too much. Especially beware of trying to teach new material. What you remember about multiplication of fractions or about parts of speech may be so different from what is taught these days that all you will do is create confusion.

Of course, if children are puzzled by their homework and ask their parents for help, parents can't very well say, "Go away." Probably the best policy is for parents to listen to the problem and see if they can find a way to help the student discover a method for solving it or identify the elements needed to solve it. But often the best thing to say, unless the school the student attends is a poor one, is, in effect, "Do the best you can now, remember just where you are confused, and ask the teacher tomorrow."

In writing, if a student wants to know how to spell a word and cannot find it in the dictionary, a parent should *write it down* (don't say it; except for very good spellers, this doesn't teach anything and the student may well write it incorrectly) on a piece of paper or in a spelling notebook. Then the student should *learn* it before using it. If a student is stuck for an idea to write about, parents can, *if asked,* make some suggestions. But they should not go over papers afterward to check the errors and require rewriting. That's the teacher's business.

In history, parents certainly can be research assistants but should not be directors; they can be a source of materials but cannot organize the paper. If there's a sentence or paragraph in a text that a student doesn't understand, a parent can have him read it aloud and can help him explain it.

Although parents should be available, they should help only on request, and then sparingly. They should try to be sure that what they are doing helps make their children intellectually more independent.

Too many parents, worried about the consequences of failure, help their children by constant checking and teaching at home. All this does in nearly every case is to shield the child from reality. If he's lazy, he should take the consequences at school. If his paper seems like a failure, let him go to school and fail—and take the consequences *at school.* Someone said, "We fail towards success."

But what if parents happen to see an atrocious paper, far below what they think is the capacity of their child? What if they know he dashed it off in ten minutes, when he's supposed to spend from thirty to forty? And what if he comes back the next day and reports that the paper was perfectly acceptable to the teacher? In other words, what if there are no consequences?

Well, again, the thing to do is to confer with the teacher. It may well be that the parents' standards are too high and that they are comparing their child's work with their own work, possibly when they were in a later grade. On the other hand, it may well be that the teacher is unaware that the student is dashing off his mediocre papers in a few minutes. He will be glad to have the information and can require a higher standard of work for that student at school. Some students can, in ten minutes, write a paper that is far better than that written by another in an hour. Also, many students are experts at convincing the teacher that they are overburdened. I've been fooled a number of times. Some good teachers will encourage parents to check homework or to help explain work that is not understood. If so, parents should proceed with caution, and only if the teacher knows what they are doing and approves.

On the questionnaire I asked, *How much do your parents help you with your homework?* The replies showed that girls in all grades ask for and receive somewhat more help than boys, but the difference isn't great. Here are the percentages, total and by grade:

	Total	*By Grade*				
		5	*6*	*7*	*8*	*9*
Do it most of the time for me	1	0	2	0	0	0
Help every night	0	0	0	2	0	0
Help me about half the time	3	3	5	5	4	0
Help me a couple of times a week	12	6	14	16	16	5
Seldom help me	67	88	69	54	64	58
Never help me	17	3	10	23	16	37

The most impressive fact is, I think, that 84 percent of the students seldom or never get parental help with their homework. You can see that it is in grades six, seven and eight where most help is received, perhaps because homework is new and still easy enough for parents to help with. By grade nine, hardly anyone reported frequent help, and 95 percent were in the seldom or never category.

In the questionnaire, I asked, *What kind of help in homework do you need most from parents?* By far the most frequently mentioned was simply "in math." Second in frequency was one or another foreign language. Also mentioned with some frequency were "help with review" or "checking for tests" and "helping me on big projects."

I also asked, *Why do you or do you not receive help?* Here are some replies from those who did not receive help:

Grades five, six, seven. "I know what I'm doing"; "I should do it myself. It's mine to do"; "I never really like getting parental help from parents."

Grades eight, nine. "I'm bright (boast!)"; "I can understand my subjects better than they can"; "they believe I shouldn't form a crutch on other people"; "if they do it, I'll never learn"; "I don't need it" (the most common response).

Here are a few replies from those who did receive help:

Grades five, six, seven. "I've got to do it and sometimes I can't figure it out"; "when I don't understand" (the most frequent reply).

Grades eight, nine. "Only when I ask and am stuck"; "I think it's good to share the family brain."

The Bad Results of Too Much Parental Help

When a parent takes a too-active part in doing homework with a child, there are four reasons, in addition to those already mentioned, why this almost always has bad results. *First,* it sets up bad relationships between parent and child. The teacher-pupil relationship at its best is a friendly but businesslike one, where there is mutual respect and often mutual affection, but where the teacher can be completely objective about the student's work and the student objective about the teacher's comments and requirements.

The relationship between parent and child cannot, and should not, be largely objective. It should be based primarily on love and on the assurance of complete support. Teachers can, if they must, set unpleasant tasks, give failing marks, keep students after school or express a low opinion of a student's work. Teachers must even be willing at times to be disliked and resented (although if they're disliked and resented most of the time, they're in the wrong profession). The teachers and students are not indispensable to each other.

This is not so with parent and child, and if a parent tries to be teacher at the same time, all too often this will arouse resentment, doubt, hostility and irritability in their children. The child will probably continue to do poorly and the parent will become more and more disgusted, until both child and parent end up rejecting each other, often with accompanying anger and tears, sometimes with quiet, grim desperation. I think parents have enough correcting and disciplining to do without taking on the schoolteaching function.

A *second* reason for parents to keep out of their children's homework is that too much help, especially when accompanied by unpleasant emotions, results in a dulling of any zest for learning which a student may have. It is a form of dependence, and it is difficult to be enthusiastic and vigorous if you are habituated to leaning. Also, as I have said, junior high school is a period when young people are struggling for independence, and they will resent any feelings of dependence, even if dependence seems to be asked for.

A *third* reason for not helping with homework is that it becomes more difficult for teachers to evaluate the progress of their students. Even an alert teacher may be fooled for a while at the beginning of the year because excessive parental propping obscures the student's true state of skill or learning. Of course, the weakness will eventually show itself on tests, but by then several weeks of useful time may have passed.

A *fourth* reason is that, especially in subjects like math, the home-taught "learning" may well be faulty and the student's sense of independence impaired. Therefore, the student is unlikely to do well on the test. He may then decide that he is nervous about taking tests, and a vicious circle can be started.

Some Ways Parents Can Help

After all this strong language about laying off the homework, a parent reader may feel like protesting: "But can't I at least show I'm interested? After all, my daughter spends hours of time on homework and often makes loud noises and even gets violent about it. Am I supposed to pretend I am indifferent to the whole thing?" Of course not. I've already suggested that you listen to your child's troubles, aid in working out methods, write down spelling words, be a research assistant and occasional procurer of materials. And of course it's important for you to show an interest in your child's work. If he's done something he's proud of and wants to show it or read it to you, be glad and enthusiastic—but be cautious about making suggestions about how it could be improved.

And another way parents can help, *if need be*, is to

work out with their children just when and where they are to do their homework. A definite time and place helps many students. Let a fairly rigid schedule provide the stimulus for getting the work done if no better source is available. Parents in some cases can be helpful by insisting that their children be in their place of study, in an attitude of study. Probably the radio and TV should be off, but there are children who can work well with the radio or even the TV on. In some cases, where drastic changes are needed, it may be well to require—after discussion—a period of one to two hours a day for homework when there will be no interruptions for nourishment or telephone conversations. (Messages may be taken, if necessary.)

Where should the homework place be? Many students will work best alone in their own rooms, away from all family distractions. However, there are others who can spend an hour in their rooms, apparently studying, and not get more than five minutes of real work done. They spend the rest of the time doodling, daydreaming, and making minor physical movements totally irrelevant to the study process. For such students (or nonstudents), there is much to be said for the parental presence in the homework situation. That is, these students work best within range of parental eye and voice. For example, a mother of three adolescent children made her two good students do their homework in the kitchen of their small house while insisting that the bedroom be reserved solely for the one boy who had difficulty keeping at his work. But it didn't succeed. The poor student accomplished little until, when the two other children happened to be away for a few days, the boy was allowed to work in the kitchen. Suddenly, under the mild disciplining effect of his mother's presence, he studied conscientiously and without interruption. In another family, the dining-room table provides an excellent small "study hall" for the brood of scholars.

To be successful, the parental presence must be exercised with great self-control lest it become parental nagging or domination. If a student has questions, it is best to avoid too many direct answers, as these discourage thought on the part of the questioner. Instead, it is better to suggest where he can find the answers for himself or rephrase the questions in new terms and shoot them right back for him to figure out. (Examples: Student: "What's the capital of Arizona?" Parent: "Wouldn't you be able to find that in the atlas?" Or, Student: "Are there two *m*'s or one in *coming?*" Parent: "What's the root word of *coming?* What do you know about adding *-ing* to words like that?")

Another way in which parents can help with their children's out-of-school learning, if they think assistance is needed, is to inform themselves about the school's homework requirements: in which subjects are students supposed to have homework on which nights? Most students should have a homework notebook, or some regular place in which they regularly write down their assignments with the due date. This notebook can be a good link between home and school.

Further, it is often a good idea, if parents aren't sure how much homework their children should have, to find out from the school how long, on the average, students are expected to spend on each subject and then to have a copy of their daily schedule so that parents will know how many study periods students have on any given day and what subjects they are supposed to have for homework.

Remember, though, that some students will need two or three times longer to do an assignment than others. Some eighth-grade classes may have individuals who read at fifth-grade level and others at twelfth-grade or even college level, and there are equally striking differences in ability to deal with figures.

Also, it's not always the ablest students who get their work done fastest. Very often students of limited ability will finish their work fast because they do not see the rich possibilities for accomplishment in a particular project or are quickly satisfied with a piece of writing in English, whereas able students will get caught up in their interest and enjoy staying with the work for several hours.

If students have no homework at all to do, they can always spend their hour or two in independent reading. There's no better, more enjoyable way to increase vocabulary, experience and general academic alertness, if the books are well chosen.

Students Teaching Each Other

Speaking of sharing brains, I think it is a healthy development that schools, especially in the middle grades, are increasingly encouraging students to teach each other. It's somewhat less common now to see the teacher at the front of the room explaining at length until the slowest student perhaps has got the idea but the brighter ones are turned off; it is more common to see the class break up into small groups or pairs, so that students can teach each other. This plan of student-teach-student can work well. Those who are very able come to understand the subject even better when they have to teach someone else. Those who don't get it the first time around are often more likely to get it on a one-to-one basis the second time around. And a much higher percentage of the class feels usefully employed. This sort of classroom procedure (and it often carries over into the halls, between classes, during study periods and even lunch and recess) needs careful monitoring by the teacher to be sure that it doesn't disintegrate into aimless chatter. However, even aimless chatter may be more productive than imposed, fruitless subjection to a prolonged explanation by the teacher. Teachers and parents should also make sure that students who have developed a less competitive, more cooperative approach to school learning do understand the distinction between a teaching situation, where sharing is encouraged, and a testing situation, where sharing is inappropriate and may be interpreted as cheating. Further, all of us—students, teachers and parents—need to be sure that students do not come to depend too much on cooperative rather than independent study.

Homework and the Telephone

Over the past few years, I have come to believe that telephonic sharing of homework problems, and the intense, interested two-way questioning and explaining that occur in the evening between earnest scholars, is usually good and profitable activity and should be permitted—provided: (1) that it is a real sharing and not a telephonic "copying" of homework answers, which short-circuits rather than stimulates learning; (2) that one student isn't imposing on the good will and intelligence of another; and (3) that the rest of the family isn't being deprived of the telephone. If the last is a problem, then an agreed time limit is needed.

School Marks

As students progress from fifth to ninth grade, the school mark or grade becomes increasingly important in their lives. Many schools give no marks in fifth grade and below, or use simplified labels like *satisfactory* and *unsatisfactory*. By ninth grade, however, most schools give marks according to an established system, and many start in seventh grade. Whether or not you—students, parents, teachers—approve of such marking systems, you will probably have to learn to deal with them and find ways of getting as much benefit from them as you can. Inevitably, many students will work and learn for marks rather than simply because of interest. Since all necessary work cannot always be made interesting, this fact is not entirely depressing. Also, inevitably, where there are marks there will be self-generating competition. This need not be bad, but it usually is hard on those who lose out and end up near the bottom. In my view, there is no excuse for schools to aggravate the bad effects of self-generated competition by such practices as posting rank-lists or reading out marks. Such activity may stimulate intense, productive activity on the part of those students who have a chance of coming out near the top, but this advantage is more than outweighed by the humiliation and damage inflicted on those who inevitably do poorly by comparison. Publicizing marks, or even blanket appeals to all students to get a good mark (instead of urging them to learn a lot—it's interesting and important, you'll be glad you did), results in conflict, unhealthy pressure, cheating and, for many, dislike of school.

However, marks do serve very useful functions. Combined with explanatory comments and given to students privately, they can be helpful in lowering anxiety: "I know where I stand," said one student, "and I know what I've got to do next." How can we make the best use of marks? The main thing is for everyone involved to consider them as *information,* not as coin to be earned. A mark has one advantage over a comment (in addition to the fact that it doesn't take long to write): it provides a possibly unsentimental element in the evaluation of a student's work. But the accompanying comment should be more important than the mark, since it explains what the mark means.

I believe, although many teachers would disagree with me, that marks should be based on the quality of the student's performance, not on effort, not on behavior. The comment can describe behavior, and it gives a chance to hazard a guess about the amount of effort. Some schools give an effort mark, which may be useful to parents, but most students know whether or not they are working hard.

Often parents will ask a question like, "What does a B mean these days?" Schools should be able to answer that question, preferably with some carefully written statement available to students and parents and well understood by teachers. If there is no such statement, ask for one.

One school I know of uses the following system:

A, A– . . . superior
B+ . . . very good
B . . . good
B– . . . fairly good
C+, C . . . satisfactory
C– . . . barely satisfactory
D . . . deficient
I . . . incomplete
NC . . . no credit

Another school uses this six-point scale:

I . . . Outstanding achievement in every area of the course
II . . . Highly competent performance
III . . . Good achievement
IV . . . Work clearly better than passing
V . . . Work just passing
F . . . Failure

If a parent asks, "What does a III really mean? Is it a B or a C?" my only answer would be that it means what it says it means: "Good achievement."

Some schools use a 0 to 100 marking system, with a certain figure, say 60, representing passing. I feel that a numerical system overestimates the teachers' ability to make accurate calculations of the quality of students' work in a course. It gives a false impression of exactness.

Ideally, I think, schools should change their marking systems every ten years or so, perhaps more often, just so that students, teachers and parents will have to think about what marks really mean and read the official descriptions of each mark to ascertain its meaning.

Just now, many schools use a pass/fail system of evaluation. Some schools give students the option of having conventional marks or taking the course on a pass/fail basis. Pass/fail does cut down competition and make the one vital distinction among students: those who passed and those who did not. If the system is combined, as it usually is, with a comment, it can work well. There are a few schools which give no marks at all, only comments. This system has the advantage of *requiring* a comment. However, it is my impression that pass/fail and no-mark plans are being found increasingly unsatisfactory because students and parents want to know where the pupil stands and don't feel that pass/fail really tells them, even with a good comment.

How Parents Can Support the Efforts of the School

There are many indirect ways in which a parent at home can reinforce the efforts of school and can strengthen the student's desire to learn. If possible, let some of the dinner table conversation be concerned with ideas, books and projects. As a parent, you can show that you yourself have a zest for learning—if you do. Don't try to fake it; kids are pretty sensitive to sham. If you read, talk about the books; keep open to new ideas, especially when they're enthusiastically held and expressed by your children. This doesn't mean you have to agree with them; you may want to challenge them. But be open to them and accept them as worthy of consideration.

Provide as many rich experiences as you can: trips to museums, visits to factories, bird-watching or rock-collecting expeditions, vacation excursions, theater. Have as many interesting visitors as you can in your home, especially people who have had unusual experiences, who are doing interesting jobs or who have traveled. If there are foreign students in your community, invite them to your house for a meal—or a weekend.

One quite specific thing you can do is to make certain that your child knows where the local library is, where the main library is, and how to use them. Unless the school has done so (and some do it year after year *ad nauseam*), go with your children to the library and get the librarian to show you how to find what's there and how the resources of the library can be used. Thousands of Americans—adults and children—have never darkened the doorways of a public library and never know what a major, helpful source of pleasure and knowledge it can be.

Another aspect of reinforcing school at home is to help the family keep complaints about school in proper perspective. Occasionally, reports from school come home in a wildly exaggerated form, sometimes quite contrary to the facts. I remember once I decided to speak privately to a boy about some notes he had passed in another teacher's class. That evening I received a phone call from the parent of a student in the same class, who expressed deep concern that the school had suspended a boy for two weeks for merely passing a harmless note. Well, there was nothing to it. The boy had been spoken to in a clear and friendly way and appeared in school the next day slightly wiser and no sadder. Perhaps it was incidents like this that led some teacher at a parents' meeting to propose the now widely quoted agreement: "If you parents promise not to believe everything your children tell you happens at school, we teachers will promise not to believe everything your children tell us happens at home."

In connection with events like these, on the questionnaire I asked: *Can you think of unfair things done to you in grades five through nine? If yes, describe them.* Fifty-five percent of the students could think of something; 45 percent could think of nothing, a figure I found remarkable given all the chances for injustice and unfairness that exist over a period of five years of school. Here's a sampling of the sorts of unfairnesses the students reported: "Being hit by a teacher"; "I get blamed for things I didn't do"; "I didn't get to be president because I wasn't smart"; "people dumping me like dirt"; "this may be stupid, but 5th graders teased me about wearing a bra and half of them need one"; "graded unfairly"; "teachers picked on me"; "I was punished by a teacher for talking *after* class because he didn't want to hear what I said"; "people hate me because I get good grades"; "people ignore me because I don't accept the ideals the group has, such as sex, being nice to people, considerate of property"; "the kid started it and I finished it and the school wouldn't listen"; "In grade 6 I had to make 1000 airplanes"; "the whole class was kept after school when only one person was at fault"; "the teacher took my cookies because a boy said they were his"; "I was accused of cheating on an exam"; "I was sent to the office for counting blocks on the ceiling"; "blamed for flooding the bathroom when I discovered it"; "being accused of stealing when the gang stole something from me."

If students feel they have been done dirt at school, it's important, of course, for parents to be truly concerned and to hear the story. They may then be able to help their children evaluate the incident sensibly (if they say they've been unjustly accused of a misdeed, ask them how many times they did something wrong and weren't caught), to calm them, to ask how it may have looked from the teacher's or principal's point of view. (It's always good training to help a person put himself in the shoes of someone else.) If, after all this, it still appears that a serious injustice has been done or a mistake made, parents should *suspend judgment* until they've had a chance to check the facts. "If Mrs. Smith really told you you cannot go to the lunchroom until you get a B in history, I cannot approve. Let me talk with her tomorrow"; or "Certainly no teacher should accuse you in front of the class of stealing if he has no evidence that you did it. I'll ask him about it," a parent can say, and then check as soon as possible.

It is always unwise to say or suggest anything like, "Well, that school! They never seem to do anything right!" or "I never did think Miss Smith understood children, and this proves it." Such remarks show children that their parents do not respect school or teacher, and it lowers their respect for school unnecessarily. The best thing to do is to confer calmly and quickly with the school to get a balanced view. By suspending judgment parents can support both their children and the school.

6

Reading and Mathematics

"5 Math is good because you get answers and reading is good because you get questions.

6 I need help and I only get homework. Help!

7 I never got taught, I mean *taught,* till I had a teacher by myself.

8 I'm afraid of math teachers and many-legged creatures that hang onto the ceiling over my head.

9 A book is the best teaching machine I know."

One of the miracles performed by every normal human being is learning to understand speech and to speak. Think what it means: learning how to gather meaning from the hundreds of voice sounds and thousands of combinations and variations of those sounds, and to produce these sounds by subtle variations in the voice box, mouth, and nasal cavities by passing air over and through them in varying quantities at varying speeds. These vastly complex processes, which linguists still do not fully understand, are learned from all the people around us but without the aid of any special teacher or school. Indeed, someone remarked recently what a disaster it would be if teachers should successfully claim the right to teach how to speak and how to understand speech.

Speech is sound. Speech sounds are symbols of meaning, symbols by which we grasp ideas in other people's minds and by which we convey to others the ideas in our minds. In their turn, letters, figures and other written signs symbolize the sounds that symbolize meaning. Thus, the written languages of reading and of mathematics are two symbolic steps removed from the ideas they represent, record and enable us to understand. Teaching or helping students to develop skill in these two great uses of symbols is probably the most important function of schools, and most other academic activities derive from or are closely related to them.

Reading

A great deal of nonsense has been written about reading, and some of it has earned its authors a lot of money. Unfortunately, the question of reading is a very complicated one, but it's the simple idea, boldly shouted, that attracts attention (and sells books). However, I can state dogmatically that no single factor or skill—not even phonics—spells the difference between success and failure in reading.

Obviously, reading is of prime importance in school. If a student cannot read accurately, he cannot even do mathematics, let alone the more wordy subjects.

Until recently, most schools assumed that by fourth grade the pupils had learned to read. Consequently, reading was seldom taught in the upper elementary school and almost never in the junior high school, except where remedial instruction was needed. Now, however, many schools have established "developmental reading programs," based on the well-justified assumption that reading should be taught and improved all the way through school. Further, teachers are increasingly aware that reading should be taught *in every subject* and not just as an isolated skill, one taught mainly in an English course. Unfortunately, however, the monitoring of the development of students' reading skills and facility is still almost forgotten in the press of other academic urgencies.

What is reading? Basically, it is getting information or pleasure or both from written symbols. Some children, if they see the people around them reading and are frequently exposed to print, learn to read almost as unconsciously and effortlessly as they learn to speak. But most need to be taught, and the methods of teaching must be varied and flexible enough to allow for children's radically different styles of learning to read. The teaching of beginning reading is an advanced skill, far too complex to discuss here.

Signs of Reading Difficulty

In one way or another, most children learn to read pretty well up to their ability without any special difficulties. Most, but by no means all. What are signs that a student, say in sixth or seventh grade, is having reading difficulty? * Here are some:

1. The student doesn't enjoy reading for information or for pleasure. Most normal middle-class students will quite frequently get absorbed in a good book.

* I mention these grade levels because this book is about middle and junior high school. However, if children in second and third grades show signs of difficulty, it is then that the problem should be investigated and treated. There is no advantage in waiting till later or blandly assuming that the child will grow out of it, even though there are some children who are not "ready" to read until second or third grade, or even later, and they should not be pushed.

2. The student avoids books or "can't find" a book to read.

3. The student obviously can't do the reading that needs to be done to deal successfully with civilized life: for instance, reading signs and directions.

4. The student can't retell a story in simple, straightforward terms—for example, the story of a TV program or movie.

5. The student gets upset or uncomfortable when reading is assigned for homework and is painfully slow in getting the assignments done. If reading homework takes two or three times as long as the time the school suggests is necessary, then there is probably trouble.

6. The student is very hesitant in oral reading, making frequent mispronunciations, saying wrong words, skipping, or reading words out of order. However, faulty oral reading is not a sure sign that a child is a poor reader. Some excellent readers get mixed up when reading aloud because of embarrassment, or because their minds and eyes go faster than their voices can. On the other hand, some fairly good oral readers may be excessively slow in normal silent reading or may not really understand the material they are reading aloud with what sounds like intelligence.

Types of Reading Difficulty

There are perhaps four main categories of students who read below their intellectual capacity:

Category 1. Those who have been poorly taught and as a result have not learned the necessary skills and may have developed a hostile attitude toward reading. These children need special work to develop skills such as phonics, word attack, phrasing, vocabulary, and comprehension methods. With such instruction the student will probably progress rapidly.

Category 2. Those who are poorly motivated, who don't care to learn to read either because they are lazy or because their parents don't read and don't, by their example, make reading seem important and rewarding. One of the ways to help such children is for the parents to try to develop their own enthusiasm for reading, to talk about books they are reading, to recommend books to each other, their friends and their children, and to have lots of books around the house.

A number of years ago, it was reported that 25 percent of college graduates said they had not read one book in the year just past; only 17 percent of adults, at any time, are reading a book; only 12 percent of houses being constructed will have built-in bookcases, and 42 percent of American homes have no bookcases at all; only 13 percent of Americans borrow books from public libraries. In such an environment, and with the quick-grabbing, mind-dulling TV ever available, it is little wonder that it does not occur to lots of young people to read except when forced.

Category 3. Those who have emotional or personality difficulties which block their learning. These children, although occasionally they may benefit modestly from remedial instruction, really need to get their deeper problems straightened out, if possible, before there will be a good return on time and money invested in remedial reading. In some cases, though, the difficulty in reading is, itself, one of the causes of emotional distress, and if the child can gain self-confidence by becoming a more competent reader, then remedial instruction may be an effective part of therapy.

Category 4. Those who have organic difficulties, who, for some physical reason or reasons, often inherited, have trouble perceiving words; or those whose central nervous systems (not the same thing as "intelligence") may mature late so that they are like prereaders as late as third, fourth, or fifth grades and are not "ready" to read. When their central nervous systems do mature, if no serious personality problems have developed, these boys and girls learn to read perfectly well, provided their difficulties have been recognized and they are taught properly from the time they have reached reading readiness, something many schools are not equipped to do.

Pupils in any of these four categories who are very bright are often able, through superior intelligence, to guess and bluff their way through reading and to obtain a degree of success, thus obscuring the fact that they are inefficient readers. They read well enough to get by (especially in the early grades), but they ought to be excellent readers, and their reading inability will inevitably cause them trouble in upper grades if they are required to do any demanding academic work.

What Causes Reading Problems?

One answer to this question is, nobody knows. Another answer is that the causes are multiple and complex, and it is a difficult task, requiring special skill and experience, to find out in an individual's case and to prescribe a set of remedies. Some people these days get a degree of satisfaction by saying that poor reading is caused by *dyslexia,* but this is no better than saying that a child can't read well because he can't read well. "Dyslexia" is a catch-all term properly defined thus: "a condition in which a person of average or better ability, who has been appropriately taught, cannot read well." What causes dyslexia? Again, nobody knows—at least, nobody knows a simple answer. The etiology is unclear and probably multiple.

Some reading problems are caused simply by low intelligence. Some people read up to their ability and read poorly, just as they reason poorly. Others, as mentioned above, were not taught well and need to be taught again. The causes of emotional blocks to reading are almost always very complex. However, when children have difficulty in the early stages of learning to read and feel themselves unable to do what is obviously an immensely important and rewarding task, they get upset, and this compounds their difficulties.

The cause of poor reading is seldom simply poor vision—that is, the inability of the eyes to see adequately on a vision chart. Much more common is seeing wrong. Some children, seemingly carelessly, read "saw" for "was," "man" for "men" or "bone" for "done," etc. Others do not learn to read consistently from left to right. Their errors are not truly careless but are honest perceptual errors. The children probably care very much (though they may deny it), but they cannot perceive and may never be able to do so without special training. People with perceptual difficulties are unable to take what their eyes see and transmit it accurately or meaningfully to the brain. Vision and perception are not the same, and it's very distressing to students plagued with visual problems, and to their parents, to find that the specialists in these matters do not agree. Most ophthalmologists (physicians who specialize in diseases of the eye) concentrate mainly on sight. The optometrists, especially those who are trained in education and who work on "visual training," say that the problem often is not sight but perception. Both groups are able to talk in learned, often complicated language, convincing to the layman, but they are unable to, or don't, talk to each other. Thus they have been unable to agree on the best ways to help problem readers.

Another physical cause of reading and learning problems may be "minimum brain damage" (MBD). In some children, this damage may have been caused by a prolonged high fever during an early childhood illness or by the lack of oxygen during a long and complex birth process. Some common symptoms of MBD are unusual clumsiness throughout childhood, difficulty in orienting oneself in space (bumping into things, not being able to walk straight easily and needing to keep touching walls or objects to maintain the sense of direction) and especial difficulty in sequencing events in telling a story or reporting an event. If the presence of MBD is suspected, parents should seek the advice of a pediatric neurologist.

What to Do about Reading Problems

If your child appears to have a reading problem, there are two things *not* to do. First, *do not attempt to diagnose his problem yourself.* Second, *do not try to teach him yourself.* Many reading problems have been worsened by parents trying to diagnose and teach via suggestions offered in books and magazine articles by authors who are not professional specialists in this difficult field.

The first positive step is to talk to the classroom teacher—probably the homeroom teacher in grades five and six or the English teacher in the upper grades. Explain why you are concerned. Ask for the teacher's impressions of how well the student reads and what the impressions of other teachers are. Also ask if there are any standardized test scores of your child's ability to read.

A commonly used test is the Stanford Achievement Test, which I described briefly in Chapter 4, page 76. Its reading section gives three measures: vocabulary (simply a multiple-choice test on the meaning of words), comprehension (a test of ability to choose the best answers to questions on a series of paragraphs, mostly on factual subjects), and a word-study skills test. An example of the vocabulary items is: A pear is a kind of: (1) vine; (2) fruit; (3) cake; (4) pet. An example of the comprehension items is: Joe is often quite tardy. This week, however, he has been on time every day. This week Joe has been: (1) worse; (2) absent; (3) on time; (4) late. Of course, most of the items on the test are much more difficult than these.

A test like the Stanford does provide these three "objective" scores, which may confirm or not confirm your concern. However, the test is limited, it does little to diagnose the nature of the problem if there is one, and it certainly is an insufficient basis for recommending a program of remedial instruction, let alone prescribing what it should consist of. Also, remember that on group-administered tests, like the Stanford, most students are trying very hard (the adrenalin is flowing), so their performance is somewhat different from what it is in an ordinary reading situation. Some students perform extraordinarily well on such tests, much better than in ordinary instructional situations; others are overexcited and disoriented and perform poorly. Too often, I think, a "good score" on such tests is taken as a sure sign that there need be no concern, when in reality the student may be reading well below his capacity.

If you and the classroom teacher agree that there is a problem, or if you still think so even though the classroom teacher doesn't, then you should seek expert help. This should come from a reading specialist if the school has one (not from a psychologist, guidance person or English teacher, unless specially trained). If the school does not have a specialist, probably the grade head, principal or guidance person can refer you to a good source of help. Most universities have a reading clinic connected with them, and they are a good place to inquire. Also, two books which list reputable reading clinics are *Something's Wrong with My Child,* by Milton Brutton, Harper and Row; and *The Waysiders: A New Approach to Reading and the Dyslexic Child,* by R. M. N. Crosby with Robert A. Liston, Delacorte Press. Two other sources of information are: Orton Society, Suite 204, 8415 Bellona Lane, Towson, Md. 21204; and Association for Children with Learning Disabilities, 2200 Brownsville Road, Pittsburgh, Pa. 15210.

Before entrusting your child to the care of a reading clinic, be sure to check with the school and, if you can, two or three people who have used it. There are many charlatans in the field of remedial reading who, capitalizing on public concern and confusion, have found a bonanza by setting up shop with a few machines, some over-simple theories, and a good line of talk. Especially avoid the so-called speed-reading clinics. One of the ways to determine whether the approach of a clinic is sound is to find out whether it considers the four major elements of any sound diagnosis of learning difficulty to be the physical, the intellectual, the educational (including what the student's teachers observe) and the emotional. If it does not include these four, it is probably not much good.

If the school has a remedial-reading teacher, unless you have good reason to think he's not competent, use him rather than someone outside. If you use an outsider, try to put him in touch with your child's teachers, so that tutor and school do not work at cross-purposes.

Special reading instruction usually costs money, but it's money well spent if the reading difficulty is clearly diagnosed as one that can probably be corrected with individual lessons. Sometimes the cost can be reduced by arranging instruction in pairs or small groups of children who need similar training. Diagnosis of a reading problem may cost $50 to $75. However, it is a bargain indeed when you consider the cost to the student throughout life if he cannot read adequately.

Promoting Book-Reading at Home and at School

Parents should never nag about reading and rarely apply direct pressure to read. If a student can read and isn't reading, it's better to ask the English teacher to apply pressure. As a junior high school teacher, I have often found that students who are well able to read but are not reading are entirely willing to work out with me on an individual basis a list of perhaps a dozen books, of which we agree they will read, say, eight, in a certain number of weeks. Usually the students will consent to having this considered "an assignment," and often they complete it with pleasure.

A good way to demonstrate the enjoyment to be derived from books is to read aloud. This is probably more acceptable to fifth- and sixth-graders than to eighth- and ninth-graders, but people of almost any age enjoy being read aloud to. A good book started this way is often finished independently by the student. If you choose an author who has written several books, perhaps by reading aloud you will stimulate the student to read others silently and alone.

Many schools provide lists of good books for students at different grade levels. If your school does not, ask the English teacher or school librarian for suggestions. Also, many public libraries have children's librarians who are well acquainted with the books available and with the interests of young readers. They are glad to suggest titles or to make out a list.*

* For those who need it, I have provided a short list on pages 275–81.

Of course, anyone who puts together a booklist needs a certain amount of courage and a willingness to be criticized, for there are hundreds of books which hundreds of parents, students and teachers will say shouldn't (or should) have been omitted, and many will quarrel with the easy/average/hard classification. For instance, many students read *Huckleberry Finn* in sixth grade, or even fifth, but it seems to me that to read it then is to miss almost everything that makes it a great book.

Some books on any list are bound to misfire in some cases. For example, some students "love" *Little Women;* some can't abide it. Some people will devour Jules Verne; others find him old-fashioned and long-winded. I always advise my students to give a book a chance for at least fifty pages, and then, if they don't like it at all, to put it back and try another. There's nothing immoral about starting a book and not finishing it.

Classics and Comics

Some academically-minded parents and teachers are not comfortable unless they are pressing upon the students books considered classics. The idea seems to be that the younger the children read them the better; it'll be good for their minds. The competition in which some schools engage to see who can have the hardest booklist is worse than foolish. The late John Mason Brown, in a chapter called "Disney and the Dane" in his book *Morning Faces,* explains why:

> No form of cruelty is more cruel than exposing the young, when still too young, to books and plays ill-fated enough to have become classics. . . . The fact that both the living and the dead are equally defenseless against such foul play is the measure of its meanness. To make a chore out of what should be a pleasure, to put the curse of obligation

on what was meant to be absorbing, is to kill in the child the willingness to be pleased, and in the classic the ability to please. Masterpieces are masterpieces not because such grim conspirators as parents or teachers have told us they are good. They are masterpieces because they tell us so themselves.

In the case of thoroughly reluctant readers, everyone should be happy when they start to read, no matter how unclassic the stuff is. The Nancy Drew mysteries by Carolyn Keene (*Haunted Lagoon, Double Jinx Mystery,* etc.) and the Hardy Boys series by Frank W. Dixon (*Clue in the Embers, Hooded Hawk Mystery*) are a way to get started, for they are exciting, action-packed and uncomplicated, but certainly not worthy of the term "literature." They can lead to better things.

What about comics?—"those polychrome termites which eat their way into every home, no matter how well guarded; into every allowance, no matter how small; into every budding mind, no matter how eager," to quote Mr. Brown again. "They cannot be kept out. No doubt, in fairness they should not be. The young ought not to be exiled from an experience, common to their generation, which will one day prove a group memory." Comic books are better than absolutely no reading at all—but not much better. They are written in such exaggerated, misshapen language that they can cause some habitués to develop bad reading habits. But they won't do a good reader any harm, except that they may tend to dull his taste for better stuff. However, most good readers lose interest in comic books (not in the daily comics) by the time they are well into middle school.

Mathematics

Most people feel they know something about reading, but about the mysteries of mathematics they are entirely willing to admit ignorance. I can remember going through what, I suppose, were for those days well-taught math courses and never having the slightest idea what I was really doing with my mind or why I was doing it. A logarithm table to me was, and would be now if I ever had reason to use one, like a sea of long numbers into which, at a certain point in the rough passage through a problem, you dived. Then you swam along under the surface and came up mysteriously with an answer, like an unidentified and probably indigestible fish.

What is mathematics? It is a group of sciences (not a single science) which uses numbers and symbols to deal with the relationships and measurements of amounts and forms. One of the sciences is arithmetic. Some others are algebra, geometry, trigonometry and calculus. I hear many people using the words "arithmetic" and "mathematics" interchangeably. This misleads. Arithmetic is a part of mathematics, the most-used and perhaps easiest part, although not for everyone, for the great Einstein was a genius at mathematics but, it is said, could not stand the boredom of balancing his checkbook, which requires only arithmetic. Also, there are students who think well and with pleasure mathematically and yet come out with the wrong answer because they cannot do, or are bored to death by, arithmetic, which is the science or art of using numbers, especially in adding, subtracting, multiplying and dividing. In the traditional organization of schools, the study and mastery of arithmetic is supposed to have been completed by the end of seventh grade, and then mathematics begins. However, good teachers know that first-graders can be taught to develop their mathematical thinking, while many twelfth-graders fall down in arithmetic. Arithmetic can be learned by rote, but mathematical reasoning is needed to understand what it's all about. A rote knowledge of how to add, subtract, multiply and divide is probably enough to get most of us through the workaday world, but not through many areas of the academic one. Pocket calculators can do the rote part of arithmetic for us, but it requires some math, perhaps, to know what to ask the calculator to do and to check whether it has done what we want or has done nonsense. If it has done nonsense, it's our fault, not the calculator's.

The other two branches of mathematics that are usually at least begun in middle or junior high school are algebra and geometry. What are they? *Algebra* is the science that uses letters and numbers in formulas and equations to solve problems, such as: "A woman had 12 coins. Some of them were nickels and the rest were quarters. The total value was 2.20. How many nickels and how many quarters did she have?" Algebra amplifies and generalizes arithmetic, but it does not change any of its principles. *Geometry* is the mathematical science that deals with lines, angles, surfaces, cubes, cones, spheres, etc., and with their measurement. Traditionally, it is based on a number of "self-evident truths" (called axioms and postulates) about points, lines and planes, etc., that a bright Greek named Euclid organized around 300 B.C. One of the things that the study of geometry may do is to teach students what an hypothesis is, how to test it out, and, thus, what the nature of proof is. A good teacher may be able to help many students see how the mathematical tasks of hypothesizing, testing and proving can be carried over into aspects of real life.

I ought to say a word about the phrase "new math," which is certainly more widely used and just as usually misunderstood as the term "dyslexia." The new math is a way of teaching the ever-developing, internally consistent system of logic called mathematics. Its main objective is not to train students to do exercises and tricky processes automatically, but rather to teach them to understand, to think clearly in quantitative terms, to enjoy solving problems in different ways. The methods of new math help give aesthetic pleasure to more students than did the old methods. It shifts the emphasis from getting the correct answer quickly to reasoning about whether or not the answer makes sense and, if it does not, checking. The new math has been overexplained and overpraised by its developers and inaccurately taught by people who do not understand it. Some students who have been exposed to it do make very simple errors that often are the result of insufficient training in the skills of arithmetic. Thus it arouses the anger of some who value simply correctness.

Types of Difficulty with Mathematics

As with reading, there are several categories of students who have difficulty working in mathematics:

Category 1. There are those who have been poorly taught and have never learned the processes of arithmetic, without which further progress is impossible, at least if one is interested in correct answers. For students in this category, some good, intensive instruction can bring quick improvement.

Category 2. Other students are just plain scared of math. They have had bad experiences with it early. They realized they weren't understanding it, so they just decided they couldn't do it. Some parents, hoping to comfort their children, aggravate this condition by saying, "I never was any good at math either," thus putting their stamp of approval on the inability to do math, as if it were an inherited characteristic.

Category 3. There are students who just haven't the intellectual power to go very far in math. It is as fruitless to try to push them into rapid progress or advanced courses as to try to get a six-year-old child to undertake abstract thinking.

Category 4. There are other students, of brilliant mind, who have been turned off mathematics by rigid teaching which discouraged them from trying out new ways of solving problems. "Stick to the textbook" or "Do it my way" are deadening commands that help develop this condition. It can be remedied by flexible, enthusiastic teachers who demonstrate that math is not just for dullards or deities but for people with good minds who enjoy the beauty and pleasure of exercising them.

Category 5. There is a special kind of dyslexia in mathematics that develops because of the nature of mathematical language. Mathematics is expressed in a language, but a most Spartan one. It uses symbols rigorously, even austerely, and it does not provide the several clues to meaning that are provided in most English sentences. Mathematical language has a special beauty for those who learn to use it, but it requires a special kind of reading. Good teaching can overcome this sort of dyslexia much more easily than it can overcome the more generalized inability to read.

Category 6. This category is made up of students who simply have never had to learn to read English closely and accurately and thus cannot do "word problems." When mathematics makes them see the need for this type of reading, they are ready to be taught it, and thus a good math teacher may be the most important teacher of reading for students at a certain point in their education.

Category 7. This category is made up of students who have skipped a grade in school or who have changed schools. Since mathematics is a sequential subject, these students often have gaps in their background and thus are unable to understand the teacher's explanations. Some of these students need only assistance from a teacher in pointing out to them in a good textbook what topics they have missed. They are able to make up the work on their own. Others catch up more easily and comfortably if they are provided with a few tutoring lessons.

The Symptoms of Difficulty in Mathematics

The symptoms are similar to those of difficulties in reading and most of them can be inferred from the categories set out just above. One is emotional distress—anger, tears, sullen or bewildered paralysis, often combined with anguished cries or groans of "I *hate* math!" Another is complaint about the math teachers, year after year. Yet another is the obvious fact that a child cannot do simple arithmetic in ordinary daily situations that require it.

What to Do about Difficulties in Mathematics

Fortunately, failure to learn mathematics is not such a disaster as failure to learn to read. Most of us live our lives satisfactorily hardly ever using mathematics, even though we are missing out on the pleasures it provides. However, a knowledge of mathematics is essential if a student is to be allowed to go on in science or in many of the professions—like medicine, psychology, architecture, computer science and engineering. Even historians these days are finding that mathematical analysis of data reveals new truths about the past.

If a student is having trouble in math, the first step is to talk with the classroom teacher, and then with others as necessary. Parents will want to know results of any tests the student has taken. Another section of that Stanford Achievement Test gives grade-equivalent scores in the areas of computation, reasoning and application. The same cautions I mentioned in interpreting scores on reading achievement apply to scores of mathematics.

If the difficulties in mathematics appear to result from some sort of learning disability, then a similar diagnosis ought to be made as that recommended in the section on reading. However, there is no large number of "math clinics," as there are reading clinics, because, as I said, one can live without mathematics. In fact, in many cases the best thing to do about difficulties in math is to stop taking it as soon as allowed.

What Can Be Done at Home

If parents enjoy numbers and problems and playing around with mathematical ideas, they can display and share this joy. Enthusiasm is catching. Talking numbers, proposing problems and looking at everything from a marketing list to a bridge under construction, from a new car's gas mileage to an old car's repair bills, as an exercise in the fun and challenge of mathematics can help develop interest and mental agility. So can mathematical puzzles, for those who like them.

But the main thing that parents can do is to exercise restraint when the kids seem to be having difficulty. Here is what an experienced, perceptive, flexible mathematics teacher says about that:

> Working independently with imagination and confidence in one's ability is at least as important as accumulating facts. The child whose parents habitually help him tends to lose part of the value of instruction in school, because attention to explanations given by the teacher seems unimportant. Also, practice in problem-solving is a poor exercise in learning when the child, on demand, is *told* what processes to use. The decision should be his own; and he can learn as much from making the wrong selection, if he checks his results, as from the correct one.
>
> Mathematics is developing rapidly, and many signifi-

cant changes are being made in the concepts taught and in the way they are taught, from kindergarten through twelfth grade. These changes are usually not understood by parents. Instruction at home, even in topics which are essentially unaltered, can be damaging. When the present generation of parents went to school, mathematics was seldom understood as an avenue to logical, pleasing, effective thinking, and as a language with which to say precisely, clearly, without verbiage, and even aesthetically, what one has to say in an area of scientific knowledge. It was rather a bag of tricks to those who enjoyed it and a source of anxiety and fear to those who did not. These attitudes are very frequent in any sampling of our present population, and instruction by parents is likely to be strongly permeated by them.

Consider equations in algebra, or reducing fractions, or adding and subtracting negative numbers. Mechanistic instructions like *transpose, cancel out, change sign, use cross products,* give quick answers, but they sacrifice understanding and thereby destroy the tree of knowledge at its root.

When one remembers that on the questionnaire "math" was the type of homework that students in all grades said they needed most help with at home, one sees what an exercise in restraint these words require of both students and parents.

7

Two Special Problems: Underachievement and Boredom

"**5** It (yawn!) moves (yawn!) so (yawn!) slow (yawn!)ly (yawn-yawn!).

6 I wish somebody would *ask* me what it is I need.

7 Teenagers get in trouble because they need attention.

8 I can't wait to get home every day and work on my discoveries.

9 I got held on the rails by force and finally I went off the track."

Students who aren't performing in school because they simply don't have the ability to do the work no matter how hard they labor over it present a difficult problem for themselves, their schools and their families. But at least their problem is an honest and straightforward one, and the solution is for the school to provide courses that are less difficult academically, or for the parents to find a less rigorous school.

More frustrating to parents and teachers, and sometimes also to the students themselves, are those who, by all measures, ought to do a good job in school but don't.

They are persistent underachievers—that is, they test high and do poorly.

The Persistent Underachiever

Most students most of the time don't do as well as they could, and they know it. They have this in common with most of the human race. But here we are concerned with the really serious cases who have superior intelligence, who score well in linguistic and numerical aptitude tests, and yet who are failing or nearly failing some of their school subjects. Most often, such students are boys. Usually, their parents have tried everything they could think of (including the suggestions in this book about homework, study habits, conferences, etc.) and the teachers have worked hard trying all their best ideas (including forgiveness, attempts at reinspiration, private talks, keeping the student after school, and all kinds of pressure). And yet the poor performance continues.

Sometimes teachers, driven by despair and rage, blame the parents unreasonably, and parents frequently thrash about and use the school as scapegoat. All too often, "more pressure" is the only answer anyone can come up with, and the student is kept longer and longer after school, comes in on more and more Saturdays—if the school is one that has such outmoded but nevertheless sometimes useful disciplines as Saturday study—is removed from sports, forbidden to use the telephone, or confined to the house on weekends.

Underachievers are almost always on the receiving end of disapproval and hostility. They seem to deserve it. We assume they are doing poorly simply because they are lazy and careless. They are bound to react adversely to the hostility they earn and which is their lot. Therefore, teachers and parents should not beat a student over the head with his high IQ. Although the purpose of a remark such as "You're bright; you can do better" is probably to compliment the student and to increase his confidence and incentive, often the effect is to attack his integrity. We are really saying: "There's something wrong with you; you're dishonest, you're lazy, you're a stinker. If you weren't these things, you'd do better." But usually the student can't do better just by being told that he can.

A better approach is to say, in effect: "We know you want to do well and you'd like to succeed. You have a good mind. Let's see if we can't find out why you aren't doing better." In other words, don't accuse; investigate.

Sometimes, persistent underachievers grow out of it as they progress through early adolescence. They may wake up in about tenth grade, when they have become more accustomed to their new selves—but sometimes it isn't until junior year in college, if they get in, sometimes not until they're in a job, if they get one—and begin to apply their capacities to the tasks to be done. However, in serious cases, it's not a good idea to count on their just naturally growing out of it.

Of course, one question we must ask is, Underachievement according to whose terms and in what fields? We have all heard of famous people who refused to let their studies get in the way of their education, who were so curious and so eager about their own intellectual pursuits and projects—as well as some nonintellectual ones—that they could not be bothered with the grind of routine, schoolish tasks. Such independence, if it involved genuine accomplishment and not just wishful frittering, should be encouraged.

The best answer is to have a conference with really able, independent academicians in order to make sure that the students aren't missing out on any essentials; then allow them to pursue their passions without requiring them to do all the practice and detailed work that most students need—provided, of course, that they can pass the tests.

What Parents Can Do about Underachievement

Here are some steps I suggest parents consider taking if they think their child is a persistent underachiever:

1. Have an unhurried talk with your child. There should be no immediate point at issue and no accusation, no nagging. If possible, the discussion should be a frank exploration together of what the student thinks might be done about the problem, if indeed he thinks there is a problem. Don't expect this single talk to solve everything, no matter what gets promised.

2. Have an unhurried and well-prepared conference with the teacher, counselor or principal and conscientiously try out any ideas he or she may have, if you are able to. It is probably good to include the student in the conference.

3. Be sure the school has given a good IQ test, a good aptitude test and several achievement tests and that you understand what these tests show. If the school has not done so, request an individually administered intelligence tests like the WISC (see page 142).

4. Have an unhurried talk with your doctor, followed by a complete physical checkup of the student if this has not been done recently. Be sure that the student's eyes are tested by an able oculist, and the ears tested with an audiometer. Many schools now provide periodic audiometer tests. (Caution: Don't accept a doctor's prescription for educational remedies any more than you would accept a teacher's for a health problem.)

5. Make sure that there's no possibility that inability to read is at the base of the trouble. (See Chapter 6.)

6. Try to make an honest self-evaluation of your role

as a parent. What are you doing that might be causing your child to underachieve? Are you too "managing"? Do you apply too much pressure? Do you provide emotional support? Do you respect him or her as a person? Do you condemn too much? Are you too punitive? Do you set a good example? Do you try to provide intellectual stimulation?

7. If none of the suggestions already made gets at the trouble, ask the school or a child-guidance expert to investigate whether some personality or emotional problem may be interfering with your child's ability to learn. Some fairly common symptoms of emotional difficulty are frequent violently aggressive behavior, hyperactive restlessness, consistent contrariness or rebellion, consistently acute shyness, consistent passivity, frequent and prolonged sullen silences, very high degree of concern with sexual exploits. I have already mentioned that a major difference in verbal and nonverbal aptitude test scores often are a symptom, as also may be a large difference in verbal and nonverbal thinking on a test like the WISC (see below). If your child shows any of these symptoms, don't be alarmed. Many perfectly normal people show them from time to time, but it may be well to check into the matter if an able child is having academic difficulty and is showing a number of these symptoms fairly often.

8. Most good schools have a psychologist available part-time. Often he is connected with a psychological clinic or guidance center which may be part of a university or hospital. This psychologist, or someone under his supervision, administers tests to students having learning difficulties. Some schools routinely give their students a Wechsler Intelligence Scale for Children (WISC) test, a measure of intelligence which is, as well, quite helpful in indicating how a student's mind is functioning; some sort of individually administered personality projective test

(such as the Rorschach or one of the apperception tests) which, expertly interpreted, can shed light on the personality and emotional adjustment of the child; and a battery of achievement tests. If the tests indicate the likelihood that some emotional factor is interfering with learning, a conference between the parents and the psychologist should be scheduled. From this often come suggestions to both parents and teachers which, if followed, may result in improved learning.

On the other hand, sometimes a more thoroughgoing evaluation of the child's problem by a psychiatrist is recommended. This usually involves three or four talks with a child psychiatrist (who will probably want to talk separately with the child and with the parents), perhaps further testing, and then a recommendation. Sometimes, after an evaluation of this kind, changed courses of action for parents, teachers and child may suggest themselves and be helpful, occasionally spectacularly so. In other cases, it is clear that some psychiatric treatment is desirable to clear away deep-rooted problems or to help deal with them.

There's nothing mysterious or magical about all of this. If a child (or an adult, for that matter) persistently worries about certain problems, problems which are so deep-seated that the individual is unconscious of them and would be unable to talk with parents or friends about them, then he is quite likely to be unable to concentrate on his lessons. He may be "careless," not because he doesn't care but because he cannot be aware of his errors on account of the strong distraction of worry and agitation. He may seem persistently lighthearted and carefree because he cannot face the possibility of failure and therefore will give himself an out, often unconsciously, by not trying. He may not be able to organize his thoughts or even spell because of emotional blocks (spelling requires inner organization of a sort, and extremely poor spelling is sometimes a sign of underlying personality difficulty).

These serious personality and emotional difficulties are certainly no easier to cure than are physical diseases requiring the attention of a doctor. They require expert attention. In not-so-ancient times people used purgatives and blood-letting as cures for many physical diseases; now we know better. But in the field of personality and emotional diseases, many people are still too ready to settle for surface treatment—"some good stiff discipline" or a reasonable punishment—or, at the opposite extreme, an expensive gift or complete permissiveness as a cure, when what they really need is to consult an expert who can get at the root of the trouble. A psychiatrist will undertake to retrain the individual to live with the reality of his emotions, of himself and of his environment (of which school and family are major parts); to teach him to use his assets and to manage his liabilities. Basic to the success of such treatment is an inviolate relationship between the patient and the doctor.

People think that such diagnosis and treatment are very expensive, and often they are. But not always. A number of communities have psychological and psychiatric clinics where expert help can be secured at reasonable cost or, in cases of financial hardship, for very little. A full-scale psychiatric evaluation costs about $150 to $200, and the cost of any further treatment, if it is needed, is determined on the basis of ability to pay. If you feel that psychological or psychiatric help may be needed for your child and are not sure how to secure it, I suggest that you consult first with the school or with your own doctor. Another possibility is to write to the American Society for Adolescent Psychiatry, c/o Mrs. Mary Staples, 24 Valley Green Road, Wallingford, Pa. 19086, briefly describing your situation. The Society will refer you to a clinic in your locality.

Yet another organization to write to is the American Association of Psychological Services for Children, 1701 18th Street NW, Washington, D.C. 20009. The AAPSC is a standard-setting organization in the field of child psychiatry, one of its major functions being to set up qualifications for the operation of child psychiatric clinics throughout the United States and Canada. Each year it publishes a list of member clinics.

For the names of qualified child psychiatrists, not of clinics, write to the American Academy of Child Psychiatry, 1800 R Street NW, Washington, D.C. 20009.

Before you commit yourself to an evaluation or a psychiatric study of your child's problem, it would be wise to see if you can find others who have used the same person or service; and be sure that the study takes into account the student's educational and physical situation as well as his emotional one.

9. If, after consulting with a clinic or a psychiatrist, you have reason to believe that the emotional problem is on the way to solution, you should consider with the school whether special tutoring or remedial instruction is now needed to fill the gap created by a period of poor learning.

The Highly Gifted Child Who Is Bored

One might truthfully say that in many schools the most gifted students are the most retarded; that is, they exhibit the largest gap between capacity and achievement. There are thousands of children in the United States today who have very high IQ scores and are being put through the same academic routine as their classmates. Since they can work two or three times as fast as the average student, since they have little need for the drill and review that take up so much time in many classrooms, and since they sometimes know more than their teachers, they frequently become weary and unhappy, and occasionally are real behavior problems. More often, though, they get along satisfactorily, enjoy good marks (for which they seldom have to work), and coast into habits of mediocrity. These exceptionally able children should be challenged with more difficult work and made to use their able minds to the fullest.

Identifying the Gifted

Is it really possible to single out those children who, say at age twelve, are gifted? In some European countries they still think it is—in fact, the bright children are separated from the dull and average well before twelve, often on the basis of a single series of tests. While there are a good many errors made, on the whole the system works tolerably well as a means of selecting those children who will succeed in an academic high school and engage in primarily intellectual pursuits. In the United States, I am glad to say, we have not adopted any such cut-and-dried plan, although there are a number of people who persistently advocate that we should. We do, however, have statistics to show that those who test high on standardized tests at ages twelve to fourteen are much more likely to go to college, to graduate and to win honors than those whose test scores are average.

The president of the Educational Testing Service, now probably the most influential test-construction organization in America, once said about tests, "They will certainly not single out for us the individual who will discover new intellectual territory, as distinct from those who will settle and cultivate that territory." They will give us, he said, "no warranted roster of Pasteurs and Einsteins." He quoted William James's statement that "individual biographies will never be written in advance," no matter how excellent the tests, but said that good tests "will tell us the pools in which to fish for the highly gifted."

What to Do about an Underchallenged Student

If you think you have a highly gifted child (and don't be led into thinking so by one or two bright remarks or the fact that he or she took apart an alarm clock at age five and almost got it back together again), check with the school to see if they agree. If they do and feel as you do that the student is not challenged by his work, encourage them to give him more difficult work: advanced reading, major research projects, a chance to teach others a special unit by himself, a program of supervised independent study. Be sure, though, that you or the teacher talk this over with the student beforehand so that he will see the reason for it and will feel stimulated rather than unfairly burdened by having a load of extra work put upon him. (Not all bright people enjoy using their minds on academic work; also, they may be well occupied with independent projects of their own.)

Remember that this souping up of courses is not as easy as it may sound. It requires extra time on the part of the teachers to find challenging work and to check on it and react to it when it's done. Unfortunately, many teachers do not have enough time to provide such individual attention; they may be so preoccupied with giving extra help to those who are having trouble passing the course that they have little time available for stimulating the gifted.

Here are some other ways parents and students and schools have found to stimulate the people with exceptionally able minds:

1. Add extra courses to their schedules. For example, instead of their taking four or five major courses in eighth

or ninth grade, let them take five or six, adding perhaps a science or another foreign language. This may require the school to make some exceptions and to complicate the general schedule of classes with individual arrangements, but it is often worth pressing for, and these days, a bright schedule-maker with the aid of a computer can perform feats of individualization that would have been impossible ten years ago. Also, school people should consider the possibility of allowing a really able, ambitious student to miss a session of a class if there's a time conflict. Such a student can often get by very well with three instead of five class meetings a week, although some teachers aren't too enthusiastic about acknowledging the tremendous capacity of students for learning without teacher aid. Another possibility is to add minor courses like art, music, mechanical drawing, typing, sewing, carpentry or cooking. If some of these sound rather unacademic, so what? Handwork is a good balance for mind work. Also, there is more academic challenge in a good art or music course than many people realize.

2. Allow the student to skip a grade. This can be done all at once or a subject or two at a time. Often, for instance, students find it quite easy to do advanced work in mathematics or a foreign language and to stay with their class in other subjects. Sometimes, some independent work is required over the summer to prepare for advanced placement the succeeding year.

It is well to be cautious about skipping grades, though, since it makes the student young for his class and quite likely socially less mature than classmates. However, you pay for everything in some kind of coin, and student and family will have to decide with the school whether they think the advantages of skipping outweigh the disadvantages.

3. Parents can try teaching their own children if they have any special field of competence. I know of parents who have successfully taught their children typing, accounting, Russian, horticulture, ancient history, advanced geography, special branches of mathematics, auto mechanics and all sorts of dance, art, crafts and music. This kind of extra teaching, if it is a desired privilege for the student and not a requirement, is much less likely to involve the psychological and academic hazards that helping with regular schoolwork does.

If parents have no special field of competence but have time to do some learning and are enthusiastic about it, they can get a good text or series of books (perhaps advised by a local academician) and put themselves through a course with their child.

4. There may be resources in the community to which parents and students can turn. For instance, many cities have excellent adult evening schools for which adulthood is not a prerequisite. Or perhaps there is a teacher in your school who would be willing to teach an extra course in the afternoons or evenings to a small group of able, interested students for a reasonable fee. Often local colleges, universities or museums have courses that will enroll really gifted younger students. Or there may be people in the community with a special knowledge or skill they'd be glad to teach: an ornithologist, a native of a foreign country or a scientist in industry.

5. Clubs, hobbies and independent projects should be encouraged. Unfortunately, many of these are just means of frittering away time, but with careful guidance and provision of facilities, able students can develop real intellectual competence, thorough knowledge and sense of purpose through them. I need only mention stamps, radio and hi fi, mechanics, nature study, physics, chemistry, creative

writing, poetry and great books, to indicate the possibilities.

6. If parents are really seriously troubled by the lack of intellectual challenge for their able children, and if the family can find no way to provide such challenge in the school the children attend, they may want to consider changing schools. There may be a public school outside the district which could do better. Sometimes, for a rather modest tuition payment, such schools will accept able boys and girls from outside their district. Or you may wish to consider sending your boy or girl to an independent school, which is what private schools now prefer to be called, since hardly any of them are now private in the sense of being run for profit and open only to a socially select group. Not all independent schools are necessarily good, but very often they offer a stimulating course of study and the challenge of the presence of other able students, almost all college-bound. Another, more radical step—radical, at least, for most families who consider it natural that children live at home while they go to school—is boarding school. You can get information about independent schools, day and boarding, from the National Association of Independent Schools, 4 Liberty Square, Boston, Mass. 02109, or from Porter Sargent's *Handbook of Private Schools,* published annually and available from Porter Sargent, 11 Beacon Street, Boston, Mass. 02108.

Parents may wonder whether they can afford an independent school. It is true that they are expensive, but many schools are prepared to give scholarship aid to really gifted students whose parents cannot afford full tuition.

I have been discussing the unusually able youngster in an undemanding school, but if you have a normally bright child in a good school, don't jump to the conclusion, the first time he or she seems bored, that a special, organized supplementary program is needed. Children probably should be bored on occasion: the effort to escape from boredom can lead them to new fields of endeavor. Not all their life should be planned and filled, at least not by forces outside themselves. They need time to be inert, to be alone, to hack around, to talk desultorily, to waste time. An all too common problem is the overcharged, over-scheduled life that so many students are pushed into by ambitious parents and schools, and by their own initiative.

8

At Home

"5 I like noise and they like quiet but anyway mostly we have fun.

6 I love my parents, they're not horrible.

7 Parents are too protective, but they should watch the activities of a young girl.

8 Sometimes I just don't feel like talking and it seems that when I don't everybody asks me questions.

9 My father keeps insisting he's right when I have proven him wrong."

I think it's easier to be a teacher than a parent, a student than a child. At school, class periods come to an end, different teachers face different children, no one is permanently responsible for anyone and everybody goes home at midafternoon. At home, although most children would rather spend their lives there than at school if they had to choose, the cast of characters remains the same, the relationships are intense, the mutual responsibilities are deep and final and there are no bells.

Reading the comments that parents and children

wrote on the questionnaires I gave them, I had the impression that quite a few people of both generations felt that their own families and their problems were worse than anyone else's. Therefore, even at the risk of seeming too negative about life at home, I start this chapter with two sets of comments about problems at home, which ought to make my readers feel they're in good company.

Family Problems

I asked the students, *What are your biggest problems with your family—parents or others?* Here's a sampling of the answers: "Being nagged and yelled at"; "not being able to do what I want"; "it's hard when your parents are divorced"; "my parents won't get my brothers to stop bothering me"; "having them leave me alone"; "blaming me for things I didn't do"; "being neat"; "Mother makes me work too hard"; "we like different music"; "they think my school work is lousy"; "I'm the only kid so I'm like the punch bag with screams instead of hits"; "my family thinks because I'm the oldest girl I should do most of the housework even though they believe in women's lib"; "I *think* my mother likes my sister better"; "I can't stand my brothers"; "I'm not allowed to express myself"; "intense sibling rivalry, which is a fancy way of saying that my sister and I are at each other's throats all the time"; "my sister domineers over me when my parents are out"; "my mother says my sister is going through a 'hate-mother' stage and this includes older sisters"; "I yell at them. The only people I can get along with are my classmates and friends. I can't stand adults, I don't know why, and adults are what we have at home"; "I have two older sisters who try to be my mother"; "I don't enjoy being with my mother and dad is always in New Jersey."

The question was put to parents in a different way:

What is the problem relating to your child(ren), aged 10–15, that you'd most like not to have? Here are some typical answers: "Giving up in a much too permissive age when adults are unsure of their own standards"; "procrastination. I dislike having to nag, but I have to do it more and more"; "the discord in our family caused by the constant arguing and bickering of our adolescent has my husband and me nearly frantic! She is at her younger brother's and sister's throats almost constantly, provoking them to battle"; "moodiness"; "emotional outbursts have just begun and without knowing anything else to credit it to I have blamed it on 'adolescence.' He has sudden periods of seeming totally irrational. Something that was clear yesterday is muddied today. He would take the opposite side in *any* argument just for the joy of being angry at us. These outbursts are followed by an hour or so of gloom and then it usually is all over"; "using *me* as a target for his bad feelings"; "I wish that they would not think that when a parent shows interest through questions, in their lives—academic, social or personal—that that parent is 'prying.' "

What Makes a Good Family?

Nothing is more important to the welfare of a child than the absolute assurance of the love and support of his family for him as a unique person, *no matter what he does.* Robert Frost, in his "The Death of the Hired Man," expresses this beautifully through the conversation of a husband and wife who are discussing why their old hired man should have come back to them to die. They say:

> "Home is the place where, when you have to go there,
> They have to take you in."
>
> "I should have called it
> Something you somehow haven't to deserve."

It is customary to state that most adolescents drastically reject the standards of their families and parents and search for an authority outside the home. In part this is true, and many adolescents make spectacular antifamily noises at home and enjoy trying out their newfound feelings of independence by challenging their parents and all that their parents stand for. Actually, some adolescents feel guilty about their seeming rejection of their parents and about their occasional feeling that perhaps they hate their parents. It seems to me that parents need to *accept* these feelings of their children. "We all feel that way sometimes," you can say. "We don't expect you to love us all the time. We've got plenty of faults."

On the questionnaire I asked: *Do you generally approve of the moral and social standards of your family? If not, what do you disapprove of?* I was surprised that 90 percent answered *yes,* they approved, and only 10 percent *no.* A slightly higher proportion of girls approved (93 percent) than of boys (86 percent). Now of course this doesn't mean that these boys and girls don't have plenty of gripes against their families, but when it comes down to their overall feeling about them, they say they approve. I suppose this is natural. After all, there's still a lot of the child in adolescents. They are not yet sufficiently independent to dare cast off their families entirely, and most adolescents, I think, after their period of apparent revolt, come back to the things their families stand for—and back to their families in a new way. I recall a story about a nineteen-year-old boy who said he was amazed at how much his father and mother seemed to have learned since he was thirteen.

Rather few girls and boys among the 10 percent who disapproved of their families' "moral and social standards" specified what they disapproved of. A number remarked, "I'm not sure" or "I don't want to say"; a scattering mentioned specific complaints: "Not allowing us to slowdance"; "Dad smoking"; "too many rules"; "too strict"; "my family ought to be more sociable and less secluded"; "I like party-goers and they don't"; "they're against my going steady." A ninth-grade girl specified a disapproval that I think others would have shared had it occurred to them: "My mother sees humor in other people's kids' misdoings, but she sees only the bad in things involving her own children." As you can see, even those who categorized themselves as overall disapprovers of standards were quite specific; none stated a blanket rejection of the standards of their families. Perhaps this simply means that most human beings—children, adolescents or adults—are not revolutionaries.

I hesitate to generalize about families, but I have the impression that the most successful ones have a framework or structure, or, to put it another way, a few firm, clear boundaries; and within the structure or boundaries the children are given as much freedom and responsibility as they can take. An example of this is in the family of Anna Perrott Rose, who, in her book *Room for One More,* describes the family life of her brood of six children, three of her own and three adopted. She says that the children expressed the code of the family by saying that you can do what you want except

You hafta be honest,
You hafta be kind,
You orta be brave,
And you gotta mind . . .

and you are punished for infringements against any of these except the one about bravery.

To establish a framework for family life, parents have

to be firm on occasion and not exemplify a young boy's definition of a parent as "something so simple even a child can operate it." Parents are permissive as far as they can be, but they are not appeasers; they don't permit their children to bully or whine them into what their children want.

Within the areas of freedom that exist in most good families, parents have to be willing to accept a reasonable amount of messiness, laziness, slouching, marks on furniture, pillows on the floor, and so on, if they don't want to lose contact with their young. They've got to be careful not to overload their children with arbitrarily imposed requirements (as distinguished from those reasonably established on the basis of discussion) about mealtimes, bedtime, going-out time, coming-in time, etc., or they will develop in their children the habit of refusal. (One parent told me that she tried jotting down all the requirements she made of her teen-ager during a week and then went over the list and relaxed as many as she could.) We can all sympathize with the eight-year-old boy in Rochester, New York, who wrote in an essay on "What My Dog Means to Me":

> My dog means somebody nice and quiet to be with. He does not say "Do" like my mother, or "Don't" like my father, or "Stop" like my big brother. My dog Spot and I just sit together quietly and I like him and he likes me.

Another characteristic of many successful families, I think, is a high degree of openness in their relationship. There is often great benefit in the frank and free expression of feelings, both friendly and hostile. Families need to be filled with plenty of mutual admiration, and parents can help set the tone in this by giving ample praise where it is genuinely deserved. And, on the other hand, I think family members should feel free on occasion to express their resentments and hostilities. It's better than bottling up rage and letting it leak out later in bitterness.

William Blake, in his "A Poison Tree," writes:

> I was angry with my friend:
> I told my wrath, my wrath did end.
> I was angry with my foe:
> I told it not, my wrath did grow.

Get Feelings Out in the Open

All parents and children are full of feelings, pleasant and unpleasant, calm and angry, toward each other and toward themselves. These feelings should be recognized and, most important, accepted. Dorothy Walter Baruch, in her book *New Ways of Discipline,* says that parents unconsciously tend to belittle the feelings of their children, starting at a very early age. They say: "It doesn't hurt very much" (when it hurts a lot); "you don't really mind missing the party; you'll have lots of other chances" (when the child really feels terrible about missing it); "you're not really angry at your brother"; "now, you know you don't hate Daddy"; "why, we all *love* the baby and are *glad* we have him!" Dr. Baruch says you should not tell your children they don't feel what they know they do feel, and you rarely should censor the expression of feelings, because that doesn't change them or eliminate them; it just drives them underground, where they can do a lot more harm. Rather, she says, feelings should be accepted, never condemned. Accepting and understanding a person's feelings is one way of keeping communications open. When teenagers (or anyone else) are being difficult and unpleasant, it usually doesn't help to cheer them, forbid them, condemn them or reason with them because these actions ignore the feelings. Help get the feelings out; then try the reasoning.

Dr. Baruch suggests a technique for doing this: that of mirroring or reflecting the feelings. First you must sincerely understand and accept the feelings as genuine and honest; then you say them back to the child in understanding recognition. She gives as examples: "I know you want to show me you can do it your way"; "I know you'd rather plan how to do it yourself"; "you don't like my interference"; "you're mad because you think I'm trying to take over"; "you don't want me to boss you"; "you hate me to tell you things to do, I know." These must be sincere expressions of understanding, not devices that are immediately followed by, "but I *have* to tell you what to do." That comes later, if necessary, when the feelings are out in the open.

Parents should accept their children's feelings, but they don't have to accept all their actions. Parents must sometimes control how their children act; they cannot control their feelings. It is absolutely impossible. The feelings are generated and exist. However, there are legitimate and illegitimate ways to express feelings. It's all right to do some griping, complaining and moaning; it's harmful to hit people or break things.

Feelings—loving and hostile ones—are natural and inevitable, and in a family, occasional feelings of resentment against parents are most natural of all. When they come, let them be expressed, and sympathize with them. On the other hand, parents' resentment of children is also natural. Possibly it will be expressed less often and less immoderately, but it's there and should be expressed rather than suppressed. Children know that their parents resent them at times. If the resentment is never expressed, perhaps the children will unconsciously conclude that it's too terrible to be expressed.

Sibling Hostility

On the questionnaire, parents said that the area at home that caused greatest concern was "attitude and behavior toward brothers and sisters," not toward parents. Here are some parent comments about this: "Our children have a high degree of competitive animosity toward each other and feel stupid and 'put down' by each other if they are unable to do well academically"; "our son puts down his younger brother and just can't see the devastating effect he has, or, if he does see, he can't control himself. This lack of self-control is *the* major problem for our son and us"; "right now our older child has decided that she would like to 'divorce' her younger sibling, for which I don't blame her, since the younger one seems to choose every opportunity to be nasty or mean to the older, who occasionally, but not always, invites it"; "we have continuous put-downs, arguments, etc., mostly verbal, some physical. I attempt to handle this by spending some time and activity alone with each child"; "these problems clearly come from someone who has a lot of new energy and doesn't know what to do with it. If he used to tease his sister, now he teases her unmercifully. If he used to be impatient, now he's furious. But all these are passing problems. His basic character hasn't changed; his basic behaviors haven't changed. These manifestations of maturation are not problems; they are merely understandable phases. The 'problem' is for me to respond understandingly and not take all the blow-ups and the restlessness and the frustrations as evidence that my son has 'changed' and that 'something must be done.' "

A wise mother, that last. After all, when several people are living closely together in a house, they are bound to get in each other's way, physically and psychologically, and everyone can take comfort in knowing that this is almost inevitable and not "something wrong with our family" about which "something must be done."

I think the idea of spending some time alone with each child is a good one if it can be done in not too studied a manner. Occasionally, it helps to ask the boy or girl to put himself or herself in the place of a sibling. "You play the role of Susan; I'll pretend I'm you," a parent might suggest. To make a real effort of imagination and to put oneself in the skin of another person, as the French say, is a good way to develop understanding and maturity. Also, I think it is a good idea for young adolescents, if they can do it reasonably good-naturedly, to try playing out a typical feeling-conflict scene with a sibling, roles reversed. Role playing, much used in schools these days, can be lots of fun, and it's a great way to replace grimness with humor. Humor, after all, isn't just laughter; it's a way of seeing things in healthy perspective.

Children as well as parents find sibling rivalry hard to take, as is clear from some of the comments of the siblings themselves at the beginning of this chapter. Many teenagers feel that their worst problem is anger, fights and arguments with brothers and sisters. It was mentioned as the worst problem on a quarter to a third of the questionnaires. While it is perhaps inevitable and often extremely unpleasant to both parents and children, sibling rivalry has its values. Children learn good methods for defending themselves emotionally, intellectually and even physically by competing with their brothers and sisters. It's a fine training ground for getting along peacefully and effectively outside the family.

Arguments between Parents

On the questionnaire, I asked: *Do your parents fight or argue? If so, over what?* Three quarters of the students replied *yes,* one quarter *no,* with most of the fights and arguments reported as verbal only. (I find it impressive that 25 percent of students perceive their parents as never having a dispute.) What are the arguments about, according to the kids? By far the greatest number are over "stupid little things": "Who did what when"; "who's responsible for certain things"; "who should do the chores"; "junk—all the things he keeps she thinks should be thrown out"; "very stupid dumb little things like my father buys marge instead of butter"; "dumb things like my grandma's age on an insurance form."

The second largest category of arguments concerns the children: "How to discipline us children"; "me"; "over what happens to me"; "my sister's clothes"; "whether my brothers should have to do whatever my brothers should have to do, or if they shouldn't and when."

Then there is a vast miscellany of other subjects for arguments: "Dad's bad day at work"; "love and a new house"; "politics"; "Dad usually tells Mom when he gets home that the house isn't clean enough and that starts it"; "finances"; "over my step-father's ego"; "over my mother's rights as a human being"; "my father has a terrible temper and my mother is very thick"; "things or politics that end in an ego battle rather than an argument"; "my father wants to do things on impulse and my mother wants to be sensible."

I suppose most people would say the less arguing in families the better, although I've always thought that the married-for-twenty-years-and-never-had-a-cross-word couples must either be scared, badly matched or liars. Anyway, I asked the students: *What is the effect of fights or arguments on you? Good — Bad — Mixed —. Explain your reaction.* Just under half of the boys and girls said *mixed;* but more boys (28 percent) said *good* than girls (20 percent), and fewer said *bad* (boys 24 percent; girls 31 percent). Here's a sampling of comments of those who felt the effects were good: "It's funny, I eat it up"; "if you didn't have arguments you wouldn't be normal, and I want normal parents"; "it means they understand each other and love each other even more"; "it helps me for when I get married"; "they are human, too"; "I sometimes learn things"; "shows me how people get along and how to give a little"; "it's crazy to raise a kid with the idea that marriage is easy and that happiness comes without being chased"; "when I see my parents argue over trivial matters it gives me perspective. I can see how silly they are."

Those who felt that arguments were bad said: "I get mad at the person who got them mad"; "when it's really bad I get kind of scared"; "I'm afraid they might get a divorce" (this is the most commonly expressed reaction of those who thought arguments were bad); "they're being bad which makes me feel bad"; "makes me feel unsafe"; "gets me all worried and mixed up"; "I get upset, worried and nervous because I wouldn't want our family to split"; "they take everything out on me"; "I feel awful when the fight is about me"; "it makes me resent my father, he gets mad so easily"; "I cry a little, mother gets sick and dad takes many sleeping pills"; "too noisy in the house"; "they always fight at the table giving me a chance to eat more than necessary"; "I just don't know what to say. I even thought if I ran away it would help"; "I end up hating my father and this makes me feel guilty because I know he loves me a lot."

The largest group, about half, who answered mixed, made comments like these: "I sometimes get upset but understand that it's silly"; "I know they won't hurt each other but I worry"; "I know they're just average parents"; "my dad yells and my mom feels sorry for *me";* "I leave and come back when they stop, as they always do"; "if they didn't fight it would mean they didn't care, but I don't like it"; "I tend to favor the side with the best argument." A sixth-grade girl had a major problem. She said, "They fight in French so I can't understand."

One gathers from these comments that one of the most damaging effects of arguments is the fear aroused in the children that their family world may break up. I think parents should keep this fear in mind. Quite often parents know that an argument is just an argument, a temporary boil on the healthy body of a marriage, but the children notice the boil to the exclusion of the body. If parents remembered that their arguments are usually noisy and conspicuous, while the predominant love and harmony of their marriage are quite possibly nearly inaudible and invisible to their children, they might find ways to make audible and visible the loving parts of the relationship. Psychologists and psychiatrists have found that some boys and girls feel guilty about the conflicts between their parents and are burdened by a heavy, if unexpressed or even unconscious, sense of responsibility for trying to keep the family together.

Divorce as Seen by Children

It's no news that well over a third of all marriages in the United States end in divorce, and many other couples are separated. In answer to the question, *Are your parents separated or divorced?* 16 percent of the students reported *yes* and 85 percent *no,* which shows that the group of families from the six schools involved in my study are much more stable than American families in general. I went on to ask, *If you answered* yes, *what was the effect on you? Good — Bad — Mixed — Explain.* Almost twice as many girls (21 percent) as boys (11 percent) felt that the effect of divorce was good, but the great majority of boys and girls (84 percent) felt that the effects were bad or mixed.

In their explanations, the children of divorced parents generally felt deeply deprived by the loss of a parent in the house (almost always the father). Here are some comments: "It's good for them and bad for us"; "it's awful not to have a mother and father to count on"; "I try not to let it get to me. It's terrible!"; "we need a man around the house for money"; "they leave bruises forever"; "wrecks up your whole life"; "at first it had a very bad effect on me, but now I feel I have learned from it and it will help me with my future wife"; "it has left most of life unhappy"; "it's really hard not knowing who your dad is!"

Most of the boys and girls who made comments preferred divorce to having to live with continuing hostility and unhappiness: "Divorce is good if you have a good reason"; "bad influence on children but better than always fighting"; "the arguments before are hard on the child"; "if they would kill each other, let them divorce"; "it's better—if they don't act snobbish to each other afterwards"; "it's fine if they hate each other's guts"; "the quicker the better if it's hurting the children"; "people do get tired of other people"; "if they stay married just to keep the family together, it's phony."

Quite a few boys and girls said they disliked their new father or mother: "I don't like my new father"; "my new mom's a sexy creep—at least she thinks she's sexy, I know she's a creep"; "why should I get stuck with a new boss?"

However, some people reported they enjoyed having a choice among four parents and a greater variety of siblings: "I got a lot of new brothers and sisters, but I think I'll be more careful when I get married"; "I'm glad they are divorced because I would never have met my stepmother or father and half brother and I love them a lot"; "I got to live with good foster parents"; "a rich choice of moms and pops and siblings."

About a third of those who commented about divorce stated that they felt strongly that a man and woman shouldn't get married in the first place if they weren't determined to stay married: "If parents rush into getting married, it's stupid, but if they plan it first, it's better"; "it's awful because they don't try, they just give up"; "it shows their original love was fake."

There's no doubt that most divorces involve sorrow, even anguish, for the children, and it's important for parents, if they possibly can, to make it easy for the young people to express their feelings. Perhaps one of the best ways of doing this is for parents to express freely their own sorrow or anguish, not in order to try to win sympathy but rather to show that the children's deep feelings are recognized and shared.

Quite a few children directly expressed the feeling that the divorce was somehow their fault. "I'd rather have them divorced than unhappy because of me" is typical of such comments. An eighth-grader gives this very sound advice to parents who are getting divorced: "Before they get married they should be absolutely positive they want to. If they get divorced they should tell the kids exactly why (if the kids are at a tellable age) and the kids should be assured by *both* parents that it was not their fault."

Moods and Temper

Earlier in this chapter I mentioned how trying many parents find the anger and unstable moods of their teenage children. In light of the commonly made generalization that teen-agers tend to be moody and short-tempered, let's look at what the young people themselves say about this. I asked: *Do you tend to be moody? What do your parents do about it if you are? What* should *they do? Yes,* I tend to be moody, said 61 percent of the students; 39 percent said *no.* Fewer boys feel they are moody (52 percent) than girls (66 percent) and fifth-graders are much less moody (33 percent) than eighth- and ninth-graders (62 percent), just as one would expect.

And how are parents reported to deal with moods? By far the largest number (59 percent) simply leave the moody person alone or ignore him. Another 15 percent are especially careful of or nice to the moody one. About 13 percent talk it over, try to find the cause and help the person get over it. Eight percent, according to the boys and girls, yell, bug or scold in their own fashion, while the remaining 5 percent try to end the mood by some minor punishment like sending the child to his room until the spell passes. In general, almost all of the teen-agers would prefer to be left alone with their moods (after all, moods, like dreams, answer a genuine psychological need; they are real feelings, not to be denied), but a few remark: "They yell at me and they *should";* "they tell me I'm grumpy and I ungrump." Many, however, would sympathize with the eighth-grade girl who wrote: "They don't understand my moods. They expect you to be good, happy and just perfect all the time. When I get in a bad mood I just take it out on everyone, and I always want to be left alone, but they just keep bugging me."

I think some teen-agers could contribute to family happiness if they would luxuriate a little less in their moods and recognize that a heavy mood is really quite a burden on parents who are saddened or annoyed, depending on their natures and the circumstances, by their children's moodiness and who often tend to take the blame for the moods upon themselves.

And what about anger? I asked: *Do you tend to lose your temper often or get very angry? If yes, what sets you off?* There was very little difference among grades or between boys and girls in the replies to this question: 54 percent said *yes* and 46 percent said *no*. Fifth-graders tend a bit more to anger (56 percent) than ninth-graders (49 percent), but not much. The things that set off a burst of anger are, in descending order of frequency, the maddening actions or words of siblings, unreasonable demands of parents, teasing ("people picking on me because I'm short and have freckles"; "when people call me the Jolly Green Giant [I'm 5′ 8″]," said two sixth-grade girls), and various kinds of unfairness at school and home or in sports.

Perhaps it is unwise to give general advice on how parents should react to angry teen-agers because the psychological chemistries of families differ so, but I think it's usually wise to avoid getting right into the dispute too often. A mother of three children, 13, 10 and 8, says, "I wish I had the calm disposition my mother had—she could ignore my adolescent carryings on—but I always react and end up right in the center of the fray!" Another writes: "I was totally unprepared for these intense emotional outbursts. When I reacted to them emotionally (as an attack on my authority) I couldn't handle it without getting upset. Now I see that if I succeed in remaining more or less objective and recognize the outbursts as not unusual for this age, it works out better." Parents, at least most of them, are experienced enough to see the situations in some sort of perspective. Another mother, who has five children, expressed the idea well: "The adult always has the advantage of knowing that for the child, this piece of reality, at least, will very soon give place to another, perhaps a more pleasant one, and just as real, so the adult can keep a basic security through the storm."

Punishment and Young Adolescents

Parents occasionally ask me about punishment for middle school children. "What do we do if we've tried reason, we've tried consulting, we've tried getting out his feelings on the subject, and *still* he won't clean his room?" —or go to bed when he's supposed to, or mow the grass, or stop teasing his sister? Or what does one do when a child has done something truly bad, such as stealing, or breaking something through deliberate carelessness, or cheating on a test? Or what if children deliberately disobey you in a major matter like not coming back by an agreed-upon time at night, or not letting you know of an important change of plan that inconvenienced the whole family?

It is safe to say that by the time people reach junior high school the need for punishment should be greatly reduced, and, if possible, the punishments should be self-administering, a direct result of the misdeed. If the punishment "fits the crime," then it has some teaching value. For example, if you force your daughter to get up in the morning, pressure her through her preschool duties, shove her off just in time to make the school bus, and say she'll have to stay in all day Saturday if she's late again, which she then is, the punishment will probably result in resentment of you and probably no great training in the values of promptness and the effects of lateness. On the other hand, suppose, after a moderate amount of encouragement from you to be on time and an explanation of the likely consequences of lateness, she is late. You decide to let the consequences happen. They may be a cold breakfast, having to walk to school or pay carfare from her own allowance, having to stay after school, displeasure from teachers, poorer marks. These follow naturally from the lateness and tend to teach the values of promptness. If the punishment really fits the crime, the girl tends to attach it to her misdeed, and to blame her own unwise action; if it does not fit the crime, she is likely to attach the punishment to you and to blame you, not the thing she has done.

If there are no nice, neat consequences for a child to suffer—for instance, of a boy teasing his sister—then what do you do? First, be absolutely sure he has a chance to understand the effects of what he is doing: help him to imagine himself in his sister's place. Can he see how impossible he is making life for her? Then, see if there isn't some way that the brother-sister relationship can't be nudged onto a new plane, either for the moment or in the longer run: have you some interesting project they might do together to lift them out of the conflict? For instance, could they go to the movies together if it's a rainy afternoon, or be interested in building a model or taking some pictures of the new dog or collecting clothes for the clothing drive or moving their rooms to the third floor?

Then, if none of this works, try to make the punishment neat and short. Sometimes telling a child to spend fifteen minutes in his room alone helps to change the situation, or withdrawing a privilege such as watching a TV show that evening or going to a football game, but *not* no more movies for a month or home from school every day at three for the next two weeks. If you are truly puzzled as to what to do, and if your teen-ager clearly knows he deserves to be punished, sometimes it works to consult with him about it. Let him figure out his own punishment.

A Few Don'ts

There are a few don'ts about punishments:

1. Don't use a punishment that brings humiliation (forced acknowledgment that you, the parent, were right; obliging the child to telephone a friend and say he can't do something because he was bad; or any public punishment), to which all children, but especially middle and junior high schoolers, are very sensitive and which often results in revolt, bitterness or a weakening of the character and personality of your child.

2. Don't spank or hit a junior high schooler. While physical punishments have the advantage of being neat and short, age twelve or above is too old for them.

3. Don't dock his allowance, which should be his regardless (except, of course, if his allowance is based on doing chores and he has not done them).

4. Don't try to get good behavior by bribing him with money or privileges. A bribe shows that you assume the child will be bad and that money must be paid to prevent this; it shows a real lack of faith in the child. Also, bribes tend to need constant increasing.

5. Don't withhold your love and appreciation of the child. Don't say, in effect, "You were bad to do that"; say, "That was a bad thing to do." In other words, "hate the sin, not the sinner."

If you find that your family life has become too filled with punishments, it's probably well to consult with an outsider to get a fresh view. A teacher, a child-guidance person, a family group therapist, an intimate relative or another parent can sometimes help get things back into their proper perspective.

I've already put physical punishment on the list of don'ts; but since these days there is an increasing interest in and advocacy of corporal punishment, perhaps some additional comment on the subject will be helpful. On the questionnaire, I asked: *Has anyone at home or at school, grades five through nine, ever used corporal punishment (spanking, hitting) on you? Yes — No —.* Of the boys, 46 percent said *yes,* 54 percent *no;* with girls it was 40 percent *yes,* 60 percent *no.* In response to a further question, *What were the effects on you?* 29 percent said that in one way or another they were good, 71 percent bad. Here are some comments in favor of corporal punishment: "Corporal punishment keeps me from doing it again"; "better because it was faster"; "it makes me respect a person very close to me. I'm glad it happened"; "at home I've been spanked several times. I think this method really helps get the message across"; "I think it is more torturous to talk it out."

Here's what the opponents of corporal punishment said: "It does not make as big an impression on me as talking"; "I felt bad"; "parents shouldn't hit their children unless they are little and they can't discuss it with them"; "it made me a sad child"; "it only hurts and builds grudges"; "it does not explain what I did wrong or why"; "I get madder and go out of the way to do bad things."

Two comments I enjoyed were from seventh-graders: "The effect was a soar rear "; and "my mother and father both think it is a hiteous idea." Another two comments are from eighth-grade girls: "My father and mother hit me up until 6th grade, when they devised other ingenious ways of making me behave"; "my mother hit me on the head with a frozen hot dog and I cried and screamed." Ah, the joys of family living! And a ninth-grade boy reports: "A certain Mr. —— used to beat us with a piece of cypress that was conveniently shaped in the size of one's gluteus maximous (ass)."

What Do They Think Makes a Good Parent?

I'm not sure how much help it is to tell parents what qualities make a good parent. Perhaps establishing some sort of model might tend to encourage us parents in whatever good points we have and help us work against the bad ones. Useful or not, it's interesting to compare how students, teachers and parents answered this question: *What are the most important qualities of a good parent?* On the questionnaires I provided a separate space for *father* and for *mother*. Generally, the students followed the lead of the questionnaire and made different lists for each parent; about half the parents made a single list for both sexes, some specifically objecting to the implied assumption that the good qualities of fathers and mothers might be different; almost every teacher made a single list and rejected the possibilities of sex differences in this respect.

By far the most frequently mentioned quality among the students is *understanding*, which means, I gather from the comments that accompanied the lists, knowing what *we* mean, how *we* feel, how it is from *our* point of view—making us feel you are with us. I should guess that those parents who listen well, who keep open minds and who succeed in reflecting the feelings of their children would rate highest in understanding.

The second quality in frequency of mention by students is that of being *loving;* it is the first in frequency of mention by parents and teachers. The third quality on the student list is that of being *nice, kind, considerate.*

The second quality in frequency of mention among both parents and teachers is *fairness and consistency,* something that I suppose boys and girls would favor but hardly any of them mentioned.

It is interesting that *understanding* did not rate on the parents' list and placed third on the teachers' list. Apparently, youngsters want to be understood above all, while adults, whether parents or teachers, see love and fairness as the key qualities.

Other qualities that students mentioned frequently as desirable for fathers to have are: having time to do things with you, spending time at home, being the leader or head of the family, and keeping a good balance of sternness and leniency. Other qualities admired in mothers are being helpful, being a good cook, spending time with you and caring.

In addition to the qualities of being loving, fair and consistent, many parents listed others: for fathers, respecting the children, having patience, being firm, keeping promises and providing a good father image; for mothers, being a good listener and being patient.

Teachers, in addition to the qualities of being loving, consistent and understanding, frequently mentioned having a good sense of self, being patient and maintaining good values.

What Pleases and What Annoys

To get at daughters' and sons' views on parents in another way, I asked two other questions: *What do you like best about your parents?* and *What annoys you most about your parents?* In general, answers to these questions were consistent with the young people's lists of qualities, but they were often expressed in more vigorous language. The main annoyance, especially at fathers, was quickness of temper evidenced by yelling. Another frequently mentioned annoyance at fathers was expressed repeatedly in the phrase, "He always thinks he's right." Mothers annoy their children most by nagging and by smoking, and a good sprinkling of the kids objected to their parents' drinking, especially their mothers. I think the best way to make the "likes" and "annoyances" of the boys and girls come alive is to give a considerable number of them verbatim.

What do you like best about your father? "He likes me"; "he doesn't punish me right away. He asks me first why I did it"; "if someone dies in the family he will cry with me"; "sometimes he will take only *one* of us camping or out to dinner"; "he's reasonable"; "he gives me confidence and courage"; "he lets me get away with things"; "he's the best skier"; "he doesn't shout and send you to your room. He talks about it"; "he works hard"; "he has almost all the answers and is a very wise man."

What do you like best about your mother? "She's a very good friend to me"; "she's more of an older sister"; "she pulls for me when dad is mad"; "she brings me up well"; "she tries very hard to be sure I can tell right from wrong"; "she works full time and still has time to love me"; "she remembers being young"; "she tells me her secrets (about her friends)"; "she *tries* to do everything she can for me (and she can be a real pest about it)."

What annoys you most about your father? "He stays at work too long"; "he gives me lectures on everything I do wrong in sports"; "when he says, 'Yes, Dear' "; "he gets far away from the subject"; "he says no and doesn't give reasons"; "my father always interrupts me but gets mad when I interrupt"; "when the stock market goes down he's mad during our dinner and bangs on the table"; "he kisses my girlfriends and tells crazy jokes"; "when I'm upset he puts on a fake smile"; "he tries to act strict in front of my friends"; "when I ask him to help with my homework he goes into detail"; "he's a male chauvinist"; "he takes comedy too far"; "he's run by my mother"; "he doesn't listen and gets mad at what he doesn't hear"; "he's so goddam smart"; "he has a flairy temper and is too honest"; "he is caught by an overbearing wife and cannot come to grips and subdue her"; "he doesn't show his feelings until he explodes."

What annoys you about your mother? "When she screams"; "she interferes with a slumber party"; "when she gets mad and starts swearing"; "she treats me like a baby"; "she calls me weird names like biddyboo"; "looking through my private property"; "she's fake nice and sweet in front of my friends"; "she's a psychiatrist and always thinks something's bothering me"; "she likes my brother more than me it seems"; "she says, 'what's your sweater doing on the floor?' instead of 'please pick up your sweater' "; "she'll call up the school at the drop of a hat"; "she's too much of a martyr. She gives up anything for anyone she thinks wants it more."

Parents, Consider Yourselves

After these comments by children on what they like and find annoying about their parents, you parents may be feeling a little shattered. Obviously, no one can be perfect. Annoying others is sometimes an inevitable part of living. So should parents take the impressions of all these kids seriously? Well, I'd say, take what you find is useful and leave the rest.

Years ago, there was a lot of good, intelligent talk and some witty comments about the "child-centered" school and curriculum. I think that some rigor-obsessed schools might well go back and read what was being said then about the importance of not forgetting that the child, or student, is, or should be, the central consideration in a school. But the same doesn't go for homes. Don't have a child-centered home! It troubles me to hear parents calling each other Mom and Dad instead of by their own names: "Well, Mother, were the children good today?"; "Oh, Dad, I'm so glad to see you!" After all, a husband and wife fell in love with each other as man and woman, each with a name. They care for each other, and their children are a by-product of their love. A child-centered home is likely to contain selfish children. Parents have needs too. An eighth-grade boy puts it:

Although my parents do a wonderful job of taking care of us children and bringing us up and help us whenever we need it and I appreciate it, I wish they would have more fun.

It's important for parents to recognize their own feelings and to be open about them with their children. Dorothy Baruch believes it's better to say frankly to a child, "Please make your bed before school because it drives me crazy to see it unmade all day," than to take a more child-centered approach: "Make your bed; it'll help teach you to be a good homemaker."

Don't martyr yourself; don't oversacrifice. It too often results in suppressed resentment and self-pity, which are likely to come out in some sort of unpleasantness later on.

Some Advice: Children to Parents

I suppose most advice in most homes flows from parent to child, whether or not it is accepted. However, it may be well for parents to consider what the anthropologist Margaret Mead said recently about who should be the teachers these days. She said that with the world changing as rapidly as it now is, the young are quite possibly better equipped to adjust to it successfully than are their parents. At least, she says, parents should listen to their young: the generation in power should listen to the generation that will inherit power. With this in mind, I asked the students the question, *If you were to write a book for parents of boys and girls of your age, what advice would you give them?*

Much of the advice is in the form of pleas—pleas for understanding, for strictness, for fewer rules, for listening, for privacy, for honesty, for patience, for good service, for less advice, for various kinds of help and for being left alone. Not much of the advice was surprising; most of it grows naturally from the same concerns and attitudes shown in answers to other questions already reported in this book.

Here are some of the most apt pieces of advice: "Be nice and understanding and don't spank, but tell them to go to their room if they're bad"; "not to curse, screw, drink or smoke"; "you have to understand that boys and girls start to love each other around age 11"; "keep up the good work!"; "talk to their children a lot and have fun with them"; "love your children. Be proud of them. We will do the same"; "always remember, when you do something your children will always hear it"; "show that you love the child openly, not hidden away somewhere under a guilty feeling"; "that we have a hard time at this age"; "make them remember that you brought them into the world and they should obey you"; "don't butt into children's business and don't tease"; "explain about sex so your kids won't be left out of a crowd"; "keep in close touch with your kids but let them handle their own lives"; "understand that there are times when your children are growing up that they go back to childhood. Instead of growing-up looking like this ⁄ it looks like this ∿∿∿ "; "don't be too protective. It leads to a spoiled kid"; "keep kids from alcohol, drugs and smoking by setting a good example"; "don't talk to your children about subjects you don't know anything about (drugs)" (this from a nonuser of drugs); "never back down on a threat"; "don't get divorced until your kids are old enough to understand and deal with it"; "RELAX —DON'T WORRY!!!"; "don't punish the first time because sometimes they don't know why they shouldn't do it"; "watch how your kids act and don't let them get too loose so they hang around street corners because they can get messed up so easily and waste their life"; "a child's room is his private domain in which he should be allowed to decide what goes on"; "hang loose. The world is too clock-conscious"; "there are some things kids would like to keep to themselves, so don't nose or snoop"; "ask questions if the kid looks puzzled"; "don't spoil a child. Kids hate spoiled kids"; "never have such a strict rule that there is not a situation where it cannot be stretched or broken"; "most of all, trust one another, trust is a two-way street."

9

Social Life at Home and at School

"5 I don't know what you mean by 'social life.' I don't think I have any.

6 One time I threw potato chips at a boy I liked.

7 There are too many creeps in our class of the opposite sex.

8 This is a very confusing time in a boy's life.

9 My parents think they're helping a lot planning my social life. I keep them thinking that way. Because what can they do once I'm out?"

The first society we live in is that of our family, and the early years of this life strongly affect the sort of social life we will live for the rest of our days. After infancy, we gradually move out from the family and our society enlarges, but until the arrival of adolescence, our parents' family is the center. At adolescence comes a rapid acceleration across the bumpy social terrain that lies between this family and the new one of our own that is the destination for most of us when we reach full adulthood. Our new family, whatever its makeup may be (mother-father-children or just a single, established person), will be strongly affected by but independent of our parental family. A few of us cross the terrain smoothly, but most are pretty jerky on the throttle, grind the gears quite a lot, squeal around corners, do some zigzagging and back-tracking, and not infrequently lose the way and need rescuing.

The Society of Home

In the social life of all families there is constant communication, much of it nonverbal and unconscious, but some of it quite conscious. In Chapter 1, I reported that two thirds of the sons and daughters ages ten to fifteen said that they found it difficult at times or always to communicate with their parents, and that it became more difficult as they grew older. And now, here is a further question I asked about communication: *Who is easier to talk to? Father — Mother — Why?* Two thirds of the students said mother, 18 percent said father, and 17 percent added that they could talk to both parents with equal ease (or lack of ease). Twice as many boys found it easier to talk to their mothers (56 percent) than to their fathers (25 percent); 72 percent of the girls found their mother easier to talk to and only 13 percent their father.

The most obvious reason that mothers are easier to talk to is that they are more often there, but another reason, reported over and over in the answer to *why?* by boys and girls at every grade is "She understands better." There are other reasons given for finding it easier to talk to the mother. Here are some from daughters: "She is my own sex"; "I'm closer to her"; "because she knows everything a girl has to do"; "Dad refuses to listen to anyone but himself"; "my mother was once a girl, my father wasn't."

And from sons: "My father's never around so problems go in one ear and out the other"; "my father makes jokes about girls"; "my mother doesn't get mad and ask hard questions"; "Mom doesn't jump to conclusions"; "she is more rational"; "she's softer"; "she is more modern, Dad is simple"; "my father has a business-type attitude. Whereas my mom can talk to me without giving me the feeling of being a little kid."

In some cases, though, the father is easier to talk to. Here are reasons for this given by daughters: "My mother thinks I'm foolish and forget it"; "he is more sort of open-ears"; "Mom gets too fussy"; "my father tries to act cool and so he understands more"; "Mom is irrational."

And by sons: "Because I like sports"; "he did practically the same things I do. My mother doesn't understand anything"; "he is more candid, and some things you just don't talk about with your mother."

On the questionnaire I asked, *What important subjects have you discussed with your parents in the past few months?* The most frequently mentioned subject, especially in grades seven, eight and nine, was schoolwork (grades, subjects, etc.; "teachers" were mentioned much less often). Next most frequently discussed was sex (and the opposite sex), again mostly in grade seven and above. But sex was mentioned only half as often as schoolwork. Other topics specified fairly often, but far less so than the first two, were social life and friends, "growing up" and career, family problems, sports, politics and world affairs (only in grade seven and up), money, drugs, and pets (grades five and six only).

Then I asked, *What subjects, if any, have you felt you'd like to talk about with your parents but have not done so?* More people specified "none" or "nothing" than anything else, but a close second was sex, which far outranked all other subjects. After sex came drugs, and then a scattering of mentions of smoking, drinking, feelings about growing up, questions about the future, and school problems. It is significant, I think, that sex and drugs ranked near the bottom of the list of parents' concerns reported in Chapter 1, while they rank at the top of the list of subjects both boys and girls would like to talk about with their parents but do not feel they can.

I asked, *If there are subjects you didn't talk about but wanted to, why didn't you talk?* The most frequently given reason was, "I'd be embarrassed." Nearly as often given were these two other reasons: "They wouldn't understand" and fear of parental anger or punishment. Other reasons given were the feeling that parents are too busy, that they wouldn't listen, or simply that there is a generation gap. Some other comments were: "They always seem to be more against me in a discussion than with me. It makes me feel inferior"; "my mother will feel differently about me if I tell her about my sex"; "I don't want them to think I'm 'boy crazy' or a hippie-type"; "they think I'm way too young to do most of the things they don't know about"; "if I talk about drugs they think immediately I'm using them and I'm usually not"; "they tease me about boys, etc., so it's a pain trying to tell them something"; "it's so personal an inner alarm goes off if you try to spill the beans"; "my parents polarize what I say and practice selective hearing."

The Desire to Talk and Be Heard

It's sad, isn't it, that there are so many boys and girls who'd like to talk to their parents and who feel they can't. But the desire to talk and be heard, and be talked to and to listen, isn't only on the side of the children. Parents feel the same way. I asked parents, *What is the main satisfaction you feel in relation to your children at home?* Many of the replies had to do with communication: "Honesty and freedom among us all"; "good, lively discussions"; "the way we deal with problems. We talk well and respect each other"; "they feel they can bring me their problems, even intimate ones"; "a very close and understanding feeling about each other's moods, opinions and needs."

On the other side, as I reported in the last chapter, I asked, *What is the problem relating to your child(ren) aged 10–15 that you'd most like not to have?* Many of the answers revealed that parents want to talk and be talked to, a desire parents would like to have satisfied. Some said: "The non-outgoingness of my child—the shyness with us"; "I wish he'd speak up and say what's on his mind"; "I have a hunger to talk and listen, but I can't get listened to or spoken to. It's like two painful vacuums wanting to be filled, or maybe two painful boils wanting to burst—our children's and ours, and both sides possess what is needed to ease the pains but, strangely, neither side can give it or even ask for it."

The School and Social Life

"The school should have nothing to do with your social life"; "schools have no right to rule our personal lives"; "I think it is a dirty, lowdown way for a school to try to ruin a teenager's life." These are eighth- and ninth-graders expressing themselves on the school's concern about their social life.

But schools inevitably get involved with the students' social life, not only at school but at home, because so many questions about it are brought to school and we are so often asked for suggestions. Also, home conditions often affect the behavior and academic work not only of the child that inhabits the home but also other children who associate with him at school and at home. For instance, if some parents allow a group of eighth-graders to drink alcoholic beverages (or are unaware that they are doing so) at their home, or if they have a teen-age party on a school night for members of a class so that no homework gets done, it quickly becomes a school problem, either because troubled parents call the school or because work at school is directly affected. However, even in rather serious cases, I think the school must be very cautious about intervening. It can state what it believes is an intelligent policy on alcohol or school-night parties; it can directly inform the parents involved what its view is and how what's done at home affects what happens at school; but after that it becomes a matter for the home to deal with, and if parents are disturbed by the social behavior of another family connected with the school, they should probably take it up directly with the family concerned, difficult and embarrassing as this may be.

Of course, any good school will get involved in social life *at school.* An experienced homeroom and mathematics teacher explains why:

Kids' friendships and their rudeness and inconsiderateness toward each other and how they feel about themselves greatly influence their ability to work. I think it bears a lot of talking about in school because they can learn, for instance, that they don't have just to knuckle under to a gang leader if they know other kids feel the same way and if the teacher can help provide the security mechanisms to try other things. I don't have any solutions except a good bit of talk and listening to help facilitate and support their efforts. When a kid hurts another, it should not be ignored.

New Roles for Parents and Teachers

When boys and girls leave elementary school and enter adolescence, their parents and teachers must play a quite different role in their social life. They continue to be providers of facilities, but they are no longer wanted as paternalistic planners of games and activities. (When I asked, *How much should your parents help plan your social life?* almost every person above sixth grade, and many fifth- and sixth-graders, answered, "Very little," "not at all" or "none.") Parents and teachers may call attention to the need for planning, but the actual planning—and more and more of the initiative for it—should now come from the young people themselves. Also, the people in any social affair become more important and the specific activities less. Further, young adolescents are much more on their own. Adults can less often directly help them out of difficult social situations, and their direct help is seldom wanted and often resented.

There is one major function that parents and teachers can have, however, and that is helping youngsters to put into perspective the eager search for popularity and friends. "Mr. Johnson," a devastated eighth-grader confided in me, "what can I do? I'm not popular. What's wrong with me? How can I change?" Another said: "I'm afraid to speak up in class. I don't like to seem to know the answer because the kids will think I'm a square." And another: "How can I change? I don't think I'll *ever* get in with the class, except for a few creeps. What'll happen if nobody ever likes me?" And, of course, for every teen-ager who works up the courage to express such worries to a teacher, there are a dozen who suffer forlornly in silence or who put up a brave front of not caring. Some become quite antisocial, seeming to try to fend off the efforts of their classmates or neighbors to be friendly, probably because they have been burned once and are afraid to expose again how deeply they care.

Still others are so preoccupied with what their classmates and friends are thinking of them that they can pay little attention to anything else. At school, a girl may seem to be looking at the text or test, but her sensitivities are all trained on her companions, and especially on the social leaders and on what sort of impression she is making on them. Many young adolescents go through a period of not daring to be themselves but trying desperately to be what they think they must be in order to win approval. These frantic efforts for popularity can, even if they succeed and especially if they are futile, result in acute suffering and unhappiness.

Adults must try to find a good moment and way to tell junior high schoolers this truth (and, kids, if you are reading, hear this!): "It's natural that you should be so worried about making friends and being popular. Almost everyone is, even those who succeed the most. It's a good thing, too, that you are making an effort because it's important to learn how to get along with other people. But don't worry so much! You're going to have friends. I know it. You're entirely too bright and attractive for people not to like you. I can remember when I was your age [if you can] feeling absolutely horrible because people didn't seem to like me. I really suffered terribly. I wish I'd known then what I know now—that everything was going to come out all right.

" 'Oh, yes,' you say, 'but how do I know it's going to come out all right with *me?*' Well, granted you don't *know,* and it is only natural for you to wonder and worry. But let me tell you: It's a funny thing the way people who are wildly popular in junior high school aren't by any means always the ones who are the most popular when they are juniors or seniors or get into college or a job. As a matter of fact . . ." and go on to point out examples of older students, now successful, who didn't fit in junior high school. I recall the boy who was so unhappy in eighth grade that he and his parents were discussing whether he should try another school, but who in eleventh grade was elected president of his class. Parents and teachers can cite the fact, observed over and over again, that when unpopular boys and girls get to college, they find that they are looked at with a fresh eye by people who never knew that they were Bobby the squirt in seventh grade or fat Sally in ninth. Another thing: sometimes it turns out that the girls and boys who are very popular in junior high school and never seem to have to make any effort to succeed socially, who have had lots of parties and dates from seventh or eighth grade on, that these envied ones may turn out to have dull marriages and to lead less satisfying lives than those for whom life wasn't quite such a carefree affair when they were thirteen and fourteen. This may be cold comfort, but it's true.

Now of course all of this doesn't have to be done in one great speech, as I have suggested. It can be done piecemeal, obliquely, as you are conversing at various times about life and people. However, I think a good strong statement like this, delivered as a whole at a receptive moment, may make the most impact.

The ideas I have just expressed can well be helpful, also, to the very popular boys and girls who are so caught up in the joy and triumph of social success and planning for further pleasures that they forget to look beyond their circle of popular people to those on the fringe who may seem beneath their notice, not quite right, perhaps even peculiar. I can remember when I was at school being completely and rather unconsciously disdainful of those in my class who didn't act the way I did and do things I approved of. It never occurred to me that they might turn out to be successful, worthy human beings, or that perhaps they would have a lot to offer me in friendship and interest. I wish someone had suggested this to me—or perhaps they did, and I didn't hear it.

Parents and teachers can help young people in another way: they can point out that *almost everyone feels insecure* some of the time in social situations, when meeting new people, arriving at a party, going on a date. They can show that they realize that it is hard to be shy and not popular and that they really understand the difficulty of the problem and sympathize with the acuteness of the misery. They can go on to say that almost no one ever minds your taking the first step to be friendly. Therefore, a girl, for example, can be urged to see how it works if she really tries to put herself forward in a friendly way. She can begin by always saying "Hi!" and smiling when she passes people in the hall—even if they don't say "Hi!" back. No one resents a friendly greeting. She will often find that a good conversation can be started by asking a question: "What did you think of the ball game last night?" Or, "What are you going to do over Christmas?" Or, "How do you like Mr. Hedges as a teacher?"; or any other question that gives other people a chance to talk about themselves and their own opinions—and then *really to listen* to the reply.

Learning to socialize requires much experimentation and hours of seemingly wasted time. Adolescents need these empty hours in which to loll around together talking, without conscious purpose. The local pizza joint, the available living room, the front steps, the basement, the main hall of the school or the lunchroom—any of these may be the place where these boys and girls will hang around aimlessly in the easy ambience of congenial equals trying out their thoughts and ideas on subjects such as love, girls, boys, war, teachers, parents, marriage, sex, careers, brothers and sisters, religion, sports, movies and cars.

The Bases for Social Acceptance

In middle and junior high school, many students glide and cavort through the social swim easily and happily, but a good many others are so miserable you'd think they were being tortured. Teachers can see this almost daily if they look out over the mass of students eating lunch. Most of the kids rush in joyously, bang down a bag or a book to save a place, chatter through the lunch line with a friend and end up contentedly and noisily ingesting their food amid a cluster of congenial classmates. Some others, not such good mixers, find their places at a table with some friends, but with less ease and joy; they are not at the top of the social heap. And then there are the unhappy several who find no ready place to sit, who are told, "This place is saved," and who wander around and finally sit alone or with a few others at a table where the only common denominator is not being accepted by any social group.

At these grade levels, the basis for social acceptance is narrow. Good clothes help (or at least the *right* clothes), enough money helps, pleasant parents help, but these are not essential. The main things are to be good at sports (whether boy or girl), to be handsome or pretty (by the standards of one's peers), and to have an easy line of chatter. Scholastic excellence, while it is respected, does not win social acceptance in junior high school.

Feelings of Rejection

How much do middle and junior high school students feel rejected by others, and is there more rejection in junior high than in elementary school? To find out, I asked this question: *Have you ever felt left out or re-*

jected by a group of your fellow students? Frequently — Pretty often — Seldom — Never —. As one would expect, feelings of rejection increase with the coming of adolescence. Fourteen percent of the fifth-graders checked the "frequently" or "pretty often" blanks; the figure increased to 42 percent in ninth grade. (Of course, the ninth-graders have more years to look back on.) Thirty percent of fifth-graders said they'd never felt rejected; only 9 percent of ninth-graders.

My question continued: *If you have felt rejected, describe generally when, how, and how you reacted. If you answered* never, *why do you think you never have?* Here are some comments from those who had been rejected: "They teased me for being near a girl and I ignored it"; "nobody answered me, they ignored me, you really feel left out and you could kill the person your friend went off with"; "I'm usually the last to get picked and I feel hurt"; "I just walk away with a smile and feel left out inside"; "I didn't say anything but I'm sure my face got red"; "what's any better about them that they should exclude me?"; "I didn't like being told to 'bug off' "; "I began to feel selfconscious and lose all of my ego"; "it's a horrible feeling, so lonely"; "I reacted pretty bad, I almost cried"; "I ignore them or attack back"; "it's done by kids I can't bear so what the hell"; "when my friends go around 'cool kids' they don't talk to me so I just stand there"; "when the kids see you they start laughing and I feel like killing myself"; "I'm not an athlete, I go to a jock school: constant rejection"; "I just thought out what I did and remembered not to do it again."

In later grades, especially in high school, it is always encouraging to see how the basis for acceptability broadens and an increasing number of boys and girls find ways to gain satisfaction in the approval of their peers. The good student becomes recognized; the musicians find their group; the science wonder-workers are appreciated. It is important that youngsters be encouraged to pursue many interests in many groups (not just at school, but in groups centering around scouts, hobbies, music, drama, church, and so on) so that they may have the maximum chance to find social acceptance and satisfaction.

The New Social Whirl

Over the years, as I have looked at junior high schoolers and their socializing, I have seen them enter seventh grade, the majority as children, and at the end of the school year leave the same grade buzzing with social activity. A few are dating, some are being invited to a party as often as once a week, but many are feeling left out. However, it is in eighth grade when things really start moving. Many of the boys, and most of the girls, are now frankly interested in the opposite sex; for a number, partying has become intense; and especially the girls and their mothers are worrying about popularity. There is an onslaught of gossiping, considerable cruelty and exclusion, and a peak of cliquishness. Since the urge of social activity is new to most parents and youngsters alike, there is usually more excitement, fear, elation, discouragement and complaining in eighth grade than ever before or ever again. During ninth grade, social life is still very active and quite fluttery, but it's settling down a bit. The boys and girls are more mature and the parents more habituated to the whole thing and thus a bit calmer.

Eighth grade is a great time for the meeting of parents at school, and one of the valuable functions of the school is to provide a place where parents can come together for mutual comfort and support and a sharing of troubles and ideas. It is very often consoling to know that others are going through the same sort of hell that you are, and it helps to give perspective to neophytes to hash things over with parents who have been through it before with children who are now older. It is often rather lonely to be a parent of adolescents, sitting isolated in the castle of your home, at the mercy of "Well, everyone else is allowed to. . . ."

Parents sometimes tell me that the teachers are organized and present a common front, the students are organized—or at least see each other every day—and present one or several fronts, but the parents aren't organized, or, if they are, they don't see each other very often. Thus, if you are a junior high school parent troubled about social problems, I suggest you arrange through the school or the P.T.A. to have a session with other school parents. It is also well to invite one or two teachers, a grade head, or the middle or junior high school principal to come so that they may add whatever information or observations they may have.

I am not advocating that the school interfere in the social life of the students or become deeply involved in activities which are essentially the business of the home. Far from it. We teachers have enough to do trying to give our pupils the best academic instruction we can. All I am saying is that the school can be the catalyst to provide a neutral, convenient place for parents to meet—preferably at their initiative and as a result of their planning—to thrash out problems.

Some Minimum Essentials at Home

How much should parents be involved in the social life of their children? I think that in most cases there are certain basic understandings that the family should try to reach. Sons and daughters should ask parents' permission before undertaking any major social activity (one which is out of the ordinary routine and will require a considerable amount of time), and parents should give permission unless they have a good reason not to. If they say no, the children have a right to know the reason.

For evening activities (parties, dates, etc.) children should tell parents: (1) where they are going; (2) with whom; (3) what they plan to do; (4) when the activity starts and finishes; and (5) how they plan to get there and back.

Most young teen-agers appreciate knowing exactly what time they are expected home, so that they do not have to make the self-belittling decision that it's now time to go home. They'd rather blame the decision on parents. While many teen-agers are happy to get home and get some sleep, there are few with the strength of character to admit it and go against the urge of the herd to stay up until the latest possible hour.

Time limits should not be absolutely rigid: that is, unforeseen and uncontrollable circumstances should be allowed for. This is especially important when young people start driving their own cars. A much-feared, absolute deadline can lead to reckless speeding.

I think there are times when, on principle, parents may feel that they need to stand alone against what may be considered community standards and take the consequences for themselves and their children. I do not favor the practice too common in America of always finding out what everyone else is doing before deciding what is right. This springs from muddy values and leads to mediocrity. But on a matter like what time to get home in the evening there's nothing absolute, no principle involved (except that of health, and there parents have to judge on the basis of their own child), and some community consultation is sensible, I think.

What to Do about Too Much Social Activity

Some happy—or socially driven—youngsters are terribly in demand and could be out at parties or visiting several nights a week if there were no controls. If parents find, for example, that their daughter is being invited out of the house too much, or is having others in excessively, they should try to find a quiet time when there's no particular social event at issue, and try to work out with her some reasonable standards. Certainly, there should be no parties on school nights, and probably only one per weekend, although no hard and fast rule can be made about this, since some children need so much less rest and sleep than do others. One intelligent family I know has the following formula for weekends: One late night only; a quiet evening to follow a big day and vice versa; a large part of Sunday quiet; same bedtime Sunday night as before any school day.

In general, most boys and girls are willing to agree that weekends should be used for fun, relaxation, some useful family chores, some family activity together (not necessarily *all* the family), and enough rest to put the student in school on Monday morning in good condition. If parents can get *previous agreement* on these as reasonable standards, then it will be easier to apply them later in specific cases. With socially-minded, popular kids, there's little doubt parents are going to have to say no occasionally. It's too much to expect any but exceptional youngsters to have the strength to turn down an attractive invitation, say, for Friday night, even when they know they will be out late again on Saturday. They'll come to parents and ask, "Please, can I go?" and parents say no, definitely, on the basis of mutually understood policies previously worked out. They may plead and groan a bit to save face, but they'll be able to go back to the telephone, or to school the next day, and say: "My family won't let me go. They won't let me go out more than one night per weekend. It's a gyp but there's nothing I can do about it."

If Your Child Is Not Invited

What about a boy, say, who is seldom invited to parties and social events and is unhappy about it? Can you help him? It's not easy. You might try investigating why he isn't succeeding by asking a teacher or the congenial parent of a classmate from whom you think you might get an honest answer. Maybe it will be because he's hard to talk to, or he's boastful, or he's a poor dancer, or he has bad manners, or he dresses queerly, or he rejects invitations when they are proffered, or everyone thinks he's a square, or he takes a superior moralistic view toward what other teen-agers consider normal behavior, or he seems to have no morals at all, or he's aggressive, or rude, or profane, or disrespectful of girls. It will be helpful for you to have a frank opinion on why your child isn't invited. Be sure you are not offended or do not become defensive when you get it. And you may find a way to relay to your son what you have learned and thus help him to overcome his social weaknesses.

Perhaps you could combine with another parent on a pair of very casual get-togethers for supper, one given by each of you, before two school parties, dances, canteens, plays, concerts or whatever. Perhaps the mother of a really popular person in the class can easily suggest to her child that yours be invited to a party. Often classmates and their parents are entirely unaware that a perfectly likable boy or girl is being left out of the social activities of the class. If you don't feel able to take this sort of initiative with another parent, at least try letting an understanding teacher in on it. He or she may be able to devise a way to help.

Friends

Fairly high on the list of concerns of parents reported in the first chapter, and near the top of the teachers' list, were the students who aren't making friends at school—and lack of friends at school usually spills over into loneliness at home unless the student goes to school outside the neighborhood. There are some youngsters who are loners at school and very social around home.

What, if anything, can or should parents do about lack of friendships at school? Is there anything the school can do? Many youngsters have little difficulty with this, but there are a number of individuals in any class—often fine, attractive people—who don't succeed in forming friendships.

Well, first let me say that I am opposed to trying to force everyone into being well adjusted and having friends. There is a place for the creative loners, happy in their thoughts and projects, perfectly willing to have friends if they want to come around but too engrossed in their own interests to make an effort to bubble around in the social pot. Perhaps they will have one or two close friends who share their activities, but that will be all. If such people seem happy for the most part, I'd support them and be thankful for them.

But what of the young adolescent who has few or no friends at school and is miserably unhappy? One thing parents can do is to talk with the teacher at school who knows the student best and whom he seems to like. There are a few slight ways teachers can help, but it must always be behind the scenes. They may be able to shift seats; they may find opportunities to get the student involved with another student they think might be congenial on a project or report (even such a minor thing as getting some extra chairs together or staying after school to help set up an exhibit can sometimes start a friendship percolating); they may—though this must be done with great caution—have a word with another student in whose judgment and discretion they have confidence to see whether he could not help provide some companionship; they may arrange to section the student with a new group next year; or they can try to see that the student gets class recognition by being given things to do he can do well. These are small matters, but they have worked.

At home, parents can be as encouraging and supporting as possible—never nagging, never urging him, as the father in the *New Yorker* cartoon did, to "get in there and *integrate*." You can try to see to it that your house provides facilities attractive to boys and girls of his age—a rumpus room, some good records, plenty of readily available food. You can try to arrange an especially interesting project or trip and let him invite one or two classmates to go along. You can be sure that he knows that your and his house is available and open to his friends and that if he wants anyone overnight he may have him. Be sure, too, that you cordially welcome any friends that turn up and that you never criticize them at this early stage. Better a little "bad influence" than no friends at all. Of course, once any friendship is launched, you should keep in the background, or out of it, as much as possible and let the companionship develop in its own way. Don't hover. One other possibility you can consider is whether there are some other groups besides the ones your child is already in or exposed to where he might develop friends. For example, is there a hobby group where his skills could find recognition? Remember, though, you cannot make or maintain the friendship for your child; all you can do is help set the stage.

If none of these things works, if your child is very unhappy for a long time and if you are truly concerned, it might be well to seek help from a counselor.

Cliques

In Chapter 3, I described the inevitable rise of and reasons for cliques. They are a major part of the social life of many middle and junior high schoolers, a help in the transition from dependency on the family for social life to associations mainly outside the family. "The clique are my best friends," said one boy. "They're like brothers and sisters to me." And a ninth-grade boy pointed out that cliques are not just a phenomenon of adolescence. He wrote: "Parents are in cliques. Everyone is in cliques. Why shouldn't we be? It's a human instinct."

On the questionnaire, I asked, *Do you belong to a clique?* I defined it as "a small group of friends who stick together and shut others out." Many of those who responded rejected this definition. We belong, they said, but we don't shut people out. Thirty-seven percent said they belonged to a clique, 63 percent did not, and the proportions were about the same for boys and girls. There was only a slight increase from grades five to nine in the percentage of clique members, the highest percentage being in grade eight, 44 percent.

I asked, *Why do you belong or why not?* The majority, who do not belong, fall into a number of categories, by far the largest being those who say that cliques are unfair to others and just plain wrong. Another fairly large category say they don't belong because they're not popular. A number of others say either that they like everybody or that they like being alone or not restricted by such group friendships. A few dismiss cliques as "childish," "stupid" or "dumb." A sixth-grade girl said, "Our clique is the whole class against the teacher," while an eighth-grade girl said, "We don't want to get to be rotten kids."

Almost all of those who said they belonged to a clique simply stated it was their way of having good friends that they could count on. A few saw the clique in a more negative way as a protection against people they didn't like or who didn't like them. ("We are shut off by others so we have a clique.")

The last questions I asked about cliques were: *What activities or experiences of your class tended most to reduce cliques and improve class spirit?* and *Which tended to increase cliques?* The activity by far the most frequently mentioned as reducing cliques was all-class projects like plays, newspapers, games, field days, camping trips, or class-vs.-class competitions. Also quite frequently mentioned were all-class parties and dances, large-group games (especially if the teacher chooses the teams or they are chosen by lot), and team sports. Gym and good assemblies were specified by a few people.

On the other side, the most clique-increasing phenomena, mentioned by a third of the students, were small-group projects, plays, games, labs, etc., especially when the group chose its own members. There is strong resentment against these by many students. The second most frequently mentioned activity is parties that are in any way exclusive. A number of people said that free working time, recess and unorganized fun caused cliques. Also, a number of people mentioned sports, gym and lunch, but no one suggested abolishing them!

I think teachers can conclude from this that arranging all-class or large-group activities is good for class spirit, hard as it might be on teachers, and that self-selected small groups are bad for it. In considering these statements, however, one has to remember that an all-class spirit is a mixed blessing in a school if it tends to stifle individuals or to lessen opportunities for people who need a small group of friends and cannot navigate socially in a large group. Diversity within unity is the ideal, and its achievement requires sensitivity and constant nurture.

Parties

An all-class party at school or at somebody's house, a party that really goes, where everyone has fun and leaves feeling good, is a blessing to a class and to all concerned. On the other hand, parties that flop, parties that exclude, parties that depend for their success on drink and pot, or on wild behavior that may be enjoyed by some attenders but which causes worry and anguish for the hosts or organizers, can be social disasters, damaging to group spirit and to individual self-esteem.

I suppose the ideal party is one cooperatively planned and run by students and parents, with teachers helping as needed but not taking the main responsibility. There are a few blessed teachers who enjoy pitching in and helping all-class parties go well, with everyone involved, but most teachers have too much to do with other aspects of school life and in their own private lives to feel able to contribute in a major way to this aspect of young adolescent social life. Certainly, though, if a party is to take place on the school premises, some school people must be present and active to make sure that agreed-upon standards and rules are maintained (like prohibition against smoking and drinking or restriction of party activities to designated areas). But it cannot possibly work unless teachers are helped by parent chaperons and, even more important, by responsible students who play a major part in the planning, arranging, running and cleaning up of the party.

I have found that in approaching large parties there is a fundamental difference in judgment between students and adults. After fifth, sixth and possibly seventh grades, most students who express themselves (let it not be forgotten that many do not express themselves) believe that the best party is one where people assemble, where there is good music, good food and little supervision, and where, in some magic way, everything goes well and everybody behaves and has fun, each in his own way, without planning but instead relying on a benign spirit casting its blessing over the whole affair. On the other hand, the adults who are involved are preoccupied with all the disasters, naughtiness, dirt, mess, breakage, loneliness and excesses of one sort or another that might result, and therefore want firm plans and guidelines to avoid all troubles. I don't think there will ever be a steady harmonizing of these divergent approaches, but when there is a nucleus of responsible students and understanding, secure adults, and when both groups are blessed with some common sense, good will, and a willingness to communicate and compromise, good large parties do happen. (One trouble is, though, that they spawn a desire for another one *next week!*)

What Makes or Ruins a Party?

Under the general heading of "Social Life at Home," I asked students a number of questions about parties. The first was: *Think about the various parties you have attended at private homes. About those you considered successful, tell what you did that made you have a good time If there were games or other organized activities that you liked, please tell what they were.* The responses to this query fell into two categories, those from people who like form, organization and activities in their parties, and those who prefer a nonorganized gathering with music, food, spaces, and nothing more provided. In general, fifth-, sixth- and seventh-graders fall into the first group and eighth- and ninth-graders into the second, but with a considerable amount of overlap: there are some sixth-graders who say they are ready for ninth-grade-style parties, and there are some ninth-graders who like the plan and form of a fifth-grade party. (But then, remember, there are some adults who love party games and others who can't abide them.)

For the *fifth-, sixth-, and seventh-graders,* here are the elements of success in order of frequency of mention: good games, indoor and out; good planning; games with a structured sexual element (Spin-the-Bottle, strip poker, Truth or Dare); good food; going to a movie; and dancing.

Some comments: "When we played Truth or Dare, we gave really sneaky, sexy dares"; "we did nice things and went to nice places"; "we played baseball and threw food all over"; "the parents didn't keep telling us to be quiet."

These same three grades mentioned the following reasons for parties not being successful: no planning; "boring"; people fooling around too much; the hostess was too bossy; the wrong people were invited; people drank wine or beer.

For *eighth and ninth grades,* here are the elements of success: just dance and talk; Spin-the-Bottle type games; a lot of sex, make-out, etc.; "booze"; good combination of people; and "lots of girls" (only boys mentioned this). Here are some comments by eighth- and ninth-graders about parties considered successful: "Boys and girls smoking and goofing off"; "the parents bugged out and we just sat and smoked, talked and listened to records. Later some making out went on"; "got real wrecked and then I laid my girlfriend. Good music, too"; "they're adult-like, we eat good, drink good, smoke good, and dance and then the important *sex* occurs. That's what really makes the party"; "I consider a party successful when I meet a girl I like and she likes me"; "good games so you always knew what to do and didn't have to hang around watching people trying to act big"; "everybody wanted to do what was planned and a lot of us helped plan it. It was mostly games, music and food."

The factors that made for unsuccessful parties in eighth and ninth grades were nothing to do, wrong combination of people, parents too strict, too few boys or girls and too much confusion. Some comments: "The host kept running around emptying ashtrays and saying 'Don't touch that, you'll get it dirty,' or 'you'll break it.' It was worse than home"; "where people are too 'cool' to make friends"; "the lights bugged me because it was so bright. You could have operated right in the middle of the room"; "my girlfriend and I didn't have dates and everyone else made out"; "all the boys were shy and sat around talking about basketball."

I realize that all this discussion of parties at home has concerned affairs for both boys and girls. I should mention that in all the grades, five through nine, boys and girls enjoy parties where only their own sex is present, and these parties don't cause much trouble or concern, to judge from the comments of students, teachers and parents. Certainly for grades five and six, and often for seven and eight, the single-sex party is most common and, at least in grades five and six, most enjoyed. I think, in most cases, it is a mistake to push youngsters into girl-boy parties until they request them and are ready for them.

The Early Sophisticate

If one isn't careful, a minority of socially advanced girls, sometimes abetted by a few ambitious—or perhaps socially insecure—mothers, and cheered on by a few of the more-developed boys who want to assert their big-wheeldom, will set the tone for a class. In their confident, often attractive way, they will succeed in persuading everyone—or in silencing those they don't persuade—that the only cool sort of party must involve smoking, drinking, sex, and no planning or chaperons. Only babies would play an organized game after seventh grade. I remember quite a few years ago, in an eighth-grade class meeting, the students were discussing whether or not they wanted square dancing. The discussion convinced everyone that square dancing was out, no one wanted it, it was for the birds. Thus, it was decided. But a sensible mother heard about this and sent in a pleasant but strong request that the class hold a secret ballot on the matter. It seemed silly at first, but we respected the mother, and the ballot was held. Result: out of a class of sixty-five, only eight voted to drop the square dances; the rest wanted them. Today, in most places, square dancing is out as a junior high activity, but the same principle holds: don't be overimpressed by the vocal, advanced few who, often without knowing it, but sometimes quite purposefully, intimidate the less-"advanced" majority. My impression is—and I can't prove that I'm right—that the lists I have given above of factors for success and failure of parties, and especially the comments I have quoted, are weighted somewhat in favor of the early sophisticates. Perhaps even on anonymous questionnaires, kids don't want to admit, if only to themselves, that they are less advanced than the leaders.

Parents at the Party

I asked students, *Where do you think parents should be at a home party?* and gave six replies to choose from.

Sixteen percent checked "out of the house"; 55 percent checked "in the house but out of sight"; 19 percent checked "occasionally mingling with the guests"; 5 percent checked "present most of the time but only as observers"; 4 percent checked "present most of the time as a part of the activities"; and 1 percent checked "never leave the rooms where the party is going on." In general, the older the students, the more removed from the party they thought their parents should be. However, 72 percent of even the ninth-graders wanted their parents at least in the house, but none wanted them hanging around. In response to why students thought parents should be where they suggested, the two most frequent comments, both of them in support of the "in the house but out of sight" category, were that parents mixing in too much makes kids uncomfortable and nervous, and that parents should be available in case there is an emergency or some serious misbehavior for which the aid of adults is necessary.

Parents and Chaperonage

I think there will inevitably be differences in many families between teen-agers and their parents about the amount of planning and supervision that should go into a party. The differences can be reduced by honest discussion and by compromise on nonessentials. But it seems to me that reasonable teen-agers will acknowledge that as long as a party is attended by minors, in the eyes of the law and other parents, the final responsibility for what happens lies with the parents—but not the responsibility for seeing that people have fun and feel comfortable and reasonably free, for that is mainly the teen-age party-giver's responsibility. Parents must make sure that no one's health, safety or welfare is endangered.

I think it should be clear that *parents cannot abdicate*. They must be present in the house, and their presence established and known. The students replying to the questionnaire make it plain that when trouble arises it is usually because adults were not present to step in when required. There is little doubt, either, that teen-agers who are hosts or hostesses want parents present to help and support them—but *only if needed.* On the positive side, parents should remember that it's their house in which the party takes place and that they can help create a congenial atmosphere. They can be present as people arrive and greet them cordially, showing they are glad to have them. If boys and girls feel that they are genuinely wanted and not just tolerated, it will help them have a good time and make the party go well. If parents possibly can, they should know the names of all those who are coming and greet them by name. If they don't know people's names, they should be introduced or introduce themselves.

Then, once parents have greeted everyone, they should probably retire, either to another room, the kitchen, or somewhere besides the rooms where the party is taking place (unless their son or daughter really wants them present and says so, or agrees that parents are to help with certain aspects of the party).

Planning the Party

At the junior high school age, especially in grades eight and nine, the kids should be encouraged to assume almost complete responsibility for the planning, with parent as chief assistant, reinforcer, facilitator and provider. Of course, usually parents have had more experience than their children and will be able to get things done and remember things that the teen-ager might not even think of, but it's his or her party, and parents should play second fiddle. Also, as several students pointed out on the questionnaires, *they* know what goes well and what doesn't at a party these days. On the other hand, parents should assure themselves that the essentials have been taken care of and that in their judgment the party is likely to succeed.

Some families have found that it works well for the teen-age host to invite two or three friends to help plan and get ready for the party. This ensures a few ready co-operators during the affair itself.

Who Is Invited to the Party Determines What Sort of Party to Plan

In most parties for adults, unless they are mass affairs, the hosts would not dream of just throwing some people together for an evening without regard to their probable congeniality. If they tried to have a party of twelve made up of two bridge players, two poker enthusiasts, three devotees of the fight on TV, four literary people and one chorus girl, the chances are the evening would flop. Yet a good many parents and teachers think that teen-agers can be mixed up in any combination and that somehow their common teen-ageness or the good social adjustment they are supposed to have been taught should cause them to mix well and have a good time. When they don't, and, being young, they stop cooperating with the hosts and start raising Cain, parents blame it on this terrible generation of adolescents.

To be successful, a party usually has to be one of three types:

1. A group of congenial teen-agers with a common interest in the main activity of the party: games, skating, dancing, or whatever.

2. A large mixed group where everyone invited is not socially expected to participate in one sort of activity but where there is a varied menu of activities probably taking place simultaneously in different rooms.

3. A mixed group where only one main activity is planned, but where it is of such compelling interest (say

an excellent film or a trip to the shore) that all kinds of boys and girls will enjoy taking part.

Much of the trouble at teen-age parties is caused by boys and girls being bored by what there is to do (games, for instance), or not really knowing how to do it (dancing, for instance), or by being actively opposed to what's being done (making out, pot-smoking or drinking, for instance). I suppose they should all be polite enough—and some are—to do their best to suffer in courteous silence, but I'm afraid there will always be a number on whom the veneer of civilization is not yet strong enough to endure an unpleasant evening with the appearance of affability.

I think that open-house parties for middle and junior high school people are likely not to work. They involve too many risks of trouble, and sometimes older schoolmates or friends show up, often with their own dates and in large numbers, and that may change the atmosphere too much to be manageable.

Lights and Territory

One of the great issues sometimes is, How much light shall there be? A junior high school girl said about a party that didn't work, "There were too many parents and little sisters around guarding the lights." The best way to avoid having the guests turn off the lights is to have them plenty dim in the first place. If there are going to be decorations and a theme for the party, have a dim theme. In a large house, you can have a well-lighted room for those who like to see what they're doing and a dimly lighted room for those who want to dance and sit around. At this age especially, boys and girls are terribly conscious of their complexions, which always look better in a dim light.

It's best to have a clear understanding among the

planners beforehand that the lights are to be kept on, and the host can pass this word along, if necessary, to his or her friends. It's much better to have the guests themselves keeping the lights on than to have parents enter the scene themselves to switch on the lights. However, if need be, I think parents have to come out and turn them back on in as firm and friendly a way as they can manage. It's not so much that terrible things are going on in the dark but rather that a "lights out" party is pretty dull for many of the guests, can be socially uncomfortable for some and can set all sorts of rumors going.

It also should be clearly understood beforehand that there are certain rooms which are reserved for the party and that the whole house is not available. For boys and girls in grade nine and below (and I'd say for older ones, too), it is giving too much freedom to allow roaming around the house and into bedrooms. This restriction may displease the ones who commented about the "all-important sex," but that is a displeasure that any responsible parent must be ready and strong enough to incur without being upset.

Making Out and Sex at Parties

As you saw from the student opinions about parties, for some boys and girls in junior high school, a party is successful mainly if it is a "make-out." In the early grades, boys and girls begin experimenting through the group-sanctioned form of kissing games (Spin-the-Bottle, Truth or Dare, etc.). By eighth or ninth grades, these games may be considered babyish, and some of those who want to kiss just go ahead and do it. Others think it's "gross" and "disgusting" and have no time for the neckers and kissers. I cannot share the dismay that many parents feel about kissing games. It seems to me they are harmless and give boys and girls a chance, without major embarrassment, to begin having a little sexual experience (although a seventh-grade kiss is usually, not always, more social than sexual). Neither can I share the disapproval of those who find it somehow disgraceful or immoral for a boy to put his arm around a girl (or vice versa) on a sofa at a party. And certainly a girl who sits on a boy's lap in a corner between records isn't engaging in psychopathic behavior. As one girl said to her mother, "You're not supposed to kiss a boy at school; you're not supposed to kiss him on a date; you're not supposed to kiss him at a party; when *are* you supposed to kiss a boy?"

Smoking

It seems to me that parents should discuss with their child and then decide clearly in advance what the policy on smoking at a party is going to be. Most parents and teen-agers (see Chapter 11) feel that seventh, eighth and ninth grades are too early for boys and girls to smoke, and I think a party is the wrong place to start. There certainly is enough evidence that smoking is harmful to the health, especially of young people, to make one feel that the fewer smokers there are the better. I think one must keep in mind, and respect, too, the strong objections to smoking that many families have. Certainly, if your conviction is that people should not smoke until they are a certain age, you have a perfect right to apply that policy to a party in your home. It should be understood in advance, and the first person who smokes should be told promptly and politely, "I'm sorry but my parents don't let us smoke in our house." Remember too that members of athletic teams often are under a regimen of training rules which outlaws smoking.

Drinking and Drugs

I'll discuss drinking and drugs more fully in Chapter 11, but here I want only to say that anyone who serves alcoholic beverages to young adolescents or permits them to smoke pot or use drugs at a party is very unwise. Even if the customs of your family include the drinking of wine or beer by teen-agers, there are so many families who feel strongly against it and so much harm can come from it that it is extremely inconsiderate to expose other boys and girls to it.

Bad Behavior

Here's a cheerful little list of the sort of bad things that junior high schoolers say they or their peers occasionally do at parties. However, 80 percent of those replying to the questionnaire said they had never participated in "rude and destructive behavior": throwing food, pillows, etc.; using the telephone to make so-called humorous calls; calling police; breaking light bulbs; accidentally breaking furniture by roughhousing; yelling and stamping; throwing snowballs in windows; locking people in rooms; doing chemical experiments with the refreshments; climbing on the roof; rushing all over the house; shooting off firecrackers; breaking into the liquor supply; leaving the party and roaming.

In general, the best way to avoid such troubles is to have plenty of interesting things for people to do and to have carefully worked out in advance decisions about what is to be done if unseemly behavior starts. It's not uncommon for it to start, but it can be stopped at once. The teen-agers expect that; they are sometimes trying out limits and are disappointed if there isn't "control" at a party. Usually it is best to have the kids themselves prepared to deal with it, say a small group of guests who will amiably squelch the prankster in a smiling but businesslike way. If measures are applied at once—not after things get going but when the first doughnut is thrown—there will usually be no difficulty. If the teen-agers and their guests cannot control themselves, then parents must step in and firmly put an end to the trouble. It usually works best to get an offender off alone and talk with him so that he doesn't have to lose face before the group. If there is a persistent noncooperator whom parents cannot manage, they should telephone his parents and ask them to come and get him. This is not an admission of the failure of a party but a demonstration that parents know what to do and have the courage of their convictions. All parents I have asked about this have said that they'd appreciate being called if their child was misbehaving and would appreciate being told at once rather than to have the report come out later by the grapevine.

A Few Other Matters for Parents

If your children are invited to a party, consult to make sure that they know what the hours are, how they should dress (this is an area where you may not have much authority), and what the transportation to and from is. Sometimes you may want to find out how the party went or check on direct or indirect reports that there was misbehavior. It can be valuable to telephone the parents involved to thank them for the party and incidentally to compare notes. Be careful to avoid rumor, escalation of rumor and gossip.

When picking up people from a party, it's better not to arrive ten or twenty minutes early, which may humiliate the young. But it's just as important to get there not more than five minutes after the time set for the party to end.

Being a Good Guest

The heading above may sound old-fashioned to readers of this book, even to parents, but I think both generations can benefit from discussing the points below.

1. Guests should go to a party with the intention of cooperating enthusiastically with the plans of the hosts. If they don't think they can have a good time that way, it's better for them not to accept the invitation.

2. They should greet the parents and host upon arrival. If parents and host aren't near the door, they should try to find them, but if they aren't to be found easily, a guest can consider his duty to be done. Guests should say good-bye and thank the hosts at the end. This may seem obvious, but many people forget it. (I am reminded of a young child, who, asked to compose an essay on good manners, wrote: "I have good manners. I say hello and goodbye, I say good morning and good night, and when I see anything dead lying around the house, I bury it.")

3. They should be nice to everyone, including little sisters and brothers, grandparents and anyone else who may be there.

4. They should avoid complaining and comparing with other parties.

5. If they should damage anything (and this often happens accidentally among gangly youngsters), they should report it at once, apologize and offer to pay to have it repaired or replaced.

10

Sexual Development and Behavior

Would you like to go steady?

"**5** In fifth grade???!!

6 It might be OK if there's no pawing and mauling.

7 I find I like a certain girl one week and a different one the next week so how can I go steady?

8 Yes. You can have a reputation and go to a lot more parties.

9 It's nice to have a girlfriend of the opposite sex."

These days, boys and girls, even young ones, know quite a lot about sex, but their knowledge is only partial, much mixed with error, and badly out of perspective. (Probably the same can be said for the knowledge of many adults.) I doubt if there are many children among the families who read this book who are ignorant of "where babies come from." The real ignorance is to think that once we have the most elementary knowledge of the physical fact, we "know about sex" and have nothing more to learn. "We all learned about it one afternoon in fourth grade," a junior high schooler reported.

But sex, or *sexuality* (the qualities and actions that arise from the fact of our being sexual), is only partly biological, and the facts about genitals are just the beginning of knowledge. I should say that sex education, whether received at home, at school or in the street, planned or unplanned, should consist much more of human relations–sociology, anthropology and psychology–than of biology, necessary as an accurate knowledge of the physical facts is.

The Need for Sex Education

The sexual situation in the United States today is not good. Our society is preoccupied with sex. We are fascinated by it; we are afraid of it; we long for it; we reject it; we ask for it; we're confused by it. Too many people fail to understand that human sex inevitably and always involves human personalities. A few years ago at an educational convention I saw an expensive plastic model of the human body to be used in biology and anatomy classes. It was ingeniously arranged so that the main organs could be taken out and examined: the heart, the lungs, the kidneys, etc. But I noticed that in the genital area the model went neuter. There were no reproductive organs. When I asked the salesman about this, he said, "Oh, we find that if we include the sex organs, most schools won't buy the model." When I expressed my amazement, he added, "Well, we have solved the problem," and he got a small package out of a drawer, opened it and showed me how for $14.95 you could buy a complete set of male and female sex organs which could be plugged into the otherwise sexless model. What sex education! Either sex is so evil that we must pretend it doesn't exist or there's no difference between a man and a woman except a $14.95 set of genitals.

Because of our confusion and ignorance, because so many of us feel that sex is either so bad that it must be given the silent treatment or that it is the ultimate of human activity, because of this lack of openness going along with blatant commercial and entertainment display—because of all of this, problems of sex are found at every level of our society. Divorce rates are high. There is vast unhappiness within many marriages. Most first intercourse between teen-agers is "unprotected" (no contraceptive is used). Too many teen-agers are getting married, hundreds of thousands because of premarital pregnancies. Over a third of a million illegitimate babies are born each year. We have annually over three million new cases of VD, many among the young.

This situation is not the result of a sexual revolution. There has been no sudden change but rather a stepped-up rate of evolution. Really, a sexual revolution is what we need—a revolution against ignorance, against sexual exploitation, against the double standard, against antisex; a revolution against the idea that there can be sex without consequences, whether they be happy or tragic, beautiful or ugly. All of us, not just young adolescents, need some good education about human sexuality.

Sex Education within the Family

In many families, even those whose members consider themselves enlightened and liberal, one great area of silence is that of human sexuality. Of course, this doesn't mean that no sex education is going on in the society of the family, for the way husband and wife relate to each other, the way they treat their children and the way they relate to other males and females are all a part of sex education, probably the most important part. However, it is futile for me to say to parents, assuming somehow that it never occurred to them, "Be loving, understanding and considerate of each other; demonstrate in your lives a beautiful relationship between a wife and a husband, a woman and a man, a female and a male; be perfect even in the open admission of your imperfections—and then your children will receive a good sex education." Saying all that will not help wife and husband one whit to live it (and certainly it won't help the divorced parent), and to try to stage a perfect married relationship for the benefit of the children is useless. Children pick up the vibes.

So, practically, what can parents do to assist in their children's sex education? They can try to be honest. If they do love each other, they can remember to show it. And they can try to deal honestly and intelligently with the questions their children ask, or suggest, starting as early as possible. I can think of four kinds of questions that kids are likely to ask:

1. *Questions of fact* ("How does a condom work?" "How does a woman know when she's pregnant?" "Does it hurt a person's body to masturbate?" "Can you get VD from kissing?"). These questions should be answered plainly, honestly and completely, but not at excessive length and never accompanied by a lecture. Also, never make up an answer if you don't know the facts, something both teachers and parents are tempted to do. If you admit there are facts *you* don't know, your kids will admit there are facts *they* don't know. Then you can look them up or ask somebody, and the result is good education.

2. *Questions of feeling* ("What does it feel like to have sexual intercourse?" "How do you know if you're in love?" "Isn't it embarrassing if a man has an erection in public?"). Here parents, if they're comfortable about it, can tell what their own feelings are and at least leave the door open for the youngsters to express theirs.

3. *Questions of opinion* ("Isn't it OK to have sex before you're married if you both want to?" "Is it OK for a boy to go as far as a girl will let him?" "Isn't it better to try out living together before you get married?"). I think questions like these should be thrown back to the questioner for sharing: "That's something people don't agree on. What do you think?" This shouldn't be a cop-out for parents, who should give their opinions if they have them, or express their doubts if they have them, but the most valuable result of such a question is to get an exchange of views going. The best way to shut off communication is to state your opinion as if it were fact. If your children ask you for your opinion and you have one, give it, but be sure it doesn't come out as an authoritarian viewpoint.

4. *Questions of values* ("Isn't an abortion really murdering a human being?" "Shouldn't a woman have the right to decide for herself whether or not to have an abortion?" "I think sex is about the biggest thing there is, isn't it?" "If it feels good, why not do it? We may all be dead tomorrow."). Clearly, these questions do involve some facts, but principally they are questions involving values. What is important in life? What standards do we use to guide our behavior? I think these questions, like those of opinion, provide rich material for discussion, but I also think that here is an area where parents, if they are confident of their values, should state them, not as commands to be imposed, but as convictions to be considered.

The Problem of Silence

Although, as replies from the questionnaire show, sex is the subject most frequently mentioned by the students as one they would like to talk about with their parents but aren't able to, I think the great majority of parents wish their kids would open up and talk and ask questions. My suggestion here is for parents to try to be open in discussion with each other in the presence of their children at times when the family is together in a relaxed situation. I don't mean that it's good to describe their own sexual pleasures and problems, but opportunities are often provided by the day's news, articles in magazines, and TV programs or movies, to talk about sexual and family relationships. Such interesting, informal, unplanned conversation will help the children feel more comfortable to ask their questions and express their thoughts.

If it is clear to parents that their children need information and aren't getting it from any reliable source, it is certainly better to strive to create an opportunity to give information, even if it means simply saying, "Come on into the next room, John; there are a few things we ought to talk about." Often, it may be just what John (or Mary) was hoping the parent would say.

Another possibility is for parents to make it clear that they would like to talk about questions of sex whenever their child would like to—that they are available. And they should keep making their availability clear from time to time, remembering that most children don't like to risk putting themselves in the position of seeming to be ignorant.

In the typical family, it will be a lot easier to talk about sex before the children pass age ten or eleven. After that, as they enter adolescence, it becomes a much more delicate matter. Few adolescents are ready to discuss with their parents their sexual feelings and their questions about sexual behavior once they themselves are having the feelings, are fumbling toward sexual experience and are, perhaps, quite scared about it. If such discussion comes easily in a family, that family can consider themselves fortunate. If it doesn't, they can know their situation is typical.

Also, most adolescents are simply not comfortable

being put in a situation where they have to think sexual thoughts about their parents or with their parents. It's rather unpleasant for them even to acknowledge that their parents are "doing it," and they don't like their parents taking too active an interest in what they themselves are feeling or doing, or not doing, sexually. The area of sex and sexual behavior is one where boys and girls want to protect their privacy and will brook no prying, even though their minds may be full of urgent questions, and their bodies and emotions are experiencing new, strange and wonderful feelings. Sexuality ought to be a subject that parents and children can discuss easily, but in our culture it isn't.

Further, the area of sex is perhaps the most important one in which the young are struggling to become independent of their families and to find their own way, figure out their own values and establish their own identities.

One good way to help break the silence barrier is for parents and children to read the same book and discuss it. This chapter itself might work as an opener for sharing points of view. Two other books that I wrote, *Love and Sex in Plain Language* (Lippincott, Bantam), for grades six to nine, and *Love and Sex and Growing Up* (Lippincott; I was coauthor with Corinne Johnson), for grades four to six, are frank and factual, and they discuss most of the issues of sexual behavior without preaching. Two other books that many parents and adolescents have found helpful are Wardell Pomeroy's *Boys and Sex* and *Girls and Sex* (Delacorte Press).

Some Facts about Adolescent Sexual Development

In Chapter 3, I described somewhat generally how boys and girls reach puberty and the striking differences in times, rates and modes of growth. It is useful for boys and girls and their parents and teachers to know these facts and to be able, therefore, to make cautious predictions about when youngsters will reach puberty—for boys, the first ejaculation with semen; for girls, the first menstruation (menarche). The chart on the facing page diagrams the average pattern of development (shown by the bars, hatches and graphs, each labeled) and the tremendous variation from person to person (shown by the range figures just below the bars and graphs).

To summarize, in boys the first sign of puberty is an increase in the rate of growth of the testicles and a wrinkling of the skin of the scrotum. Then appears the first downy pubic hair. Next begins the overall growth spurt and the growth of the penis. The first ejaculation with semen usually occurs about four to six months after the appearance of pubic hair, but in many boys it comes somewhat later. A boy usually first ejaculates with semen while he is fairly early in his growth spurt, somewhat before its peak. Growth of underarm hair and beard usually come well after the first ejaculation, as does the change of voice, which is gradual.

Most people do not realize at what an early age boys commence erotic sexual activity. According to the Kinsey reports (1948, 1953), 8 percent of boys experience orgasm with ejaculation by age eleven, 28 percent by age twelve, 57 percent by age thirteen, and 82 percent by age fourteen. In terms of school level, this means that by the end of seventh grade about 38 percent of the boys have ejaculated, 63 percent by the end of eighth, and 86 percent by the end of ninth. After the initial ejaculation, reports Kinsey, almost all males become sexually active, in the early teens mostly through masturbation and nocturnal emissions. It's interesting, too, that in boys, sexual activity (not necessarily sexual enjoyment) reaches its peak, as measured by the number of "sexual outlets"

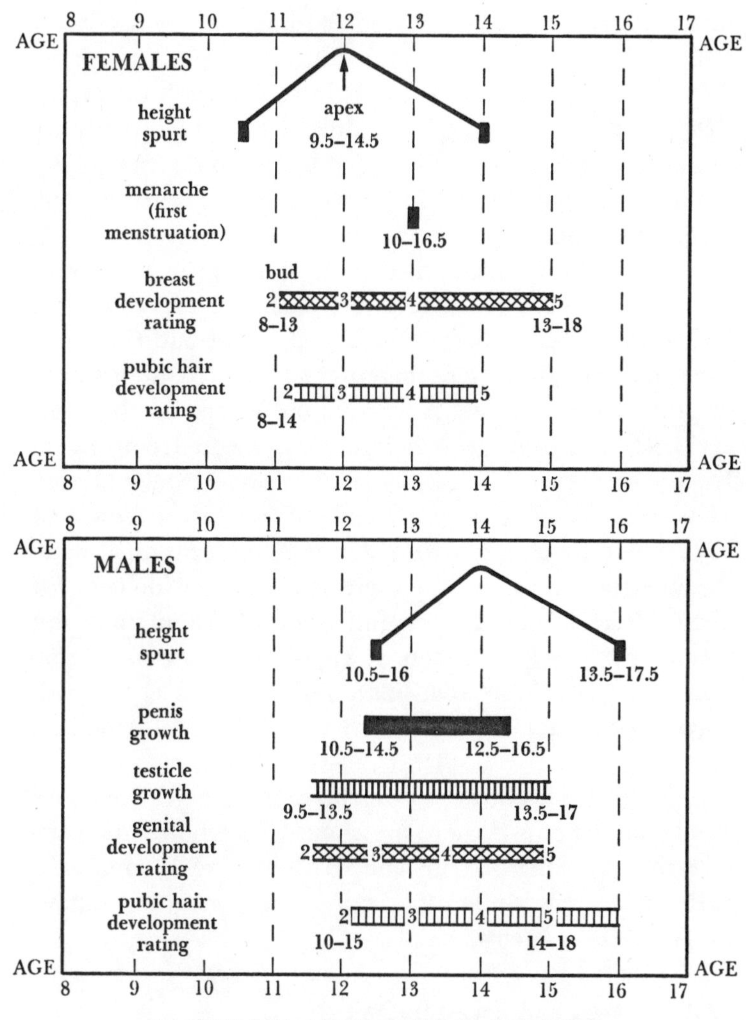

SEQUENCE OF PHYSICAL EVENTS IN ADOLESCENT DEVELOPMENT

The average age is represented. The age range within which each event may begin and end is given by the figures directly below the start and finish of the bar or graph (except for the female height spurt, for which the age range of apex is given).

(ejaculations) per given period of time, only a few years after the first ejaculation and, other things being equal, declines gradually from then on into old age. This means that the male reaches his maximum sexual performance most often in his late teens. Since there are no thoroughly approved sexual outlets for boys at this age in our culture, there is obviously a problem.

In girls, the first sign of puberty is the beginning of the growth spurt (see the chart again). Next come the appearance of the breast buds and, at about the same time, sometimes earlier, sometimes later, the appearance of pubic hair. The first menstruation occurs, on the average, *after* the peak growth rate has passed. According to Kinsey, 4 percent of girls have menstruated by age eleven, 21 percent by age twelve, 50 percent by age thirteen, and 79 percent by age fourteen. Only 21 percent first menstruate after fourteen, but there is no reason for concern about those in the 21 percent, some of whom may not menstruate until seventeen or eighteen. If the menstruation comes later than that, it would be well to check with a gynecologist for assurance that the girl's development is normal.

In most girls there is no ovulation for a year or more after menarche, *but* there are some girls who ovulate before they first menstruate and, if they have become sexually active very young, they can become pregnant before they have ever menstruated.

Erotic Interest and Social Interest

An interesting fact of which many people are unaware is that although girls look mature about two years before boys do, they have their first menstruation, on the average, at about the same age as boys experience their first ejaculation. Thus males, who, if we judged by their appearance, do not look at all mature in sixth, seventh and eighth grades, are already ejaculating rather regularly, in most cases, except among sexually precocious groups, by masturbation or nocturnal emissions. They are capable of impregnating a female. All this happens quite some time before all but a few girls are having an active sex life.

Thus, in considering the development of boys and girls during adolescence, we must distinguish between purely sexual and erotic activity on the one hand and social interest in the opposite sex on the other. By age fifteen, Kinsey says, "92% of the males have had orgasm, but at the same age less than a quarter of the females have had such experience; and the female population is 29 years old before it includes as high a percentage of experienced individuals as is to be found in the male curve at 15."

Most boys are sexually aroused at a much earlier age than are most girls, but their voices haven't changed, they have no whiskers and they look at the "mature" girls with interest, curiosity and a certain amount of fear. In girls, social development and interest in associations with boys come earlier than does the social interest of boys. Thus, very often, girls in junior high school consider boys their own age with some disdain. Boys are thought to be loud, dirty and small (quite an accurate assessment in some cases); they are babyish; they won't dress up; they won't dance. By age eleven or twelve, girls start admiring older boys, although they're scared of them and might well turn down an invitation to go out with one of them. They have long telephone conversations *about* boys, less often *with* boys.

What is the explanation of the commonly unrecognized fact that boys are generally ahead of girls in sexual performance and erotic interest, while the girls are ahead of the boys in desire for boy-girl association? Probably, it is a part of the general feeling still prevalent in most parts of our society that it is desirable for a girl to be popular, to have dates, not to be a wallflower, whereas we consider it more acceptable for a boy to be independent of all that. Isn't it still true—though illogical—that the label "old maid" is a somewhat damning one, while there's a certain romance about "bachelor"?

I have the impression recently, though, from my discussions with junior high boys and girls and from seeing them together that the idea that the eleven-to-thirteen-year-old boy "hates" girls and that the eleven-to-thirteen-year-old girl "loves" older boys is less true than it was. Girls and boys of the same age, but of quite different degrees of maturity, are more often ready to associate closely, even romantically. It is now considered OK for a girl to be turned on by a good-looking guy her own age, and girls are becoming much more interested in looking with frank pleasure at a boy and in the plainly erotic aspects of sex.

Where Did You Get Your Information?

On the student questionnaire I asked, *Do you have all the information you want now about sex?* Seventy-nine percent of the fifth-graders said *yes,* but only 58 percent of the ninth-graders said yes. It may seem strange that more fifth-graders than ninth-graders feel they know all they want. However, if we compare the knowledge they have to an island in a sea of unknown, we understand that the larger the island the more of the unknown it touches. Fifth-graders don't feel the need to know, and don't know or particularly care about what they don't know; ninth-graders are more aware of all there is to know and realize they'd like to know it. As an eighth-grader wrote to me a few years ago, "I don't know how much sex education I've had until I know how much there is."

My question continued, *If not, what would you like to know that you don't know?* The most frequent responses by far had to do with intercourse—How do you do it?; what does it feel like?; when can you do it? (I think the best policy is to answer these unsimple questions as plainly and factually as possible. With such answers, the young are less likely to feel pushed into irresponsible, uninformed experimentation.) Many others replied, in effect, "Just everything"; and there were a number, including both boys and girls, who wanted to know about homosexuality; others had questions about the feelings and emotions involved in sex; some asked about petting; and some asked what various terms meant, especially slang terms.

Here's a sampling of other replies: "How to do everything the right way"; "I know all I have to know at my age"; "I know everything there is to know—menstruation and sexual intercourse"; "patting"; "the parts that are forbidden—*everything!* about fucking and the bases"; "birth control, not for me, I'm too young and old-fashioned, but just in case"; "whether my girl wants to have it or not"; "how do you intercourse with someone?"; "if I don't know how can I ask it?"; "I'd like to know how to (ask) (get) (have) sexual intercourse"; "how to make advances"; "mutual masturbation and such"; "I always wonder whether people do the same things I do sexually and if they think about the same things"; "how does a girl become a slut or a whore?"; "what do you do when a guy tries to go all the way?"; "boys' feelings"; "I'll never know all there is to know, so when the time comes and I do have sex with someone, I'll probably be wondering again."

I also asked, *Where did you get whatever information you have about sex?* I give the replies in order of frequency of mention. The figures after each item represent the proportion of the total number of responses. Most students listed more than a single source.

Girls		*Boys*	
school course	24%	parents	19%
mother	21%	school course	19%
friends	19%	books	16%
parents	13%	friends	16%
books	11%	experimenting	7%
picked it up	3%	the street	11%
the street	3%	other	12%
other	6%		

Thus we see that girls think most often of a course at school as a source of information, with their mothers as second, friends third and "parents" (presumably mother *and* father) fourth; whereas boys recall parents and a school course with equal frequency, books and friends next, and "the street" next (compared to a much lower number of "street" responses from girls). One boy said, "I learned the hard way, if you know what I mean." It is interesting, especially given the popular stereotype of the father taking his son off to a private place to tell him the facts of life, that hardly any boys or girls mentioned their fathers as sources of information, except that father may have been included in the label "parents."

I next asked, *Which source of information was the most valuable?*

Girls		*Boys*	
mother	29%	books	25%
school course	27%	friends	19%
friends	13%	school course	19%
books	10%	experience	16%
parents	10%	other	21%
other	11%		

It's interesting what a high value girls put on their mothers as sources of information, while boys consider books the most valuable (a couple replied "the dictionary"). The school course and friends rate high with both boys and girls. Among those who responded "other," a girl said "graffiti" and a boy said, "Figuring out jokes kids tell at school."

If I were to draw conclusions from these responses, I'd say that school sex-education courses are valuable and there should be more of them; that books are useful and should be provided in school, at home, or both; that girls should be thankful for their mothers; and that fathers need to find ways to take part in the home-based sex education of their sons and daughters, for I don't think it's sound for the information to come so predominantly from the female parent.

What about "Going Steady"?

Although I supposed that "going steady" is something that not many fifth- and sixth-graders are likely to be doing, I asked this question of all grades: *Do you go steady? Why?* (The term "go steady," I was told, is a bit out of date, but it didn't cause more than a very few kids to object.) No fifth-graders said they went steady; 14 percent of sixth-graders said they did (19 percent boys, 12 percent girls); and the figures increased to 40 percent of ninth-graders, 33 percent of the boys and 47 percent of the girls. I judge from the responses that "steady" is a relative term, meaning that at a given moment now or in the recent past, or, in some cases, in the immediately anticipated future, the individual did, does or will "go with" a person of the other sex exclusively—for a time, length undetermined.

The next question I asked was: *Would you like to go*

steady if someone you liked asked you to or you could find someone you liked who wanted to go steady with you? Yes — No — Maybe —. Why? At all grades, given these ideal conditions, the majority answered *yes* or *maybe.* The noes steadily decreased: fifth grade, 35 percent; sixth grade, 27 percent; seventh grade, 21 percent; eighth grade, 15 percent; and ninth grade, 7 percent. More girls (24 percent) said *no* than boys (16 percent).

The answers to *why?* demonstrate a widely held desire for a deep relationship with another person, a desire for the security of a companion, and an appreciation of the status that goes with being known to have a steady boyfriend or girl friend. Here are some comments:

From girls who don't want to go steady. "I'm too young"; "I'd have to wait and see if he's OK (no drug or sex freak) cause later maybe he'll drop me"; "I hate boys!!!!"; "going steady doesn't mean much nowadays"; "not at 13. I want to meet a lot of boys"; "I'm only 13½ and I'd rather go with different kids"; "going steady is pretty boring. It reminds me of marriage."

From girls who do, perhaps or certainly, want to go steady. "I'd like to see how it's like"; "he might be nice"; "you get a warm nice feeling inside that somebody likes you"; "would be fun" (most frequent answer); "I think to have someone who makes you happy and you can do different things with is very important"; "I'd be flattered but I'd talk about the advantages and disadvantages of such a heavy commitment"; "*maybe* I could tell him some of my problems and have fun"; "it would keep your mind off other problems you have"; "because you feel secure, warm, wanted and fulfilled."

From boys who don't want to go steady. "It would take up too much time"; "I'm only in 5th grade"; "I like sports more than girls"; "I'd like to but I'd feel embarrassed with everyone"; "if I cared about girls it would take time away from studying, relaxing, reading and watching sports"; "8th grade is sort of young"; "I went with a girl for 5 months and got sick of being tied down"; "I don't want to get stuck with one chick."

From boys who do, perhaps or certainly, want to go steady. "Maybe because I'd feel like doing what I wanted"; "I'm somewhat *go* for sex"; "females are a natural reaction to males"; "good for one's soul and spirit"; "it would be nice to be able to kiss a girl, and it would give you a member of the opposite sex who is not related to you to talk to"; "depends if the girl is intelligent or not. She must also have some 'assets' "; "because that's what they do where I live"; "I dig chicks"; "I've been in a boys' school all my life so I like to keep a girl as long as I can"; "I need the satisfaction of lust and intimacy feelings."

My advice to parents would be to try to make sure that their children understand the disadvantages of going steady (limitation of acquaintance, possibility of being pushed into going too far sexually, missing out on a variety of fun) and to suggest that junior high school is too early to start. The years from eleven to fifteen are good years during which to associate with many different boys and girls. Being able to be with a variety of members of the other sex is an experience all its own, and during the teens is about the only time a boy or girl is likely to have it. If young people cut themselves off from this opportunity they may later regret not having had more experience with all sorts of people. After junior high school there is time enough for deeper boy-girl relationships.

However, it is impossible to enforce absolute rules about the matter. I know a few mature boys and girls who have gone steady during junior high school and for whom it has apparently been a good experience. Anyway, as the comments above show, a "going steady" arrangement is much less steady than one is led to expect from the term. Therefore, if the boy and girl are normally sensible and have been taught the facts of sex and good attitudes toward it, I do not think going steady need be harmful. Certainly parents should show that they appreciate the desire of many boys and girls to feel a special kinship with someone of the other sex, or to have an assured companion for social events. After that, the decision is up to the young people.

Let me add, though, that most seventh-, eighth- and ninth-graders have never been on anything that could be called a date, let alone going steady, and are happy, or, at worst, not miserable with that state of affairs.

What Do Young People Think about Sexual Behavior?

A good many surveys have been done of the opinions and experiences of adolescents in relationship to sex, most of them rather fragmentary.* I was in no position to make such a study. I debated giving a sexual behavior and opinion checklist as a part of my questionnaire, but I was afraid that teachers, parents and students, seeing the checklist, might object to it as an invasion of privacy and possibly as "putting ideas into people's heads," and that the students checking the answers might tend either to exaggerate the amount of their sexual experience or to deny it. Therefore, I decided on this rather general, open query: *Boys, girls, parents and teachers are interested in the sexual behavior of young people. Think about such matters as dating, petting, and sexual intercourse, and try*

* By far the most comprehensive one that I know of is Robert Sorensen's *Adolescent Sexuality in Contemporary America, Personal Values and Sexual Behavior, Ages 13–19,* published in 1973 (World Publishing).

to explain some of your main ideas about them. Obviously, the replies to such a broad query cannot be tabulated. Therefore, I have had to be satisfied with trying to make a fair selection of replies to quote. Some are typical, some are especially wise, and some illuminate the attitudes and opinions of the young these days.

Fifth grade. In this grade the opinions tended to be at one pole or the other. Many made comments like these: "I'm just too young for all that"; "I'm only in fifth grade"; "Sick-o!"; "No Way!" Others, with a splendid, detached freedom from experience, said, "They're all great!" or "I love them!"

Here are some other comments (G after a comment indicates a girl; B, a boy): "They are all OK after 16 because if you can drive you certainly can have sex (besides your parents had to do it to have you so they shouldn't be upset or worried)" (B); "I don't think you should get into it too young. Maybe at fifteen or so is nice" (B); "I don't really think too much about it. Kids should be told about them so they know what they are" (G); "If you're not serious they're dumb" (G); "I know everything. We saw a movie in science. I already knew but they said nothing about love" (G); "Groos'm" (G).

Sixth grade. There is still a good deal of simplistic all-against or all-for opinion: "I'm only 11!!!!" (B); "in sixth grade??? Bleah!!!" (G); or "they are great!!!" (B); "I think sexual intercourse is groovy!!" (B) (Sixth-graders go in for multiple exclamation marks.) But there is a larger number of more-considered comments: "Dating is good, sexual intercourse is also fun from what I read" (B); "*everybody* has sex so why not *use it,* but don't *abuse* it" (B); "dating: a good idea. Petting: I'm not sure. Intercourse: I'm not saying" (B); "well, it's a touchy subject" (B); "dating and petting are all right but don't have sexual intercourse until you are married if you really want to" (B); "dating is fine, petting is disgusting. Sexual intercourse is bad if you do it in the back seat without being married. I guess it feels nice though and is lovely if you're married" (G); "I have only had sexual intercourse once and it wasn't that great" (G); "It's all right for kids over seventeen and a half" (G).

Here are comments from the other grades:

Seventh grade. "Sexual intercourse—I intend to try it in the future" (B); "if they are mature enough to take it seriously, O.K., but if they giggle when they get near a girl they are too immature" (B); "dating, not bad if you're old enough. Sexual intercourse, vulgar. Petting, I don't know what it is" (B); "I don't see what is very wrong with it. It is just showing affection" (G); "sure maybe a kiss or two but never anything that perverted" (G); "when will they happen to me?" (G).

Eighth grade. "We're all animals, aren't we? The only thing that needs explaining is the technical part" (B); "sexual intercourse is not too much fun if she gets pregnant" (B); "it's a very important way of finding oneself" (B); "I feel that sex is the most natural thing in the world, it's almost the most important and people, whatever age, should be able to practice it without some ass standing around saying 'You shouldn't do that, that's dirty' " (B); "we should be free about it because if we aren't all of us will grow up with sexual tensions. Also contraceptives should be made more available" (B); "I think America is too uptight about sex" (B); "dates and kissing are OK but that other stuff is just for status or rebellion" (B); "it's fine *except* when people use others as objects instead of people, with feelings" (G); "kids today are often rushed into sex by their peers and their parents who think that letting yourself be used gains you entrance into the popular set. Sadly enough this is true. The great majority of the 'status group' are known to have had a lot of sexual experience. I think teenagers who abstain from heavy sexual relationship are going to be happier that they are not all tangled up in a web of guilt, curiosity and shame" (G); "I feel very strongly that too many young teenagers use another person for their pleasure or social advancement, and it upsets me, but when two people have an affection for each other, I think it's nice for them to express it in another way than words" (G); "if you love somebody a whole lot I guess you should have sex" (G); "feeling somebody up if you don't like them is disgusting and whorey" (G); "sexual intercourse isn't right unless you have a great excuse" (G); "dating gets you to know the personalities of boys. But petting is disgusting, dumb, and germing" (G).

Ninth grade. "Petting is good and makes both people feel for each other. But not too young (age twelve). I've had intercourse and I enjoyed it but I think I was too young and I feel guilty because I didn't really love the girl. It won't happen again for a long time" (B); "if you have a good meaningful relationship with someone you should go as far as you and your girlfriend want to" (B); "face it, sex is enjoyable, so long as no one gets hurt it's great" (B); "they are good if you are emotionally involved but can become traps later on in life" (B); "I'm unclear about sexual intercourse. I am a virgin although I have engaged in sexual activity, and I've turned down quite a lot of offers. Virginity isn't something to be lost at the first opportunity. If I had a strong relationship with someone and the desire was there and I cared beyond infatuation, I would most definitely make love to them. However, this is extremely idealistic and I may well go to bed with someone before I reach this stage. I don't really know. I swing back and forth" (G); "if it's love, it doesn't matter but how do you know it's love?" (G); "petting and making love should be up to the people involved. Young people are really pretty sensible. Abiding by your own moral code isn't easy because you have to know where you stand. It would be much easier to have somebody else's rules to abide by, but that would be a cop out. I think when other people impose their moral code on young people it makes it easier for the young people to do what they are told not to, just because they aren't forced to make their own decisions" (G).

A School Program of Sex Education

One reason why I quote the students so extensively is to give an idea of the sorts of opinions and ideas that kids these days have that need to be discussed, argued, refined and challenged, not with the idea of finding a single right answer but in order to help each student develop his or her own sense of values and to give each one all the information needed to make responsible choices. We should not leave such education to chance. While there is much that can be done at home, I do not believe that home is the ideal place for all sex education, for several reasons. First, many parents don't know enough. Second, many parents are not aware of the issues and questions that the young people need and want to talk about. Third, as I've already said, the adolescents' need for independence makes deep discussions of sexual feelings and behavior almost impossible. And fourth, it is important for the kids to have opportunities for discussions with their peers under the guidance of a knowledgeable, nonjudgmental adult. School (or perhaps institutions like the church or the "Y") is about the only place where such discussions can take place.*

* A useful pamphlet on this subject is *A Guide for Parents: How to Relate to Sex Education Programs,* Bantam Books, 666 Fifth Avenue, New York, N.Y. 10019; $1.00.

Some Acceptable Values for a School Program

As I have talked with parents, teachers and students about sex education in schools over the years in different communities, I have heard strong opinions expressed about what such a program should and should not do. I have tried to distill from these conversations and public meetings a set of values which it seems to me are acceptable to people of otherwise quite different convictions. I believe that most parents in most communities can support a program based on these values, and that teachers can use them as a guide to their classroom work. They are also useful for parents to keep in mind.

1. The value of *information:* that correct information is better than ignorance or error; that information leads to the possibility of responsible action, while ignorance can lead to irresponsibility. We need not fear that sound knowledge will lead to experimentation and trouble. Those who get into what we call "trouble" are not generally those who are truly and fully informed.

2. The value of *responsibility:* that actions, sexual or otherwise, undertaken in the light of knowledge of all their consequences, good and bad, present and future, can be called responsible.

3. The value of *control:* that sex is a power and, like any other power, can be used for good or bad, and that it needs to be controlled by the individual for good purposes.

4. The value of *consideration:* that the welfare and needs, short-term and long-term, of oneself, of the other(s) involved, and of society should be considered in whatever a person does.

5. The infinite value of each *individual person:* every person is worthy of our loving consideration.

6. The value of *communication:* that it is good to

have opportunities to talk over our questions and ideas, to test them out against the ideas of others, to make our feelings known and to know the feelings of others through discussion and conversation (and in school this means discussion in the presence and under the guidance, but not the domination, of a knowledgeable teacher).

The Results of Sound Sex Education

The results are not a panacea. Selfish, exploitative people will not be suddenly transformed into unselfish, considerate ones; insecure, fearful people will not all at once become secure and confident—although a good program can help toward these ends. I think the main result can be stated quite briefly: it is the development in boys and girls of knowledge and attitudes that will enable them to make sound *choices* about the use of their sexual powers—choices that are *intelligent* (based on information), *responsible* (undertaken in the light of knowledge of their consequences), and *moral* (good and not harmful to themselves and all others involved, now and in the future). They will learn not to be afraid of the sexual part of their natures, but to understand and gladly accept it and to be prepared to control it and enjoy it as a part of life and for the good of life.

11

Trying to Feel Better: The Use and Abuse of Drugs, Alcohol and Tobacco

"**5** I hate it!!!!
6 Ugh!
7 They can change your whole life. I like my life.
8 Don't knock it if you haven't tried it.
9 You've got to be a STUPIDASS to try drugs."

Human beings throughout history have tried various ways to make themselves feel better. The forces of life have always impinged upon us, forces outside us and within us. A splendid quality of being human is that we are conscious of a gap between what is and what should be, between how we feel and how we would like to feel. And, being an inventive and experimental species, we work hard to make things better. The subject of this chapter is some of the ways we have discovered to make ourselves feel better.

Food will do it, making love will do it, a good talk will do it. Being praised for success, or just our own sense of accomplishment, will do it. A beautiful morning, an inspiring landscape, or the sudden sense of wonder at the marvel of a flower or a tree, or even a beetle or an ant, will do it. And, for many, drugs—which include alcohol and tobacco—will do it.

Those who write and talk about the lives of teen-agers too often lump drugs, tobacco and alcohol together with sex, as if all were menaces that we wish would go away—at least for the young. I can understand why this is done, for any of them, used without control, without a sense of the worth of people, and without responsibility, can lead to tragedy. But there is a difference: our use of the gift of sexuality within loving relationships and to enhance the quality of life is a blessing, something precious, good and immensely rewarding. We cannot be nearly so enthusiastic—well, most of us can't—about drugs, alcohol and tobacco, which involve special health and behavior problems, tremendous social costs, and without which, it could be argued, life would be better for most people.

Although I have carefully separated the discussion of sex from the discussion in this chapter, I think that the values I suggested as acceptable guides for our education about sex apply equally well to education about drugs, alcohol and tobacco: information, responsibility, control, consideration, the worth of the individual, and communication.

The Use and Abuse of Drugs by Students

You will remember that drugs was one of the subjects that boys and girls often mentioned that they wanted to talk about with their parents but did not feel able to. On the other hand, it is one of the problem areas that parents felt least concerned about, according to responses on the parent questionnaire. On the student questionnaire, I asked: *Have you ever used "drugs"—marijuana, speed, heroin, LSD, etc.? Yes — No — If yes, when, what kind, and how much? Why? If no, why?* The proportion of those who had used drugs steadily increased as the students were in higher grades: fifth, 0 percent; sixth, 7 percent; seventh, 18 percent; eighth, 24 percent; ninth, 58 percent. (These figures were gathered in May of the school year.) The biggest jumps in the amount of drug use were between sixth and seventh grades, and between eighth and ninth. It is striking that by the end of ninth grade, well over half of these boys and girls have tried drugs—48 percent of the boys, 70 percent of the girls.

What kind of drugs do the students report using? Of all those who said they'd used drugs, 78 percent said they used or do use marijuana, 13 percent "uppers" (amphetamines), 4 percent "downers" (barbiturates) and 4 percent LSD. There were no reported heroin users.

As to *when* the drugs were used, the answers were: only at parties, 47 percent; regular use, 23 percent; as an experiment, once or twice, 13 percent; rarely but on occasion, 7 percent; other, 10 percent.

There were three main *reasons* given for the use of drugs: it feels good, 55 percent; everybody else was doing it, 36 percent; I did it to be cool, 9 percent.

In answer to *why do you* not *use drugs?* (and the replies of those who had tried it a time or two and quit are included here), nonusers gave the following reasons:

It's stupid, hateful, foolish, horrible, etc.	30%
It's bad for you, can kill you, etc.	25%
It wrecks up your life, messes you up, etc.	24%

The remaining 21 percent said they feared addiction, or thought they were too young, or were afraid to try, or felt no need for drugs, or had tried it once but never would again, or never had a chance to try, or thought it was too expensive.

Some comments on why people don't use drugs are: "They'll kill or damage you for life"; "gets to be a habit like cookies or potato chips"; "I see no reason if I'm going to feel good for a few minutes and then get sick"; "I don't want to be one of those cool people who go crazy"; "makes you sick, weird and crazy"; "I'm not *that* dumb"; "a big cop-out"; "just living gets *me* high"; "life is so precious that tampering with your own for the sake of feeling good for a couple of hours is dumb."

Some Facts about Drugs

Several students stated that "pot is not a drug." Well, is it? Most people are not clear what a drug is because the word is used in so many senses. Traditionally, we define a drug as "a chemical substance, other than food, used to treat or prevent disease." In that sense, pot is not a drug. As far as I know, it is rarely prescribed by doctors and is not established as a cure for diseases.

So we need another definition of "drug" that will include the serious problems we are discussing in this chapter. Let's use this definition: "A drug is a chemical substance that can alter perception, consciousness or behavior, that is used with the intent of obtaining pleasure or avoiding pain, and that has the potential for abuse so as to harm individuals or society." * In this sense, marijuana —pot—is a drug, a rather mild one; coffee is also a mild

* From *The Dope Book, All about Drugs,* by Mark Lieberman, which I recommend to students, parents and teachers. It is a factual, sensible, up-to-date treatment of the subject, presenting all the information and points of view a person needs to make intelligent decisions about the use of drugs. The policy of the publisher is to keep it up to date by revision. It can be obtained for $1.95 from McDougal, Littell & Co., Box 1667, Evanston, Ill. 60204.

drug, but its excessive use can have harmful effects and cause users to become dependent on it; and heroin is a drug, a heavy and disastrously harmful one that almost certainly leads to addiction. Alcohol and tobacco, too, are drugs—"socially acceptable," yes—but both can be very harmful to their users. Most drugs have multiple effects, some good and some bad, which are different for different users. Some people drink in moderation and smoke most of their lives without apparent harm. Others become alcoholics or die of lung cancer. Measured solely in terms of the total damage done to health and welfare in the United States, alcohol and tobacco would head the list of harmful drugs.

"Problem" drugs can be classified into four groups according to their effects on the human body. The first is *narcotics.* (The word comes from the Greek *narkotikos,* "benumbing.") These are drugs that make people drowsy, relieve pain, can give a floating feeling of well-being and removal from the problems of the real world. Such a feeling is called euphoria. Many people think that the words "drugs" and "narcotics" are synonymous because federal and state governments have narcotics laws which actually cover all drug abuse, not just the use of narcotics. These laws were passed originally to control the use of opium and, later, heroin. Today the use of substances that are not narcotics, like marijuana and the amphetamines, is an offense under the narcotics laws.

A second class of drugs is the *stimulants.* The main stimulant drugs today are the amphetamines ("speed" and various pep pills). They have few important medical uses, and they can be extremely harmful, even fatal, when used to excess over a period of time. Caffeine, the substance in coffee, tea, cocoa and cola drinks that peps up the user, is a stimulant drug.

A third class of drugs is the *sedatives,* mainly barbiturates and other sleeping pills. These are drugs that induce drowsiness and have a calming effect, but not the same as narcotics. They can make users feel pleasantly "out of it" or high. Properly used with a doctor's prescription, they are valuable for relieving insomnia. Misused, they are very dangerous.

A fourth class of drugs is the *hallucinogens.* They cause people to have hallucinations—that is, to see, hear and feel things that are not really there, or to perceive them in an unreal way. People can feel very good when they escape into hallucinations, and they can have the impression that they are great, have great ideas, are conscious in new and beautiful ways, can even see God. (Hallucinogenic drugs are also called *psychedelic,* from the Greek words *psyche,* "soul," and *delos,* "visible.") They can also make people feel lost, shaken and alarmingly detached from reality, as if they were going crazy, a frightening experience. The principal hallucinogen is LSD, a dangerous drug that can bring on and aggravate (not exactly cause) mental disorders and which sometimes has long-term repeat effects—flashbacks. An LSD "trip" can provide temporary ecstasy, but it can also be a grim and terrifying "bummer."

Many drugs do not fall neatly into any one of these four classes. Take, for example, alcohol. It is a sedative all right, but it first sedates—puts to sleep—the cerebral cortex, that part of the brain which, among other functions, makes us feel shy and inhibited. Therefore, taken in moderate quantities, alcohol causes many people to feel stimulated, lively, talkative and friendly. Taken in large quantities, however, it really does knock people out, sometimes in rather uncomfortable ways. Alcohol also acts as a hallucinogen; it causes some people to see and hear things in unreal ways.

Another drug that is not easily classified is tobacco, the active ingredient in which is the chemical nicotine. It gives some people a lift and makes others feel relaxed and comfortable, and it can have both effects on the same person in different circumstances and at different times.

I shall say more about alcohol and tobacco later in this chapter.

Addiction, Physical and Psychological

There is another set of fundamental facts about problem drugs that it is important to know—the facts about addiction, that is, "getting hooked." This is a legitimate fear of people using or considering the use of drugs. Edward Brecher, in his excellent Consumers Union Report, *Licit and Illicit Drugs,** defines an addicting drug as "one that most users continue to take even though they want to stop, try to stop, and actually succeed in stopping for days, weeks, months or even a year. It is a drug for which men and women will prostitute themselves. . . . It is a drug which most users continue to use despite the threat of long-term imprisonment for its use."

Addiction can be classified in two types, physical addiction and psychological addiction. They are not, in fact, distinct, for the mind is a part of the body and affects, and is affected by, it. Thus it is often impossible to tell whether the symptoms of addiction are physically or psychologically based. Probably they are usually both.

Physical addiction is a craving for a drug, a need for it so overpowering that it becomes the addict's most important concern. He feels he cannot live without the drug, and his life becomes committed to the quest for it. A part

* Published by Little, Brown and Company, 1972. I highly recommend this lively, complete and accurate account of the drug problem. It can be obtained for $4.95 from Little, Brown and Company, 200 West Street, P.O. Box 902, Waltham, Mass. 07154.

of physical addiction is *tolerance,* which means that the addict's body adapts so that it can tolerate increasing doses of the drug without the desired effects; thus he needs constantly larger doses. Another aspect of physical addiction is *withdrawal symptoms.* If the addict does not get the doses he needs, he experiences severe physical and mental reactions such as vomiting, pain, convulsions, hallucinations and delusions. These symptoms are so hard to bear that the addict is driven to almost any lengths to get relief by obtaining more of the drug. Physical addiction and withdrawal symptoms result from alcohol, the amphetamines (speed), narcotics and barbiturate sedatives, *not* from LSD or marijuana. There is some question about tobacco. To see why, read this excerpt from psychoanalyst Sigmund Freud's account of how he felt when, warned by his doctor that his heart problems were caused by cigar smoking, he tried to give up tobacco: "There came . . . a severe affection of the heart, worse than I ever had when smoking. . . . And with it an oppression of mood in which images of dying and farewell replaced the more usual fantasies. . . . It is annoying for a doctor who has to be concerned all day long with neurosis not to know whether he is suffering from a justifiable or hypochondriacal depression." * Freud never succeeded in kicking the tobacco habit, not even after over thirty surgical operations for cancer of the jaw and mouth. However, most smokers do not have such extreme difficulties, and many do succeed in quitting smoking, but usually not without considerable mental and physical stress.

Perhaps a better term for *psychological addiction* is *psychological dependence,* that is, having a habit so deeply established that it is impossible to break it without great

* Quoted in Brecher, p. 24, from Ernest Jones, *The Life and Work of Sigmund Freud,* Basic Books, N.Y., 1953, pp. 309–310.

mental stress, often accompanied by physical discomfort and agitation. The user comes to depend on the feeling of improved well-being, or lack of tension, that he experiences from using the drug. However, with psychological dependence there is not the phenomenon of tolerance or such grim and terrifying physical withdrawal symptoms.

People whose use of drugs causes them to become physically or psychologically addicted to them are engaging in *drug abuse;* that is, they are using the drug to the point that their health and social activities are damaged. It is not possible to say at what point use becomes abuse. Probably most users do not know that use has merged into abuse until it is too late to stop without experiencing major pain and stress.

Why Do People Use Drugs?

Probably the main reason that people use drugs is to try to get rid of bad feelings or to experience good ones, or both. We all have bad feelings, some more, some less, and we all would rather feel good than bad. Further, we live in a society in which most of us, especially adults, use drugs—coffee, alcohol, tobacco, stimulants, tranquilizers, pain-killers—to try to feel better, not simply on doctor's orders to cure diseases. We are told daily on TV and radio, in magazines and newspapers, that such and such a pill will calm us down, pep us up, stop pain, reduce worry. Drugs are a part of our lives. Little wonder that many of us are pushed toward overuse, if not abuse.

Also, there is the persuasion to use drugs that comes from people we know who have tried them and liked them. They want us to try too. Well, drugs may work for *them* now; but they may cause *us* trouble. They may also cause them trouble later on. Therefore, a prudent person will not start using drugs, except mild ones that are approved by doctors, without first thinking about it carefully. And the pressure from our friends to do so, especially among teen-agers, may be very strong.

Then, of course, there is the normal human desire to experiment. We want new experiences; we want to know for ourselves, to find out what it's like. In most areas of life this desire to explore is good. In the matter of drugs, it is probably better to read about it, but not to do it. At least that's how I feel about taking these sorts of new risks that are not necessary.

I have mentioned persuasion. Another sort of persuasion is from the person who is making money out of selling drugs—the pusher and the pusher's friends. There is a lot of money to be made from selling drugs, and some sellers are compelled to push in order to keep up their own drug habit, to meet the needs arising from their addiction. Also, many drug users feel somewhat guilty about their use and puzzled by it. They feel better if they can get others to go along with them.

Lastly, I suppose one can say that people with bad problems that cause them pain are more likely to turn to drugs for escape or relief than those whose problems are more manageable. Parents and teachers can help teen-agers with problems by being ever ready to listen, to share, to advise if asked, although all of this is not as simple as it sounds. Also, teen-agers can help each other in the same way. Someone said, "A good spouse halves your troubles and doubles your joys." The same can be said about a good and trusted friend.

A Special Word about Marijuana

The vast majority of drug users use only marijuana—also called pot, grass, dope. How many? Nobody knows, but an educated guess would be from six to twelve million regular users in the United States. In the six schools I surveyed, 45 percent of ninth-graders said they had tried pot, but I judge from their comments that most of them are not regular users. By twelfth grade I'm sure the figures are higher. Some people get no effect from smoking pot; some feel wonderful in a variety of ways that defies brief description. The vast majority of marijuana users do not go on to using heavier drugs, but most users of heavy, harmful drugs did start with marijuana. Marijuana does not cause physical addiction, but many users become psychologically dependent upon it. However, it cannot cause a person to become mentally ill, although it occasionally brings out a mental condition that was hidden or controlled before. Therefore, people who have doubts about their mental stability should be wary of marijuana.

No adequate studies have been made of the effects of long-term use of marijuana and therefore no one knows for sure whether or not it is harmful in the long run. *Probably,* not certainly, the effects are less likely to be damaging than those from the long-term use of alcohol or tobacco.

If all this is so, why not use marijuana if you want to enjoy the pleasant feelings it induces? Well, millions of people do. But it's against the law, and potential users need to decide if they are willing to break the law. Users and sellers of marijuana can and do receive heavy fines and long jail sentences, as much as $20,000 or forty years. Also, users of marijuana come into contact with lawbreakers, some of whom may try to persuade them to try more powerful drugs, drugs which make an even better profit for pushers.

Some observers report that frequent users of marijuana tend to lose ambition—to be less interested in doing well in school, in keeping up friendships, in engaging in active recreation. So, in a way, using pot may be a cop-out from the challenges, satisfactions and accomplishments of life. However, probably some regular marijuana users are showing, consciously or unconsciously, that they reject the commonly accepted values and standards of society, and it is this rejection, rather than the marijuana, that looks like a cop-out. In any case, it's a lot easier to start using marijuana than to stop.

Discovering and Curing Drug Abuse

A question parents frequently ask is, "How do I know if my child is on drugs?" Often it is not easy to tell. In the ideal family situation, the children would talk about it with their parents, but such a situation is rare, and in matters of drug use (as well as sexual behavior), easy communication is rare. Young people, if they want to start, want to do so on their own. If they get in too deep, they are very reluctant to admit it. This is too bad, and certainly teen-agers who are troubled about their use of drugs, or even those who have questions that have not yet become troubles, should find a responsible, mature, informed person with whom to talk over the situation. Talk among teen-agers themselves is good, but it may be just a trading of experience and of ignorance. Also, adults who are approached by teen-agers wanting to talk about drugs should be very careful not to maintain an authoritarian, negative stance. We just don't know enough to justify such a position, and it's no way to get at problems.

Some signs that may indicate to parents or others that a person in the family has started using drugs are fairly sudden and marked changes in the person's life-style—changes in eating patterns, sleeping patterns, relationships with others, attitudes toward friends, school and outside activities. Rapid loss of weight, long unexplained absences from home or a marked increase in irritability or nervousness also may be signs. Now of course the normal processes of going through adolescence may involve the same sorts of changes and shifts, so parents should not "jump to conclusions," a tendency among parents and teachers that young people say they especially fear and object to. Parents should not go into a flurry of concerned activity just because they have heard of an incident or two of pot smoking.

If parents believe that their child may be on drugs, I suppose the best thing in most families is simply to ask, not accusingly, but as a matter of concerned interest in someone they love. If that doesn't satisfy, then parents can try checking with a teacher who is respected but also knows the scene. Other parents and their children can also be sources of information, but it is very important not to act like a spy.

If the person suspected of drug use continues to show disturbing symptoms—health problems, strange antisocial behavior, lethargy or odd vivacity—then it would be good to arrange with the family doctor for a general checkup, being sure to share with the doctor in advance the reasons for concern.

If drug use is established, then the family has to decide whether it is use or abuse. If it is the latter, so much depends on the individual circumstances that it is impossible to prescribe a single course of action. A frank talk is desirable, if possible. If parents think that the drug use represents an attempt to escape from serious emotional problems, then they should seek advice from a psychologist or psychiatrist about how to get at these problems. The school may be able to put families in touch with good professional people. If not, in most communities there are agencies that can do so. Major universities often have guidance clinics attached to them, as do many hospitals.

Most large cities and many state governments have programs to help people who have questions about drugs, are afraid, or are involved in drug use. The addresses and telephone numbers of these government programs can be found in the telephone book under "Health" or "Public Health," or under the name of the city or state and then "Health" or "Health Department." Also, in the Yellow Pages of the telephone book, agencies are likely to be listed under "Drug Addiction Information and Treatment Centers." Often there will be a hotline, like "HELP," where trained people are on duty seven days a week, twenty-four hours a day. The people in these agencies will not tell you what to do or ask any personal questions. Instead, they will give all the information you need to make your own decisions.

The Use and Abuse of Alcohol

I've already stated that alcohol is a "drug," a physically addictive one involving tolerance and withdrawal symptoms. But it is also a drug that is "socially acceptable." Probably, most of the adult readers of this book are social drinkers and find moderate drinking a source of pleasure and relaxation. The question is, What about boys and girls in fifth through ninth grades? Do they drink? Should they drink? What should family policies be with regard to the use of alcohol by minors?

On the questionnaire I asked, *Have you ever drunk alcoholic beverages (beer, wine, whiskey, etc.)?* I was surprised at the high percentages that said *yes,* ranging from 78 percent to 96 percent over grades five through nine, with a slightly higher percentage of girls than boys.

The next question was, *If yes, when, what kind, and how much?* It is clear from the answers that the vast majority who said they had drunk first did it by having a sip of their parents' drink or a bit of wine at family dinner. About a quarter of the users described themselves in one way or another as regular users. The preponderance of "occasional sippers" is in fifth and sixth grades; all the regular users are in seventh, eighth and ninth grades, most in eight. Here are the percentages of types of use, classified rather roughly, according to their own descriptions:

Occasionally at family dinner	17%
Have tried, and say they now use, a variety of alcoholic beverages	15%
On family or religious holidays, or special occasions only	14%
An occasional sip from parents	14%
At teen-age parties (several said "to be cool")	13%
Only one try, just to see	10%
Regular user of beer or other single specified beverage	9%
Once in an effort to get drunk, as often unsuccessful as successful	5%
Pushed into it once or twice by friends	2%
During travels abroad	1%

In general, there is much more openness about drinking than about the use of drugs, even marijuana. Many parents appear not to object to moderate family drinking. However, drinking at teen-age parties is another matter. According to the comments of students and parents, students drink at parties without the approval, and often without the knowledge, of their parents or their adult hosts, and there is very little conversation about this in families, except about how *other* kids drank.

Here are a few interesting comments about the occasion of drinking: "When I was a little kid I went around asking people at parties for a sip and I got so many sips I got drunk"; "champagne on New Years"; "half a pint of vodka because we wanted to"; "twenty-two glasses at a friend's bar mitzvah"; "once, threw up all day"; "makes the party more exciting if I am depressed"; "I fell in love with gin and tonic at seven"; "I tried to get drunk but I got sick"; "you name it, I drank it. I like to get a little high once in a while"; "New Years I tried to get smashed but I couldn't"; "washa matter with a shmall ship?"

The last question I asked about alcohol was, *What is your opinion of drinking?* The proportions of favorable and unfavorable opinions were pretty much the same in all the grades, with a slightly higher proportion of "it's bad" in fifth and sixth, and of "OK in moderation" in eighth and ninth. Here are the main categories of opinion:

OK in moderation, at special occasions, etc.	39%
Bad (horrible, YUCK!, ugh!, disgraceful, dumb, etc.)	38%
OK without qualifications	21%
Afraid to do it	1%
It's illegal*	1%

A considerable number of boys and girls, both on this question and on the questions about what makes a good father or mother and about aspects of family life, commented that they did not like it when their parents drank, especially when they drank too much. They found it disturbing and embarrassing. Also, when I asked what ac-

* Serving alcoholic beverages to minors, even to one's own children at home, is illegal. People are minors up to eighteen in some states, twenty-one in others. The law is seldom applied, but upon complaint it can be.

tions of parents tended to affect the children by example, a great many specified drinking. There were comments like: "My Dad drinks and that means to me that I'll never drink. I've seen from experience." Others said in one way or another, "They drink, why shouldn't I drink?" which is an appealing argument to the young and should be considered.

Discovering and Curing Alcohol Abuse

The same things can be said about alcohol abuse that were said on pages 250–52 about drug abuse. The main difference is that in general parents are familiar with drinking and its effects and know more about the subject than they do about drugs. Therefore, they are less afraid and probably better able to communicate about the subject with their children. One of the major difficulties comes when parents serve, or allow to be available, alcoholic beverages to other people's children. (See the section on teen-age parties on pages 201–14.)

I think there is little question that most middle and junior high schoolers are too young to manage the effects of drinking, except for the sip or the occasional ceremonial serving, and that the best rule is no alcohol for the kids while they are minors.

The Use and Abuse of Tobacco

Tobacco is another "drug" that most adults are familiar with and therefore not really afraid of. The kids have no more information about it than their parents do. However, one great advantage that many of the kids have is that they haven't yet started to smoke and so still have the chance not to start, while a lot of parents are hooked on a habit that they find too painful to break now. But they wish they hadn't started. I think this fact should be explained to boys and girls, especially by parents who smoke. An even stronger "fact" is the example of parents who feel so strongly that smoking is unhealthy and a public nuisance that they have gone through the painful process of breaking a habit of years' standing. Many students specified this as an action of parents that strongly influenced them.

I asked the students a number of questions about smoking. The first was, *Have you ever smoked?* By grade nine, 86 percent answered *yes;* at grade five it was 32 percent, with a steady increase from grade to grade. About the same proportion of boys and girls have smoked. However, boys tend to have their first puff earlier than girls. That a person "has smoked" doesn't mean he is a smoker. A great many try it as a lark, and that's it.

I asked, *If you have smoked, when and how much?* The great majority of *yes* answerers have simply tried a puff or say they smoke "only a little bit." However, about 13 percent of all the ninth-graders say they smoke "a lot" or regularly. These include people who smoke regularly at parties, and there are a few, perhaps 6 percent, who smoke *only* at parties. In general, one can say that smoking has not become an established habit in more than 10 to 15 percent of the students who have completed ninth grade.

The last question I asked was, *What is your opinion about smoking?* Here are the answers:

Smoking is bad	69%
OK, fun, I like it	12%
A bad, expensive, harmful habit, but I do it because it's cool, calms my nerves, etc.	8%
It's up to the individual to decide for himself	7%
It's OK if you don't inhale or smoke very little	4%

Many of the following comments illustrate what strong feelings some junior high and middle schoolers have about smoking and how much conflict others feel about it: "I used to like it but now I hate it"; "makes you die sooner"; "I don't like it at all and I made my parents stop"; "I took two puffs and choked"; "if it relaxes or gives pleasure do it, but I wouldn't because it's unnatural, expensive and habit-forming"; "I enjoy both a pipe and cigarets and I don't have any regrets"; "you're a jackass if you smoke today because today kids know what it can do to them but *your* parents didn't know when they were kids"; "it bothers other people, if that's the only way to be cool I'd rather not be"; "it's a lousy hangup but I get very nervous at a lot of parties when the status group has gone off to the bushes and my friends are eating up the refreshments, and smoking is an escape that gives my hands something to do and calms me down"; "I like it because you get respect from younger kids"; "I smoke now and then to remind me how stupid it is"; "it's ugly to see pretty young people with a cigaret hanging out of their mouth."

I think that parents, whether or not they themselves are smokers, should make sure, without preaching, that their children know the facts about smoking: that tobacco is a drug; that it does not cause acute physical addiction but, once the habit is established, does create a very strong psychological dependence; that there is a tolerance effect —people tend to need more and more tobacco to get the effects they desire; that people who try to quit may suffer nausea, nervousness, bad temper, aches and general discomfort that many consider to be intolerable; that therefore it is much easier not to start; that our society has somehow promoted the idea, strongly maintained by advertising, that smoking is "cool," mature, and associated with the good things of life; that if you become a regular smoker, moderate or heavy, your chances of getting lung cancer and a host of other ailments are greatly increased;

and that many nonsmokers are bothered and annoyed by smokers (although they seldom have the courage to say so) and that even they, when they breathe the smoky air in a room or other enclosed area, are more subject to disease than if they breathed clean air.

There's no doubt that drugs, including alcohol and tobacco, do help many people to feel better, at least for a time. There's also no doubt that all of them involve risks to health and welfare. The least we can all do is to know the facts and discuss the problems openly. In some families, it may be possible to agree that the children will not use drugs, alcohol or tobacco until a certain age. If this is possible, I strongly recommend it. But if the rule is imposed against the will of unconvinced teen-agers, it may backfire and make them more likely to use the forbidden substances. Most families will settle for a full exposure to the facts and the best possible parental example. Then they will have to trust whatever common sense family members are endowed with.

12

How to Live with Parents and Teachers

"5 I just keep telling myself they're human too because they often are.

6 It's hard to get started talking with them but when I get started it's easy.

7 Our teacher gets so wrapped up in being mad that he doesn't explain why he's mad.

8 With my parents I used to be embarrassed until I realized they understood my personal problems.

9 At times I feel they're so far away from me that we really aren't related. They seem too old to know what I mean."

"Why can't you write a book for us?" asked one eighth-grade girl on her questionnaire. "We need it as much as the parents and teachers do!!!!!" Well, this chapter is addressed directly to students. Up to this point in the book, I have concentrated on what you students are like, how you came to be the way you are, what your opinions on various questions are. I have made suggestions for dealing with your problems and making the most of your opportunities. Possibly, a lot of the information and suggestions I've given are more interesting to your parents and teachers than to you, because, after all, you do know about yourself, and they don't—at least not as much. What I've tried to tell parents and teachers is things that they may not already know.

You know about you, but how much do you know about parents and teachers? About a hundred years ago, the American poet James Russell Lowell said, "If youth be a defect, it is one that we outgrow only too soon." However, if adulthood be a defect, it is not one that we outgrow. Most of us grow more and more adult and less and less youthful. But, to judge from the adults I know best, including myself, most of us still feel like the same person we were when we were children, except, as a witty little kid said about adults, "They've stopped growing at the ends and started growing in the middle." Scratch an adult and you'll find a child—below the adultlike surface.

Many of you, when asked for your advice to parents and teachers, made comments like: "Try to remember what it was like when you were young, and do what you would have wanted done to you"; or "we're all people, so don't put us in the 'teenage' package. What you feel, we feel, and don't forget it"; or "think of *your* youth in present terms. Then think of the best thing your parents could have done in the present case to make you a better human being, and then do that"; or "try to put yourself in the kid's position." My guess is that most parents and teachers do try to put themselves in the kid's position, but it's difficult to do because the "kid" we adults tend to imagine is the kid *we were,* rather than the kid *you are.*

To Close the Gap

What is needed then is, as an eighth-grade boy said: "Communication! Communication! Communication! Kids, don't be afraid, just stick out your necks and communicate." What other way is there for parents to understand you than to hear from you on how you feel, what you think, what you need? But sometimes this communication is very difficult for parents, as it is for you. They want to know about you, but they know you hate prying. Of course, you have a right to your privacy and to your own thoughts; you want to be yourself and to enjoy at least a degree of independence from your parents. But there must be parts of your life that you can share with your parents. If you can volunteer some information and sharing, you will probably find that the parental urge to pry will be less. However, if you discover that sharing experiences and feelings leads to even more questions and to what you feel are invasions of your privacy, say so frankly. An open statement like, "I don't feel like talking about that," or "That's something I can't tell you now," will be respected by most parents and teachers. But a near-total and puzzling silence, which to parents and teachers often looks like sullenness and dislike, leaves the adult with only two choices: either to accept the silence and the communication gap or to keep asking questions.

A number of boys and girls on their questionnaires gave these sorts of advice to other kids—to you: "Try to put up with your parents and *make* them understand how you feel"; "feel free to tell your parents about things"; "be able to talk to your parents about anything and be able to understand them"; "if you love your parents, *show* them; if you don't, try to understand them, and make them understand you." So, even if it's hard, maybe even risky, try to get your feelings out and to share as much of your life as you can.

To Keep from Being Annoyed

In Chapter 8, pages 174–76, I listed the things about parents that most annoy their children. High on the list were a know-it-all attitude, lectures and yelling. How can you avoid these things?

To avoid lectures and yelling, listen hard and responsively before your parent or teacher starts to yell and then try to show that you understand what is concerning the adult. A good way to do this is to repeat it in your own words: "I get it. You don't like it when I drop my things around"; "oh, I see, you wish I'd asked you before I did that"; "it annoys you when I tease Timmy"; or "yes, I see how my whispering in class bothers people." Just to know that they've gotten through to you is a great help to parents and teachers. If you can possibly go one step farther and say something like, "I'll try to do better from now on—but it's hard, so don't expect me to be perfect—but I *will* try," that is a great comfort to adults. And if you think the adult criticism is not fair or right, say so, calmly if possible, loudly if necessary—but *say what you think; get it out.*

To avoid the know-it-all attitude, try to admit that you don't know it all, listen well and respond, be sure you understand, and if you don't, ask questions. And if you are quite sure you know better than your parents (as in matters of your own friendships, how to behave at school, how to dress at parties), say so in as friendly a way as you can and explain why. It's really worth it to try to do some explaining.

The Worries and Problems of Parents

You are doubtless aware that parents have problems and worries. Have you ever actively encouraged your parents to talk about them with you? I know that most parents would like to feel that you're interested. On the questionnaires, some students urged other students to consider the situation of their parents: "Try to understand your parents"; "understand that your parents have hard times too"; "I find it hard to get mom and dad to talk about what they really feel. They seem more likely to tell me and my brothers what they think I ought to think they ought to feel. But now and then when I really ask them I get good results, and it *helps* me to know what they feel. I'm always amazed they seem to have even more worries than I have. In your book, tell other kids to get into the worries of their parents and maybe it will make the worries of the kids seem only medium size."

Well, what do parents worry about? On the parent questionnaire, I asked, *What would you say are the two or three things about your life that worry you most?* The thing most frequently mentioned was *"the pace of life":* "The pressures of living prevent my being enough involved with my children"; "life is going by so fast I don't have a chance to look at it"; "I'm too busy to think about my life and its direction."

The worry next most frequently expressed was *"our financial future":* "The economy"; "how can I make enough money to pay for all that we need to do?"

Next was *"anxiety about my own career":* "My job doesn't make life better"; "I like my work but it keeps me away from the rest of my family both physically and psychologically"; "can I be a good wife and mother and still do my career?"

Coming close after career was *"the health of all of us"*: "My health"; "is my husband working himself to death?"; "can my wife hold the family together without falling apart herself?"

Next was *"death"* or *"that some great harm will come"* to self, spouse or children: "Loss of spouse"; "will we live to see them all into adulthood?"; "the uncertainty of life: can we go on?"; "will I live long enough to spoil my grandchildren?"; "a terrible accident. We've almost had several."

Then comes "Will the kids succeed and be happy?": "That my boys won't be as happy as we are"; "are we giving our children the skills they need to succeed in this rapidly changing world?"; "I'm afraid the children won't have a chance to lead happy, productive lives."

A great many parents say they worry about *"my worth as a human being":* "My lack of self-confidence"; "will I be anything when the children have grown up?"; "I may be a failure"; "my shyness with adults"; "my worth as a parent"; "that I'll not be a good parent."

Other worries quite a few parents mentioned were: "How can I [or we] be happy?"; "I want to be loved more than I am"; and "the way relationships are in our family."

Another question I asked parents was, *If you could change two or three things about your life, what would they be?* I was surprised that the most often mentioned was *"I'd like to be better educated"*—to have gone to a better school, to know more, to have an advanced degree, to be better prepared for advanced jobs, to have a richer cultural life, to be able to share more education with the children.

Close behind this in frequency was *"I'd have a better marriage"*—that I'd never gotten married, that my husband shared more with us all, that my wife could do what needs to be done and still be happy, that *I* didn't have all the drudgery, that we argue too much.

Then, as you'd expect after reading the worries, next came *"I'd be less busy and have more time."* This is mentioned by fathers and mothers and by a good many people who were trying both to work at a job and to be parents.

Next was *"We'd have more money"*—so as not to have to worry, so as to be able to travel, to buy things, to be more generous with the children, not to have to make such a sacrifice to send the children to school.

Also high on the list was *"I'd have the love of a good man."* This was mentioned in one way or another by almost every mother who was divorced: "There would be a strong, loving man on the scene"; "I'd be happily married to a man who would be a good father to my children."

If your parents are typical, probably they worry about some of these things and would like to make some of these changes. If you understand that your parents have hard times too, perhaps you will find that you will all enjoy each other more. You might even try discussing this chapter with your parents.

How Teachers Get Their Satisfactions

So far, this chapter has been mainly about parents, and that is as it should be, since living with parents is a much bigger part of your life than living with teachers. But you do spend a lot of time in the presence of teachers, and the following ideas may help you to try to understand them a little better.

One way to understand them is to know how they get their satisfactions out of life and out of teaching. Now, obviously it is not a student's obligation to satisfy teachers but rather to get an education. However, you may be able to make the lives of teachers more rewarding and find it easier to live with them if you know how they answered this question: *Explain the main satisfactions you feel in relation to your students at school.* Here is what some of them said: "When I feel I am reaching most of the students one way or another; when it's not just like white-washing a wall, but deeper"; "I love to talk with them about what they think or feel. And I love to be sought out for serious discussion. I like knowing they like and respect me at the same time"; "I love knowing them. I gain a rejuvenating happiness"; "when they come into class looking interested, not dejected"; "good, sound relationships with the kids"; "respect and affection of students"; "watching them grow, especially seventh and eighth—gain in self-confidence, suddenly take on a new challenge and meet it well"; "helping kids help themselves straighten things out—emotionally and academically"; "when they try hard to write good papers and respond to each other's papers"; "the light bulb!"

Obviously, you can't fake understanding and growth if you don't understand and aren't growing. But when you do understand, when the idea suddenly comes clear, don't be afraid to let the light bulb shine; if you think a lesson was well taught or if you got a lot out of a unit of study, take the trouble to say so (even if you don't particularly like the teacher; it's much more important to like and learn the subject than to like the teacher). If you notice things that teachers have done for you or others that are especially helpful or thoughtful, say so. You can make a teacher's week, or even month, by taking the trouble to say how much you got out of the class. I'm talking about genuine appreciation. If it's not honest, it doesn't mean much.

Also, if you feel you might get some help by talking over a problem with a teacher during a free period or after school, take the initiative to do it. Most teachers like to have you talk things over with them. Don't assume because they seem busy and rushed that they don't want to see you, or that if they are very businesslike they aren't warmly interested in you and your life. A lot of students in school miss rich opportunities for friendship and personal help by not seeking out their teachers and talking with them.

What Makes a Good Daughter or Son?

In Chapter 8, pages 173–74, I gave some student responses to the question, *What are the qualities of a good parent?* The first three qualities were "understanding," "loving," and "nice, kind, considerate, etc." I feel quite sure that parents would rate very high those same qualities for children. So, if you want to live well with parents, you might put to yourself these queries:

> *Do I try to be understanding of my parents?*
> *Am I loving of my parents?*
> *Am I nice, kind and considerate?*

As I write down these three questions, I realize that they sound corny, maybe so corny that your reaction is: "What?! You want us to be perfect? No way!" Of course, it would be ridiculous to want you to be perfect, to pretend to be perfect, to try always to act loving when you sometimes feel quite full of hate, to force yourself to act nice when you feel angry and depressed. In other words, not to be yourself would be false and, in the long run, harmful. I'm sure most parents would want you to be yourself—and to share yourself, your real self, insofar as you are able to. But it does come as a wonderful reward to parents, I know from having talked with many of them and from my own experience, when their daughters or sons show they really do understand, not science or math or English, not the need to take out the trash or the desirability of keeping their room neat, not the importance of letting the family know where they are and what they're doing—but do understand how it is to be a parent, understand how it is to love like a parent, understand that a parent is a parent second and a human being first, sharing all the needs that other human beings have.

Three Specific Suggestions

Here are three suggestions of actions you might undertake that would make it easier to live with parents and teachers:

1. *Be polite when it doesn't go against your principles.* To be quite specific, how delighted parents are when they hear a spontaneous, unasked, enthusiastic: "Thanks!"; "Gee, thanks!"; "I really liked that!" Another kind of politeness is the offer of help beyond arranged duties and chores: "Let me unload the groceries"; "I'll finish the vacuuming"; "We'll do the dishes, you go read the paper"; "I'll erase the board"; "We'll put those books back and rearrange the room."

2. *Acknowledge that your parents and teachers are right when you really think they are.* This does *not* mean being an apple-polisher or a yes-person. It means that if you see that people are right, even if you opposed them, you simply say so. It gives the people great satisfaction, it makes them feel good, and it removes the necessity for them to keep insisting that they are right or to say the revolting, "I told you so." If you admit they are right, they don't have to prove it. It also puts you in a much stronger position when you're sure, in an important matter, that *you* are right. You can say so and will be listened to with respect.

3. *Take the lead, when you can, in talking, opening up, expressing your feelings, keeping your parents up-to-date with your life and informed about how things are with you.* I can't think of anything that is more rewarding and satisfying to parents and teachers than to feel that their sons and daughters, or their students, are trying to keep the flow of communication open.

13

Adolescence and the Future

“5 If you learn as much as you can, you'll have something later.

6 I sometimes think if we could stop thinking, it would be better, I think!!

7 I don't know where the world is going, but I want to be here to go along with it.

8 Teenagers just don't care any more. They've seen too much to feel they can do anything about it.

9 The world is really fu--- up and no one really understands anyone, now do they?”

Perhaps to every generation since man began, our earth has seemed, as the Scottish poet Alexander Smith described it, "a maniac world, homeless and sobbing through the deep," a place where vast forces beyond our control are acting. I think that seldom in the known history of humanity have the forces of turmoil and potential destruction seemed to us more threatening or the pace of life or the rate of change more frantic than today.

Certainly, a major requirement for humanity in the period just ahead will be the skill and resilience not only to adjust to change but to help control and direct it. I should guess that the changes of the fifty years just past, radical as they have been, will seem modest compared to those to come. But still, in our schools we tend to teach: What is, will be. But the truth is: What is, will change.

A Forward Look

What rough passages of change are today's young teen-agers likely to have to negotiate in the years ahead? I should guess that the world will not much longer tolerate a situation in which we in the U.S.A., who constitute only 5 to 6 percent of its population, consume perhaps 40 percent of its resources—about seven times our share. It is unlikely that the growth of population, the production and worldwide distribution of food, the possession of nuclear weapons and power, and the sending of pollutants into the air, water and soil can much longer remain uncontrolled. Unless humanity is to starve, kill or poison itself, these problems must be grappled with. No one knows (although we should all be trying to figure out) how they will be solved, but it is inevitable, I think, that their solution is going to necessitate radical changes in our habits of eating, in the ways we house and transport ourselves, in the ways we use energy and cope with waste, and in our liberty to have children. We shall certainly have to delegate to world authorities, of which we will be only a part, much of our national and individual independence.

Even as I suggest a few areas of change which it appears to me we must be prepared to face, I, too, may be bound by the idea that what is, will be. I like the story which is told about Dorothy Parker, who went to an afternoon party and was given two baby alligators. She returned home to get ready to go out again for an evening party, and, not knowing what to do with the alligators, she put them temporarily in the bathtub. When she came back, she found a note on the hall table written by her housekeeper. It said: "I am leaving. I cannot work in a house with alligators. I would have told you this before but I never thought the subject would come up."

We do not know what subjects will come up, or whether, in the house that is our world, we shall have to work with alligators or something else now quite inconceivable to us.

New Emphases on Education

Thus, our schools must give students experience in dealing with change, both in class and outside. There will be less justification for the fixed curriculum and fixed schedule. Also, we must teach people to rely less on physical possessions and surroundings and more on inner resources that they carry with them—ideas, values, ways of personal renewal and pleasure. To be ready for change, we need to learn to be considerate of others rather than to try to beat them out in competition. Such consideration requires that we know how to observe them, to hear them, to sympathize with them, to imagine ourselves into their situations, and to communicate our own situations to them.

Today, most of our education is still limited to the view from the U.S.A. and to what is good for America. Instead, we must habituate ourselves to look at all questions—historical, economic, mathematical, scientific, anthropological, linguistic, artistic—from a worldwide point of view. For example, we should redesign those big classroom maps so that the U.S.A. doesn't always stand at the center of the world. We need to teach history so that events and developments are not presented as if American democracy were the end result, with materials chosen mainly because they explain the rise and progress of the West. We need to show that the welfare of each Bushman of the Kalahari is as important as that of each American. True, our responsibility for action will usually lie where we live and work, but our concern for welfare must become worldwide.

We need to teach confidence in the importance of the right actions of individuals. These days, Americans are rather depressed by the state of their nation and the world. Many of us feel that the big guys run it, that they run it for themselves, and that there's nothing much we little guys can do but struggle and complain. Too often we allow ourselves to submit to a feeling of futility—"Eat, drink and be merry, for tomorrow we die"—and to sink into inaction. When I feel that way, I like to remember Colonel Abraham Davenport of the Connecticut Assembly. It was the famous Dark Day of New England in 1780, when the sun scarcely appeared at all. Thousands thought the end of the world was at hand, including many of the members of the Assembly in which Colonel Davenport was sitting. But when adjournment was proposed, Davenport said: "The Day of Judgment is either approaching or it is not. If it is not, there is no cause for adjournment; if it is, I choose to be found doing my duty. I wish therefore that candles may be brought." No individual is too weak to bring a candle, to do a constructive act by which he demonstrates his faith in the power of such acts.

Finally, in schools, where we have the greatest opportunity to gather groups of people together to interact, one of our main concerns should be to teach and give experience in the skills of moral decision-making and of decision-postponing. This requires presenting to students situations where it is necessary to make decisions, where their decisions will be challenged, and where they will have to defend them in the light of moral principles that they will be developing for themselves. What kind of moral principles? Our schools should create an environment in which as many students as possible move as far as possible up Kohlberg's scale of moral reasoning. (See Chapter 2, pages 34–38.)

I stated the importance of having one's ideas and decisions challenged, but challenged not simply so that the challenger can win an argument, because more win-or-lose debates are certainly not what the world needs. They should be challenged so that the whole group must work hard, with mind and spirit, to move as near as possible to the best truth that can be known by those people at that time. In this sense, challenge-giving results in sharing.

The Need for Adolescence

Isaac Newton, who lived around the end of the seventeenth century, made all his revolutionary discoveries about gravity, light, color and calculus in an eighteen-month period in his early twenties. He had been a poor student, a school dropout, but an avid reader and experimenter. I have the impression that, famous and honored as he was toward the end of his life, he never stopped being an adolescent, for shortly before he died he wrote:

I do not know what I may appear to the world, but to myself I have been only like a boy playing on the seashore, and diverting myself in now and then finding a smoother pebble or a prettier shell than ordinary, whilst the great ocean of truth lay all undiscovered before me.

When we think superficially of that state of body, mind and spirit called adolescence, most of us tend to think of its awkwardness, intemperance and instability. We would sympathize, perhaps, with Ogden Nash who, in a long verse addressed to an adolescent, recited the disorienting actions and foolishnesses of teen-age boys and girls that he found both comical and exasperating. He closed his poem with this couplet:

> Still, I'd like to be present, I must confess,
> When thine own adolescents adolesce.

An understandable sentiment from a puzzled and loving father. But we forget that in the most important sense, as I reported in Chapter 2, almost half of all Americans (and doubtless it is the same with other nationalities) never reach adolescence. They all reach puberty, yes. They become sexually mature. They feel ready to establish families and to a greater or lesser degree settle down. But they never develop the capacity for abstract thought and for an order of moral reasoning higher than Stages 3 and 4, where convention dominates. Convention will not suffice for the fifty years ahead. More of us all over the earth need to move beyond convention to the ever-renewing challenges of the postconventional levels.

How to live through junior high school? The key word in this question is *live,* and the qualities of worthy living during middle and junior high school years or during any other period of life are not essentially different. One of the qualities is the readiness to examine and reexamine our lives, to discover and rediscover truths, to seek to know ourselves—and, by extension, the world and all its peoples. This seeking to know again is the special quality of adolescence.

The French philosopher-novelist André Gide said, "Ordinary people have only one adolescence, geniuses several." The world requires more geniuses, and both our families and our schools should be arranged to evoke the genius that they now too often stifle in the name of order and convention, and for the sake of short-term comfort.

List of Suggested Reading

If the school or children's librarian doesn't have a list of books to suggest, students and parents can use the one that follows as a starter. Many of the books will appeal to fifth-graders and to ninth-graders. A good book is good because of what's in it, not because of the grade level it may be judged suitable for. Therefore, I have not tried to rate the books by grade, but only as *easy, average* and *hard* for, say, a reasonably competent seventh-grader. I recognize that these ratings are somewhat arbitrary and open to challenge, but they may be of some use. A dot (•) placed in front of an entry means that it is especially easy, while an asterisk (*) means that it is especially challenging. A plus (+) after a title indicates that there are other good books by the same author. In general, *but not always,* books in the "easy" group will appeal more to fifth- and sixth-graders and those in the "hard" group to seventh- and eighth-graders.

EASY

Aiken, Joan. *The Wolves of Willoughby Chase* +
Almedingen, E. M. *Stephen's Light*

Anonymous. *Go Ask Alice*
Armstrong, William H. *Sounder* +
Beatty, John and Patricia. *Holdfast*
• Blume, Judy. *Deenie* +
Bonham, Frank. *Durango Street* +
Bradbury, Bianca. *Those Traver Kids* +
Buck, Pearl. *The Big Wave* +
Burnford, Sheila. *The Incredible Journey*
Byars, Betsy. *The Summer of the Swans* +
Christopher, John. *The White Mountains* +
Cleaver, Vera and Bill. *Where the Lilies Bloom* +
Collodi, C. *Pinocchio*
Colman, Hila. *Claudia, Where Are You?*
Duncan, Lois. *A Gift of Magic* +
• Edwards, Julie. *Mandy* +
Eyerly, Jeannette. *A Girl Like Me. Escape from Nowhere*
Farley, Walter. *The Black Stallion* +
• Fitzgerald, John D. *The Great Brain* +
• Fitzhugh, Louise. *Harriet the Spy* +
Forbes, Esther. *Johnny Tremain*
Fox, Paula. *The Slave Dancer.* +
George, Jean. *Julie of the Wolves* +
Gipson, Fred. *Old Yeller*
Green, Bette. *Summer of My German Soldier* +
Greene, Constance C. *A Girl Called Al* +
• Hamilton, Virginia. *M. C. Higgins, the Great* +
Head, Ann. *Mr. and Mrs. Bo-Jo Jones*
Henry, Marguerite. *Brighty of the Grand Canyon* +
Hinton, S. E. *The Outsiders. That Was Then, This Is Now*
Hunter, Kristin. *The Soul Brothers and Sister Lou* +
• Johnson, E. W. *The Stolen Ruler. Escape into the Zoo*
Kerr, M. E. *The Son of Someone Famous* +
• Klein, Norma. *Mom, the Wolf Man and Me* +

- Konigsburg, E. L. *From the Mixed-up Files of Mrs. Basil E. Frankweiler* +

Lee, Mildred. *Fog*

- Lewis, C. S. *The Lion, the Witch and the Wardrobe* +

Lipsyte, Robert. *The Contender*

Lofting, Hugh. *Dr. Dolittle's Zoo* +

Meader, Stephen W. *Whaler 'Round the Horn. Who Rides in the Dark?* +

Means, Florence. *Great Day in the Morning* +

Neville, Emily. *It's Like This, Cat*

- O'Brien, Robert C. *Mrs. Frisby and the Rats of Nimh*

O'Dell, Scott. *Island of the Blue Dolphins*

Offit, Sidney. *Not All Girls Have Million Dollar Smiles*

Peyton, K. M. *The Beethoven Medal* +

- Platt, Kin. *The Boy Who Could Make Himself Disappear* +

Reiss, Johanna. *The Upstairs Room*

- Rodgers, Mary. *Freaky Friday* +

Sachs, Marilyn. *The Truth about Mary Rose* +

Sewell, Anna. *Black Beauty*

Snyder, Zilpha Keatley. *The Egypt Game* +

- Sobol, Donald. *Encyclopedia Brown, Boy Detective* +

Sperry, Armstrong. *Call It Courage*

Vining, Elizabeth Gray. *The Taken Girl* +

Waltrip, Lela and Rufus. *Quiet Boy*

Wilder, Laura Ingalls. *Little House in the Big Woods. Little House on the Prairie. Farmer Boy. On the Banks of Plum Creek. By the Shores of Silver Lake. The Long Winter. Little Town on the Prairie.*

AVERAGE

Abrahams, Peter. *Tell Freedom*

Adamson, Joy. *Born Free. Living Free. Forever Free*

Alcott, Louisa May. *Little Women. Little Men* +

Axline, Virginia. *Dibs: In Search of Self*

Bonham, Frank. *The Nitty Gritty* +
Borland, Hal. *When the Legends Die*
Braithwaite, E. R. *To Sir, with Love*
Buchan, John. *The Thirty-Nine Steps* +
Craig, Margaret. *It Could Happen to Anyone*
Dizenzo, Patricia. *Phoebe*
Donovan, John. *I'll Get There, It Better Be Worth the Trip*
Fast, Howard. *Freedom Road* +
Forbes, Kathryn. *Mama's Bank Account*
Forester, C. S. *Mr. Midshipman Hornblower* +
Frank, Anne. *Diary of a Young Girl*
Freedman, Benedict and Nancy. *Mrs. Mike*
Gallico, Paul. *The Snow Goose* +
Gibson, William. *The Miracle Worker*
Gilbreth, Frank, and Carey, Ernestine. *Cheaper by the Dozen*
Godden, Rumer. *An Episode of Sparrows. The Diddakoi* +
Graham, Robin. *Dove*
Grahame, Kenneth. *Wind in the Willows*
Green, Hannah. *I Never Promised You a Rose Garden*
Griffin, John H. *Black Like Me*
Hansberry, Lorraine. *A Raisin in the Sun*
Hemingway, Ernest. *The Old Man and the Sea*
Hentoff, Nat. *Jazz Country. I'm Really Dragged but Nothing Gets Me Down*
Herriot, James. *All Creatures Great and Small. All Things Bright and Beautiful*
Heyerdahl, Thor. *Kon-Tiki* +
Kate, Elizabeth. *A Patch of Blue*
Kingman, Lee. *The Peter Pan Bag*
Kipling, Rudyard. *Captains Courageous. Stalky and Co. Just So Stories*

Kjelgaard, Jim. *Big Red* +
LaFarge, Oliver. *Laughing Boy*
Laing, Frederick. *Ask Me If I Love You Now*
Lee, Harper. *To Kill a Mockingbird*
L'Engle, Madeleine. *A Wrinkle in Time* +
Llewellyn, Richard. *How Green Was My Valley*
London, Jack. *The Call of the Wild. White Fang* +
Lord, Walter. *A Night to Remember*
McCullers, Carson. *The Member of the Wedding. The Heart Is a Lonely Hunter*
Mathis, Sharon Bell. *A Teacup Full of Roses*
Maxwell, Edith. *Just Dial a Number*
Miller, Warren. *The Cool World*
Neufeld, John. *Lisa, Bright and Dark*
North, Sterling. *Rascal. The Wolfling*
Orwell, George. *Animal Farm*
Parks, Gordon. *The Learning Tree*
Peck, Robert N. *A Day No Pigs Would Die*
Rawlings, Marjorie Kinnan. *The Yearling* +
Richter, Conrad. *The Sea of Grass. The Light in the Forest*
Ross, Leonard Q. *The Education of H*Y*M*A*N K*A*P*L*A*N*
Saroyan, William. *The Human Comedy. My Name Is Aram*
Shaefer, Jack. *Shane*
Sherburne, Zoa. *Too Bad About the Haines Girl*
Smith, Betty. *A Tree Grows in Brooklyn*
Speare, Elizabeth George. *The Witch of Blackbird Pond*
Stanger, Margaret. *That Quail, Robert*
Steinbeck, John. *The Red Pony. The Pearl. The Grapes of Wrath. Of Mice and Men. Travels with Charley*
Stevenson, Robert Louis. *Treasure Island. Dr. Jekyll and Mr. Hyde. Kidnapped*

Stewart, George. *Fire. Storm.* +
Stirling, Nora. *You Would If You Loved Me*
Stolz, Mary. *A Love, or a Season*
Swarthout, Glendon. *Bless the Beasts and Children*
Tolkien, J. R. R. *The Hobbit* +
Twain, Mark. *Tom Sawyer. The Prince and the Pauper*
Wells, Rosemary. *The Fog Comes on Little Pig Feet*
Wersba, Barbara. *Run Softly, Go Fast*
West, Jessamyn. *The Friendly Persuasion*
White, E. B. *Charlotte's Web. Stuart Little. The Trumpet of the Swan*
Wibberley, Leonard. *The Mouse That Roared*
Wilder, Laura Ingalls. *These Happy Golden Years*
Williams, Beryl, and Epstein, Samuel. *The Great Houdini: Magician Extraordinary*
Wodehouse, P. G. *Brinkley Manor* +
Wojciechowska, Maia. *Tuned Out. Don't Play Dead Before You Have To*
Wright, Richard. *Black Boy*
Wyss, Johann. *The Swiss Family Robinson* (abridged)
Zindel, Paul. *The Pigman. I Never Loved Your Mind*

HARD

Asimov, Isaac. *Fantastic Voyage* +
Bradbury, Ray. *The Martian Chronicles. Fahrenheit 451. The Illustrated Man*
* Brontë, Charlotte. *Jane Eyre*
Buck, Pearl. *The Good Earth* +
* Clarke, Arthur C. *Childhood's End*
Dickens, Charles. *Great Expectations. Oliver Twist.*
* Dickens, Charles. *David Copperfield. A Tale of Two Cities.*
Doyle, Arthur Conan. *The Adventures of Sherlock Holmes* +
DuMaurier, Daphne. *Rebecca*

Ellison, Ralph. *The Invisible Man*
Golding, William. *Lord of the Flies*
* Heller, Joseph. *Catch-22*
* Hemingway, Ernest. *A Farewell to Arms* +
Hersey, John. *Hiroshima. A Single Pebble* +
Herzog, Maurice. *Annapurna* +
Kipling, Rudyard. *Kim*
* Kipling, Rudyard. *The Light that Failed*
Nordhoff, Charles B., and Hall, James Norman. *Mutiny on the Bounty. Men Against the Sea. Pitcairn's Island*
Paton, Alan. *Cry, the Beloved Country*
Poe, Edgar Allan. *Tales*
Potok, Chaim. *The Chosen*
* Remarque, Erich Maria. *All Quiet on the Western Front*
* Rolvaag, O. E. *Giants in the Earth*
Salinger, J. D. *The Catcher in the Rye*
Sayers, Dorothy L. *The Nine Tailors* +
Shelley, Mary. *Frankenstein*
Shute, Nevil. *On the Beach* +
Stoker, Bram. *Dracula*
Sutcliffe, Rosemary. *The Eagle of the Ninth. Outcast. The Silver Branch* +
Twain, Mark. *Huckleberry Finn. Life on the Mississippi* +
Uris, Leon. *Exodus. QB VII*
Verne, Jules. *Around the World in Eighty Days. Twenty Thousand Leagues Under the Sea. The Mysterious Island* +
Wells, H. G. *The War of the Worlds. The Time Machine* +
White, T. H. *The Sword in the Stone*
Wiesel, Elie. *Dawn. Night*
Wilder, Thornton. *The Bridge of San Luis Rey* +
Wouk, Herman. *The Caine Mutiny* +

Index